Discovery Travel Adventures™

AFRICAN SAFARI

Melissa Shales
Editor

John Gattuso
Series Editor

Discovery Communications, Inc.

Discovery Communications, Inc.
John S. Hendricks, *Founder, Chairman, and Chief Executive Officer*
Judith A. McHale, *President and Chief Operating Officer*
Judy L. Harris, *Senior Vice President, Consumer and Educational Products*

Discovery Publishing
Natalie Chapman, *Vice President, Publishing*
Rita Thievon Mullin, *Editorial Director*
Michael Hentges, *Design Director*
Mary Kalamaras, *Senior Editor*
Rick Ludwick, *Managing Editor*
Chris Alvarez, *Business Development*
Jill Gordon, *Marketing Specialist*

Discovery Channel Retail
Tracy Fortini, *Product Development*
Steve Manning, *Naturalist*

Insight Guides
Jeremy Westwood, *Managing Director*
Brian Bell, *Editorial Director*
John Gattuso, *Series Editor*
Siu-Li Low, *General Manager, Books*

Distribution
United States
Langenscheidt Publishers, Inc.
46–35 54th Road, Maspeth, NY 11378
Fax: 718-784-0640

South Africa
Faradawn cc
PO Box 1903, Saxonwold 2132, South Africa
Tel: 27-11-885-1787. Fax: 27-11-885-1829
email: faradawn@icon.co.za

Worldwide
APA Publications GmbH & Co.
Verlag KG Singapore Branch, Singapore
38 Joo Koon Road, Singapore 628990
Tel: 65-865-1600. Fax: 65-861-6438

Discovery Communications produces high-quality nonfiction television programming, interactive media, books, films, and consumer products. Discovery Networks, a division of Discovery Communications, Inc., operates and manages the Discovery Channel, TLC, Animal Planet, Travel Channel, and Discovery Health Channel. Visit Discovery Channel Online at www.discovery.com.

Although every effort is made to provide accurate information in this publication, we would appreciate readers calling our attention to any errors or outdated information by writing us at: Insight Guides, PO Box 7910, London SE1 1WE, England; fax: 44-20-7403-0290;
e-mail: insight@apaguide.demon.co.uk

Printed by Insight Print Services (Pte) Ltd,
38 Joo Koon Road, Singapore 628990.

Library of Congress Cataloging-in-Publication Data
African safari / Melissa Shales; John Gattuso, series editor.
    p. cm. -- (Discovery travel adventures)
    Includes bibliographical references (p.   ).
    ISBN 1-56331-935-7
    1. Wildlife watching--Africa--Guidebooks.
2. Safaris--Africa--Guidebooks. 3. National parks and reserves--Africa--Guidebooks. 4. Africa--Guidebooks.
I. Shales, Melissa, 1958-
II. Discovery Communications, Inc. III. Series.
    QL336 .A45 2000
    333.95'4'096--dc21   00-060201

African Safari combines the interests and enthusiasm of two of the world's best-known information providers: **Insight Guides**, whose titles have set the standard for visual travel guides since 1970, and **Discovery Communications**, the world's premier source of nonfiction entertainment. The editors of Insight Guides provide both practical advice and general understanding about a destination's history, culture, institutions, and people. Discovery Communications and its website, www.discovery.com, help millions of viewers explore their world from the comfort of their home and encourage them to explore it firsthand.

About This Book

This book reflects the contributions of dedicated editors and writers with extensive knowledge of life in the African bush. Series editor **John Gattuso**, of Stone Creek Publications in New Jersey, worked with Insight Guides and Discovery Communications to conceive and direct the series. He turned to London-based **Melissa Shales** to oversee the project. As a child in Zimbabwe, Shales spent her holidays on safari living out of a beat-up saloon car and tatty tent. Moving to England, she translated her roving lifestyle into a career as an award-winning travel writer and editor, returning to Africa to write numerous articles and guidebooks, including titles on Kenya, Zimbabwe, and South Africa. "I have dreamed for years of drifting in a mokoro through fields of water lilies," she said, "and finally, by writing the sections on the Okavango Delta and Chobe, I have realized my ambition. It more than measured up."

"To live awhile in the sun and wind, to sleep under canvas in a land of lions, to smell the grass and touch the wild. Freedom – that's what Africa means to me," explains **Brian Jackman**, Britain's foremost writer on wildlife and safaris. Now freelance after many years at London's *Sunday Times*, he has traveled widely across Africa, from Kenya to the Cape, writing powerful accounts of the lions of the Masai Mara in *The Marsh Lions* and *The Big Cat Diary*. For this book, he has written the impossibly difficult but succinct "Web of Life," and has chosen to return to his beloved Masai Mara in Kenya and Serengeti in Tanzania.

Over the past 20 years, award-winning newspaper and magazine journalist **Jack Barker** has explored Africa on foot, by motorcycle, Land Rover, Canadian canoe, inflatable raft, camel, and Citroën 2CV, also writing guides to Kenya, South Africa, and Mauritania. His keen interest in African flora and fauna, the continent's diverse cultures and societies, and the need to reconcile the needs of the natural world with the local population are clearly reflected in his chapters on the Selous in Tanzania, Tsavo and Amboseli in Kenya, Mana Pools in Zimbabwe, and the introductory discussion about the safari experience.

Michael Woods first visited Africa 15 years ago and has been on safari several times a year ever since. He writes and broadcasts about African and European wildlife, teaches courses about observing mammals, and has led a number of safaris. "I love both the vast space of Africa and the accessibility of its wildlife; for me the Namibian landscape and the gorillas in Bwindi are the epitome of both." Woods was the ideal person to write the introductory chapters on wildlife watching and conservation as well as those on Bwindi and the game reserves of Namibia.

Based in South Africa, travel writer **Philip Briggs** has traveled widely across Africa since 1986. The author of 10 travel guides to African destinations, including South Africa, Tanzania, Uganda, Kenya, Ethiopia, Malawi, Mozambique, Ghana, and, most recently, Senegal, he also contributes regularly to a number of leading South African and British wildlife periodicals. His encyclopedic knowledge of Africa is reflected in the range of destinations he covered in this book, from the Zululand Reserves in South Africa to Bale National Park in Ethiopia.

South African born and bred, **Melissa de Villiers** wrote about Kruger National Park. She traces her love of the bush back to family holidays. "Like many South Africans, I got my first taste of the bush at about age five on a family trip to Kruger. Although I've been back many times since, it's never lost its magic." De Villiers' first job in journalism was producing an anti-apartheid newspaper for a township civic group. Now living in London, she writes for a range of national newspapers and magazines, has edited and written several guidebooks, including Insight Guides to South Africa and Namibia, and has been editing a travel website.

An institution in travel publishing, both as a writer and publisher of the groundbreaking Bradt Travel Guides, **Hilary Bradt** has an ongoing love affair with Madagascar. Since her first visit in 1976, she has returned more than 20 times as a tour leader and an author, writing four books about the island – and the Madagascar chapter of this book.

David Else has been working and traveling in Africa since the early 1980s, crossing the continent several times by every conceivable form of transport. Along the way he has written numerous guides for Bradt Publications and Lonely Planet. Just home after several months in Malawi, he was the ideal choice to write the Malawi chapter of this book.

Among writer and photographer **Nick Hanna**'s many guidebooks are the highly acclaimed *Greenpeace Book of Coral Reefs* (with Sue Wells as coauthor) and a guide to beaches, snorkeling, and scuba diving in 22 countries. He is also consultant on the best-selling diving guides, *Dive Sites of the World*, which he helped develop, and has written extensively on sport diving and the marine environment for the international press. He writes here on diving in the Red Sea.

Born in Kenya, writer and photographer **Claire Foottit** has specialized in African tourism, land use, and environmental issues since 1991. She is keen to portray the positive aspects of a much-maligned continent and is particularly interested in the role tourism can play in conservation. Foottit was given the difficult task of summing up the many reserves that, through lack of space or difficulty of access, did not make it into the main body of the book.

Finally, and crucially, the authors would like to thank the following people and organizations for their generous hospitality and expertise during the writing of this book: Chris McIntyre of Sunvil; the World Conservation Monitoring Centre; the Environmental Investigation Agency; Lee Vincent of the KwaZulu-Natal Conservation Authority; South African Airways; Wilderness Safaris; CC Africa; Bill Adams of Safari Consultants Ltd; Nigel Crofton of Outposts; UTC; Retosa; Moremi Safaris; Air Botswana; Afroventures; Tafika Lodge, Zambia; Kapani Lodge, Zambia; Ghost Mountain Inn, South Africa. Thanks also to Judith Dunham and Glen Martin for invaluable editorial assistance and to the staff at Stone Creek Publications – Sallie Graziano, Nicole Buchenholz, and Edward A. Jardim.

A gray meerkat (above) keeps a beady eye out for predators from the vantage of a termite mound.

A reticulated giraffe (opposite) browses the high branches of an acacia tree; its long neck helps it reach new growth.

A tree frog (below) perches on the stalk of a carnivorous Madagascan pitcher plant.

Preceding pages: Hippos spend the daylight hours in water in order to avoid the sun and keep their body temperatures low. They emerge at night in search of forage.

Following pages: Cheetahs are quick to take advantage of a new lookout point, even if it's atop a game-viewing vehicle.

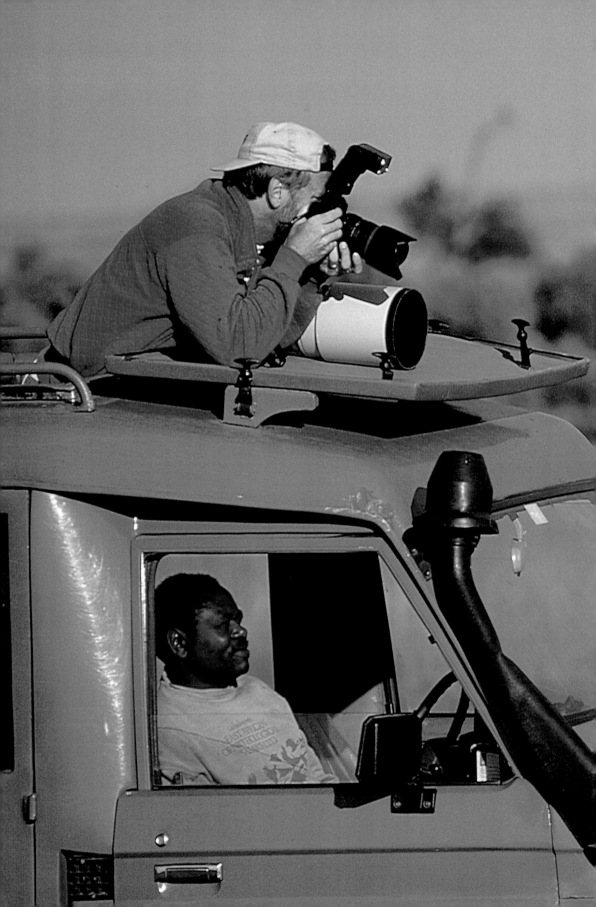

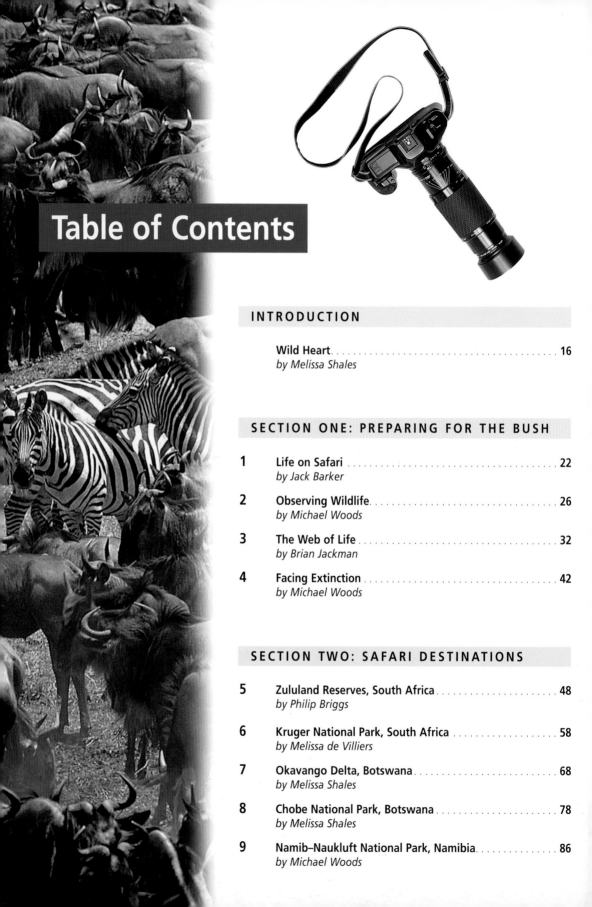

Table of Contents

MAPS

Africa is dangerously addictive. Few people visit only once. Most are drawn back again and again, venturing ever farther into remote tangled corners, searching for the peace that comes only from immersion in the natural world. ◆ This is a continent that inspires passions – some dark, some euphoric. It is subtle, complex, anguished, exotic. It is starkly and startlingly beautiful, from the Sahara sands to the Mountains of the Moon, the Congo rain forests to the flowers that carpet the Cape of Good Hope in the southern spring. It is the cradle of humanity, filled with charismatic, beautiful people, and the last great refuge of wildlife forced from the rest of the world by the incursions of man. As Beryl Markham put it in her wonderful evocation of 1930s Kenya, *West with the Night*: "Africa is mystic; it is wild; it is a sweltering inferno; it is a photographer's paradise; a hunter's Valhalla, an escapist's Utopia. It is what you will and it withstands all interpretations." ◆ To go on safari is to enter an enchanted world. There is nothing more thrilling than the bone-rattling roar of a male lion at dusk and nothing more peaceful than the sound of a Cape turtle dove cooing you to wakefulness at dawn. Sit huddled in a blanket under a coral sunrise, while around you impala stretch and bound as they work out the kinks of the night. Watch as a last, late hyena slinks home, greasy-jawed after a night's scavenging. Listen at a water hole as elephants slurp up great trunkfuls of water and spray them across their backs. ◆ While the animals are undoubtedly magnificent,

From the Zambezi to the Sahara, the Great Rift Valley to the Skeleton Coast, Africa is a continent of vast proportions and exciting diversity.

San art is a vivid reminder of Africa's earliest residents; it is scratched onto the rock or painted with mineral and plant dyes.

Preceding Pages: A lion brings down a zebra in the Serengeti, Tanzania; the migration of the wildebeests in Masai Mara, Kenya; cheetah and cubs in Phinda Resource Reserve, South Africa.

Bat-eared fox cubs (left) use their large, sensitive ears to detect insects and other prey beneath the ground.

Malachite kingfishers (below) are solitary predators, perching low on vegetation around rivers and lakes.

Black rhinos (opposite) use their hooked upper lips to grasp the branches of bushes and trees. They are famously bad-tempered.

there is much more to a safari. It is important to leave behind your preconceptions and your fears of the unknown and look beyond the headlines to see the entire world of the African bush, down to its smallest inhabitants. The dew glints like spun silver on the vast web of a golden orb spider hung like a curtain across the road. Below, an energetic dung beetle, an essential street cleaner, creeps laboriously backwards up an incline, rolling a ball of dung several times its body weight between its back legs. The grasslands are studded with the skyscraper cities of termites, ingenious architects whose mounds are constructed with ventilation for cooling and heating. Many of the plants, from the humble wildflower to the pendulous fruit of the sausage tree, have medicinal properties only now beginning to be fully understood.

This book distills the very best experiences to be found in the African bush, drawing a vivid portrait of its wonderful wildlife and the extraordinarily varied ecosystems that it inhabits. Faced with the magic of an entire continent, it is difficult to choose which national parks and game reserves to visit. Some fine reserves are sadly out of bounds due to the political turmoil that all too frequently ravages the continent. Others are so difficult to reach that only the most dedicated and resourceful traveler will make the journey. Those that are covered in this book encompass mountains, rain forests, wetlands, woodlands, grasslands, desert scrub, dunes, and even the underwater world of the Rift Valley lakes and Red Sea coral reefs. They are all accessible and have sufficient tourist infrastructure to make a visit safe and simple to organize. They also represent an extraordinary wealth of wildlife, from the wildebeest herds of the Serengeti to the gentle mountain gorillas of Uganda and the colorful chameleons of Madagascar. Most of the parks offer birders several hundred species to choose from in an aerial extravaganza unheard of in the Northern Hemisphere.

They are all beautiful islands of serenity away from the hubbub of daily life. Enjoy the dream as you read, enjoy the journey as you head off on safari.

◆

Preparing For the Bush

◆

Your journey into the African bush will be more rewarding if you review proven wildlife-watching techniques, develop an understanding of animal behavior and habitats, and learn about conservation issues.

t wasn't so very long ago that the whole of sub-Saharan Africa teemed with game, from the open veldt of the east to the lush jungles of the west's great river basins. Inexorably expanding human populations and their works – agriculture, development, poaching, war – have taken a dreadful toll. The great tide of African wildlife is now at an ebb, restricted to reserves and sanctuaries.   ◆   But it is still possible to see great seasonal migrations of wildebeests and elephants, to witness lions and cheetahs at their kills, to lie in a tent at night and feel a delicious frisson of apprehension from the not-so-distant cough of a leopard. And you do it the way it's always been done: by going on safari.   ◆   The word *safari* is Swahili for *journey*, but European explorers and settlers in East Africa adopted it as a description for a certain **Do your homework carefully** type of hunting trip: one that **and choose the style of safari** involved dozens of porters, gunbearers, **that best suits your dreams,** and personal manservants, as well as **ideas of comfort, and budget.** civilized niceties such as single malt scotch and folding canvas bathtubs. The concept of the safari still exists, but in considerably streamlined form, and for different purposes. No longer is the quest for ivory but for the simple opportunity to see, and perhaps photograph, the animals that carry the tusks.   ◆   Safari options are many, ranging from the plush to the rough, covering all of southern and eastern Africa's diverse habitats. For those who demand creature comforts with their creatures, the Sabi Sand area near Kruger National Park in South Africa is ideal; the leopards are particularly inured to visitation here and preen agreeably in front of pampered humans. In Kenya's popular parks, game viewing is down to a science – or, at least,

African elephants can be tamed: these adult orphans near Victoria Falls, Zimbabwe, take visitors on daily safaris.

Preceding pages: A red-billed ox-pecker cleans ticks and fleas from the thick coat of a Grant's zebra.

Reed and thatch huts (right) stay cool and airy through the midday heat, but nothing keeps mosquitoes at bay like a traditional net.

a business. Range Rover caravans regularly sally out on the veldt, affording a relatively cheap safari with good sightings guaranteed. In Botswana's Okavango Delta, adventurous trekkers can explore the game-rich sloughs, islands, canals, and upland thickets with local guides in dugout mokoros. For those disinclined to walk or drive, there are always the bore-fed water holes of Zimbabwe's Hwange National Park. During the dry season, it's the only source of water for miles, and everything from sand grouse to lion shows up for a drink sooner or later.

From Camel to Car

If you went on safari in the 19th century, you walked. You can still do that; walking safaris have remained popular with that segment of the tourist population that is adventurous and robust. In Zambia, particularly, walking safaris, usually accompanied by an armed escort, have become a popular option. You don't get as close to the large game on foot as you do in a car – undisguised by the stench of diesel exhaust, the human scent screams "carnivore!" to herbivorous species – but you do get to examine the insects, reptiles, birds, and flora up close. Walking safaris often extend for days, and on many of these jaunts, nights are spent in permanent camps outfitted with sturdy tents, metal cots, and bucket showers. Others are more basic in their amenities.

In addition to walking, a wide array of alternative transports is available. For the cheapest safaris, rather cramped minibuses are standard. In East Africa, all safari vehicles are enclosed for safety, with viewing panels cut in the roof. Land Rovers fitted with tiered seats hold sway farther south. Cars are also available for self-guided safaris, but they are

The Golden Age of Safari

Far from being dressy affairs, early safaris were usually practical expeditions whose main business was killing lots of animals. Early women explorers – of whom there were surprisingly many – generally broke this rule by shooting less frequently and donning full Victorian dress, which several found useful against thorns.

Safaris in the 19th and early 20th centuries had traces of luxury, with bottles of champagne and vintage wine often the only drink. The wine would, however, be drunk warm. And changing for dinner did little to improve a meal in which freshly shot game was often plentiful but the accompanying vegetables, usually pressed in London, were insipid. Even the lavishly funded safaris of Theodore Roosevelt and George Eastman of the Eastman Kodak Company found luxury easier to claim than attain. Contrary to popular belief, the golden age of safari, with damask tablecloths, cut glass, and silver service, is not a thing of the past but of the present.

Luxury living (left) in the heart of the bush: the golden age of safaris is now.

Flooded trees (right), drowned when Kariba Dam was built, offer safe nesting places for fishing birds on Lake Kariba, Zimbabwe.

often too low to the ground to afford either good visibility or maneuverability on rough roads.

But transport choices are no longer restricted to shank's mare or the internal combustion engine. It was once thought that the African elephant was impossible to tame, but several outfits in Botswana and Zimbabwe have proved that conventional wisdom dead wrong. They offer elephant-back explorations, often accompanied by baby pachyderms gamboling along at their mothers' sides. In Botswana's Okavango Delta as well as parts of South Africa, Malawi, and Zimbabwe, horses are available for either day trips or multiday safaris. In many respects, horses are the best way to explore wild Africa: the game views the rider and mount as just another herbivore on the veldt and often allows them to approach closely.

In Kenya's arid northern regions, camels are the way to go. These indomitable desert beasts are ideally suited for exploration of this sere region, providing a relatively comfortable ride as long as a gentle pace is maintained. Samburu or Masai guides usually escort these caravans.

Africa's many rivers and lakes offer other alternatives. Mokoros – long, slender dugouts – are standard transport along the narrow watercourses of the Okavango Delta. On the Zambezi River's Mana Pools, two-man canoes are used for close encounters of the hippo kind. And for those who don't wish to exert themselves, sundowner cruises explore the Zambezi's calm stretches, the vast expanses of Lake Kariba, and the Chobe River in Botswana.

Silver Service

No matter the mode of travel, a secure and comfortable bed is essential for a sense of well-being on any safari. The ideal accommodations for many travelers are private camps, arrayed in the classic East African style: commodious walk-in tents, sometimes outfitted with twin beds, tables, and lights. Dinners are often ambitious, multicourse affairs, complete with cocktails and wine. Some of the top-end camps have wooden decks, thatched roofs, flush toilets, and showers. Expect to pay dearly for these amenities.

As with all real estate, location is all-important. Lodges built over floodlit water holes bring game almost to your table, and river settings add hippo serenades to the evening meal. Some are built into huge granite outcrops overlooking game-strewn plains. Wherever they are situated, small is beautiful with African lodges; the safari ideal is quiet, intimate evenings in the bush while a decanter of port circulates around the bonfire.

But even those without deep pockets can enjoy superb game viewing. Zimbabwe and South Africa in particular cater to the shoestring wildlife enthusiast by situating large hotels and lodges around many park boundaries. And except for Botswana, virtually all the African nations with renowned game preserves offer cheap, self-catered accommodations. For those prepared to fend for themselves, many of the game parks can still be done on the cheap.

Africa's game parks are not zoos. Though animals in some parks are habituated to the presence of humans, you'll need both dedication and a little luck to score a sighting of many species. As with most endeavors, wildlife watching requires a certain set of skills and some crucial equipment. ◆ First, the gear. At the top of the list should be a good pair of binoculars – the best you can afford. Choose 7 to 10 magnification; anything more powerful will wobble when you attempt to hold them steady. Go for large object lenses (the fat ends farthest from your eyes), as these admit more light and give a clearer picture. A pair with roof prisms rather than porroprisms is likely to be lighter and less cumbersome. Spend your money on a reputable make with high-quality optics, avoid fancy gimmicks such as zoom or antishake features, and don't forget the option of buying a good second-hand pair. Always pack your binoculars securely in your luggage to avoid damage, but keep them around your neck, uncased, when in the field.

Dress sensibly, keep your binoculars and camera handy, and stay alert. A leopard may be lurking in a tree above you.

Wildlife often comes and goes in a flash, and you need to be ready when an animal reveals itself. ◆ Practice with your binoculars before leaving home, so you can bring them up to your eyes and focus on target objects at varying distances with minimal difficulty. Old Africa hands always look at the game, never the binoculars; they stay sighted on their quarry, bringing the binoculars up and "inserting" them between the animal and their eyes. ◆ Spotting wildlife is only half the challenge; the other half is making sure it doesn't spot you. Khaki, gray, or olive green fabrics are good choices. Avoid white or light colors, which signal your

A wood-poled mokoro, a traditional dugout canoe, is a silent, atmospheric form of transport through the narrow channels of the Okavango Delta.

Giraffes (left) like to keep their distance from intruders, cantering slowly away from approaching vehicles.

Elephants (below) will charge to assert their supremacy. This photographer may be concentrating on getting his shot, but his driver will already have the engine running.

Bush babies (right), nocturnal primates, are often spotted close to lodges and camps; flashlights reflect brightly in their large eyes.

presence to game like a beacon. Long-sleeved shirts are best, as sleeves can be turned up or down depending on temperature. It's nice to have shirts with breast pockets for pens, notebooks, and sundries. Shorts or long pants? That's strictly a matter of preference. Long pants can get a little sticky on a hot afternoon, but they protect against insects and sunburn. Take a light jacket even during high summer. Predawn mornings can be bitterly cold on the veldt.

Choose desert boots or other light, rugged footwear. Even four-wheel-drive vehicles get bogged down in sand or mud once in a while. You may have to get out and push or walk back to your lodge.

Perhaps most important: wear a hat. The sun can kill, or at least make you miserable. Baseball caps are best in open vehicles, where bush hats may be blown off. But when the sun is beating down and you're trekking through the veldt, only a broad-brimmed hat will provide adequate protection. Also bring polarized sun-

glasses, a 30-SPF sunscreen, lip balm, and a reliable insect repellent.

Making a Record

Though cameras are de rigueur, it's also a good idea to bring a notebook and – if you're of an artistic bent – a sketchbook. Journal entries will greatly augment the pictorial record, and provide an account of the trip that can be enjoyed for years.

Compact cameras are gaining in popularity on safari, but they should be equipped with built-in telephoto lenses. Because wildlife photography invariably entails telescopic shooting, it's best to bring a standard 35mm camera and some "long glass" – good telephoto lenses. Professional wildlife photographers use lenses in the 500mm to 800mm range, but this is generally impractical for the casual visitor. Two zoom lenses – one in the 28mm to 100mm range, the other 100mm to 300mm – should suffice. Whenever possible, shoot from a blind, a motor vehicle, or on foot, bracing the camera with whatever support is available. A tripod is best, but a door frame, tree, or rock is better than nothing. Some photographers bring along a beanbag or small pillow to rest the camera on. For obvious reasons, shooting from horse or elephant back is generally unsatisfactory.

Always take more – much more – film than you think you'll need. Africa inevitably

Night Dwellers

A night drive, under huge, starry skies, reveals another side of the bush, one that's alive with scurrying nocturnal creatures. The person behind the spotlight swings the beam back and forth, checking under bushes and trees and among the branches, looking for shining eyes. A knowledge-able guide should be able to identify the owners of those eyes, passing quickly over the diurnal species who need their sleep.

Small eyes, bobbing about under bushes, are likely to be those of an elephant shrew, while those that seem to bounce may belong to a spring hare, a rodent resembling a small kangaroo which slips into an underground burrow when disturbed. Large eyes close to the ground probably belong to small cats – African wild cat, genet, and caracal – or a large member of the mongoose family, the civet. The huge eyes of bush babies and owls can be seen shining from high branches. A lucky few may catch sight of a scaly anteater called a pangolin, a honey badger, or even an aardvark.

But the biggest thrill is spotting one of the big cats or other predators. Lions, usually seen lazing around during the day, pace menacingly through the bush at night. Hyenas whoop and jackals yap as they prowl around the fringes of a kill. Most exciting of all is an encounter with that quintessential denizen of the night, the leopard. Rarely seen in daylight, it will completely ignore the interruption, moving purpose-fully along, lithe muscles rippling under its magnificent coat until, with a haughty flick of a white-tipped tail, it slips silently into the dark.

stimulates a shutter-snapping frenzy in even amateur photographers. Transparencies provide better clarity than prints and are essential if you plan to give slide shows. Otherwise, print film is the best choice. Try to take pictures in the early morning and late afternoon, when the canted light is, in the professional photographer's parlance, "sweet." Faster film – from 200 to 400 ISO – is best in these low-light situations, particularly if you're using a telephoto lens.

Video cameras are increasingly seen on safari. They're

a good choice, because they usually have powerful telephoto lenses, they're easy to use, and they perform well in low light.

Animal Behavior

Seeking wildlife on foot is the most intimate way to experience Africa, because you're on the animals' level. It's important to remember, however, that if you're walking – or on horseback – you're engaging wildlife on its own terms. Some precautions are in order.

Imagine the world from the wildlife's point of view.

Most mammals rely on scent and sound rather than eyesight to gather information about their environment. Keep your voice down and avoid perfume and scented sunblocks and insect repellents to enhance your chances of approaching game closely. Watch your step and where you put your hands. Breaking twigs and rolling rocks disturb game as well as venomous snakes and scorpions. The latter, by no means uncommon in Africa, can be very venomous indeed and naturally get testy when they are trod upon or othewise threatened.

Though many animals have poor eyesight, they can still detect movement, which they invariably find alarming. Like people, they resent having their private space invaded, especially if the intruder appears suddenly. Most species will flee in panic, but a few will react aggressively and attack. Animals in this category include lions, rhinoceroses (particularly black rhinos), lone bull cape buffalo, hippopotamuses (especially those encountered away from water), and elephants, particularly cows with calves.

It's generally possible to escape from all these animals

Trash (above) can be harmful to wild animals like these vervet monkeys.

Dung beetle crossing: warning signs (right) are meant to protect both wildlife and visitors.

Mountain gorillas (top) may allow you to approach if you're patient.

Horseback safaris (opposite) are ideal for getting close to herbivores, who see the horses as kindred spirits and let them walk among the herd.

The Rules of Survival

Human beings have destroyed wildlife habitats and ecosystems the world over, and now all that remains of wild Africa are its national parks and game reserves. The only way to preserve them for future generations is to treat them with respect.

● As the saying goes, "Take nothing but pictures, leave nothing but footprints." Carry out your trash and campfire ashes (better yet, forgo the fire and use a portable camping stove). Resist the temptation to collect natural objects. Every feather and seedpod is food or a home to some creature.

● Animals can be easily stressed, especially those with young or predators at a kill. Keep your distance and always carry binoculars. They permit safe viewing without intrusiveness.

● Protest if your driver leaves the prescribed roads to get a better view of wildlife (in some areas they anticipate larger tips in return for close encounters) and resist the temptation to do so yourself.

● Above all, remember that wild animals are unpredictable. Don't try to pet or feed them and never try to herd them into a better position for viewing or photographing.

– except lions – by climbing a tree, or hiding among rocks or the tangled branches of a large windfall. Few animals will pursue a charge once they've determined that an intruder has been driven off or is in hiding. Lions, however, can be problematic. Never run from a lion, as that merely excites its predatory instincts. Instead, face the animal, stretch out your arms to look as large as possible, shout loudly, and slowly back off.

Professional guides should keep you perfectly safe, but Africa isn't Disneyland; wildlife is unpredictable, and unexpected things do happen in the bush. To a significant degree, you are responsible for your own safety. Determine wind direction regularly by kicking up dust to see which way it drifts; this will tell you where your scent is going. Regularly check the surrounding terrain for refuges and escape routes. Generally speaking, if an animal is aware of your presence from a distance it will not attack, unless provoked. That's why people sleeping in tents are seldom molested.

Not every outing will produce sightings of large, charismatic species. But one of the great joys of walking in Africa is the opportunity to appreciate all the small things you would otherwise miss from a vehicle: the clacking call of guinea fowl, the various tracks and scat of different beasts great and small, termites constructing their massive mounds, dung beetles rolling balls of dung. Ultimately,

these are the greatest pleasures of safari: immersing oneself in a land that has to an appreciable degree remained unchanged since the end of the last ice age.

The Change of Season

To everything there is a season, including African wildlife. A safari in the rainy season is a wondrous experience – the bush vibrant with new foliage, the grass electric green and knee high, and panoramas of wildflowers to the horizon. The animals are plump and fit, and most of the herbivores give birth at this time. Birds breed and nest during the rainy season, and often display extravagant

breeding plumage. One drawback: the dense vegetation tends to conceal animals, making sightings difficult.

Once the rains stop, water sources begin shrinking. The game concentrates at water holes and along rivers; the vegetation desiccates, making it easier to spot animals. By the end of the dry season, virtually all the animals in a given area gather around the few available sources of water. A great variety of species can typically be seen in a short period of time, and predator and prey interactions are common, making this the most exciting time of year for wildlife viewing.

Dawn comes up fast in Africa. The sun, a huge red bubble on the rim of the plains, catches a line of wildebeests in sharp silhouette, horned heads erect, alert for danger. Sound carries far in the clear highland air. Already the ring-necked doves are calling from the flat-roofed acacias, begging the world to *work-harder, work-harder,* and from somewhere in the sea of grass, as the plains turn to gold in the morning light, there comes the sudden rumble of lions. ◆ By mid-morning the dew is just a memory, and the skies are full of soaring birds. In the distance, a vortex of vultures indicates the presence of a kill. A cheetah has pulled down a Thomson's gazelle. Out in the open with nowhere to hide, the hungry cat feeds as fast as it can. But little escapes the sharp-eyed vultures, and the sight of them falling from the sky summons other scavengers. Spotted hyenas come loping over the skyline, grim jaws agape as if in anticipation of the feast to come. The cheetah

Dramas large and small unfold in a wide range of environments, from savannas to rain forests, deserts to wetlands.

gives way. An hour passes, and nothing is left but a stain on the grass and soil. ◆ In the vastness of the African savanna, life and death march side by side, but there is nowhere else on earth so vibrantly alive. Every horizon is a moving frieze of animals – giraffes and zebras, elephants, buffalo, wildebeests, and antelopes by the score. And always the spine-tingling presence of the big cats: leopards, cheetahs, black-maned lions. For them the savanna is an ideal hunting ground. This is their land, their kingdom of the grass.

Cheetahs feed on an antelope at Masai Mara National Reserve in Kenya; the lightly built cats need to eat quickly before lions or hyenas chase them away from the kill.

Wildebeests (left) are found in grasslands throughout southern and eastern Africa.

recycle the droppings left by animals – a vital task when you consider that an elephant produces some 220 pounds (100kg) of dung every day.

Besides beetles, Africa's grasslands are alive with butterflies and grasshoppers. During the rains, termite mounds erupt, sending fountains of flying ants into the air, to be snapped up wherever they land by all kinds of creatures, from bat-eared foxes to migrating storks.

The abundance of food – seeds, insects, mice, and snakes – guarantees the presence of large numbers of birds, from button quails and tiny cisticolas to Kori bustards, the world's largest flying bird. The sad cries of larks and pipits, the shriek of crowned plovers, the booming of ground hornbills – these are the sounds of the savanna.

Thorny acacia trees are another feature of the savanna landscape. Moisture-loving fever trees with lemon-yellow trunks grow beside rivers and drainage lines. But the quintessential thorn tree of the savanna country is the umbrella acacia, whose flat-topped crown is as much a symbol of the African plains as the lion or wildebeest.

Feeding Ground

Grass and rain, these are the engines that drive the savanna ecosystem. In East Africa, the long rains of April and May nourish savanna grasses, among them the red-oat grass that grows in rolling, waist-high waves across Kenya's Masai Mara National Reserve.

The grasses transmute the sun's energy into food for a host of herbivores. During their migration from the Serengeti plains, zebras chomp down the coarser stems. Wildebeests follow, and after them antelopes and gazelles with their slender muzzles, selectively nibbling tender leaves and shoots. The grazers in turn become food for predators such as lions and cheetahs, and the scavengers – vultures, jackals, spotted hyenas – mop up the leftovers. Such is the economy of nature; nothing is left to waste. Even dung beetles

Desert Sands

The classic savanna parklands of East Africa lie within 100 miles (160km) of the Equator, but they enjoy a glorious climate because much of Masailand lies 5,000 feet (1525m) above sea level. As you descend into the dry country north of Mount Kenya, the scene changes yet again. Instead of green and parklike savanna you find a semi-desert of thorny thickets threaded by red dusty game trails, with here and there a mighty baobab tree. This is the home of dry-country animals not seen elsewhere in Kenya, such as the beautiful reticulated giraffe and Grevy's zebra, with its big bat ears and pinstriped coat.

To see what a true desert looks like, you must venture south, into the Namib – "the Place where there is Nothing." Here the sun beats relentlessly upon an emptiness of gravel

plains. Cindery mountains seem to quiver and dissolve in the furnace heat, and searing winds hiss over the dunes of Sossusvlei, whose crests reach 1,000 feet (300m), the highest in the world.

These barren thirstlands offer a glimpse into the far-distant future, a vision of what our world may look like millions of years from

now. What you see here in Namibia is the oldest desert in the world, the burnt-out carcass of a dying planet, a landscape of unrelenting hostility. Some places have had no rain for a century. Yet, even here, life persists.

Black rhinos wander the wastes of Damaraland. Desert-dwelling elephants migrate through the dunes.

Dwarf mongooses (left) keep watch from an old termite mound.

Grant's gazelles (opposite, bottom) are found in either bachelor herds or harems. This female with her young could be one of up to 30 other females impregnated by a single male.

Baobab trees (below) flourish in arid regions; some giant specimens are several thousand years old.

Pangolins (left), nocturnal anteaters, roll into a ball if attacked; their sharp scales deter most predators.

Sometimes they leave their giant footprints in the sands of the Skeleton Coast; and often, when you think you are alone, you look up and see a troop of gemsbok – handsome antelopes with rapier horns – cantering over the horizon.

The drought-proof gems-bok is uniquely adapted to a world without permanent water and can survive for months without drinking. Everything about it is designed to conserve fluid. Its pale coat helps deflect the sun's fierce rays, and instead of losing precious water by panting or sweating, it allows its body temperature to rise from a normal 96°F (36°C) to levels that would kill other animals. Its secret is an ingenious heat-exchange system in which the blood is cooled by a maze of veins in the muzzle before it reaches the brain.

To the east of Namibia in neighboring Botswana lie the sandy soils of the Kalahari, one of the harshest environments on earth. The Kalahari isn't everyone's idea of a true desert. For a start, much of it is covered with grass. In places, camelthorn trees and the shepherd's tree create pools of shade. Wild cucumbers and Tsamma melons provide food for desert animals, and spring rains bring a sudden flower-ing of vlei lilies, wild hibis-cus, and devil's thorn.

But desert it is. Drought is the norm, and the animals who live here have evolved ingenious strategies for sur-vival. Sand grouse cope by flying 37 miles (60km) in search of water. Desert beetles draw breath only once every 20 minutes to conserve mois-ture, and ground squirrels use their tails as sunshades. Some animals, such as the meerkats of Kgalagadi Transfrontier Park (formerly Kalahari Gemsbok Park), avoid the heat by burrowing. Others – leopards, genets, Kalahari lions – are mostly nocturnal. But all desert life follows one unbending rule: adapt or die.

In the northern Kalahari and in Namibia's Etosha National Park, cruel mirages hover over vast salt pans – the white ghosts of lakes that died in prehistoric times. The Makgadikgadi Pans of Botswana are the largest salt pans in the world – 14,286

square miles (37,000 sq km) of glittering saline crust. For most of the year they are as dead as Mars. But during the rains a miraculous transformation occurs. Here and in Etosha, for a few brief weeks the pans come alive, their shallow waters shimmering with the pink reflections of greater and lesser flamingos in the hundreds of thousands.

The flamingos feed on algae and brine shrimps, whose eggs lie buried in the salt mud through the long hot months of drought. Using their inverted bills as vacuum cleaners, the birds sweep up the brine shrimps by the billions and stay on to breed far out in the Sua Pan, one of the two main pans of the Makgadikgadi, where no predators can reach them.

The Rift Valley Lakes

Flamingos also occur in huge numbers on the soda lakes of the Great Rift Valley. The volcanic escarpments of this giant fault line extend 3,520 miles (5,660km) from the Red Sea shores of Ethiopia to Mozambique, dividing the savannas of East Africa from the tropical rain forests of the Congo Basin.

Until the 1970s, Kenya's Lake Nakuru regularly attracted more than one million

Meerkats (right) are always alert. At the first sign of danger, they utter a shrill bark and scatter for their burrows.

Gemsbok (top) are uniquely adapted to desert life. They can survive for long periods without drinking, relying on moisture in bulbs and wild fruits.

An elephant (opposite, below) in the dry Kaokoland region of Namibia stands on its hind feet to pull down fresh vegetation.

flamingos. Pollution has now caused numbers to dwindle, forcing the birds to move on to Lakes Bogoria and Elementaita. But Nakuru National Park is still worth a visit, although nowadays mammals, including lions, leopards, and black rhinos, are the main attraction.

Not all Rift Valley lakes are soda lakes. One notable exception is Lake Naivasha, less than 40 miles (64km) from Nairobi, whose clear waters attract large numbers of herons, fish eagles, black crakes, jacanas, and a half dozen kinds of kingfishers. In all, more than 400 bird species have been recorded here; and nearby, in Hell's Gate National Park, colonies of griffin vultures and Verreaux eagles nest on the dizzying cliffs.

Other, much larger fresh-water lakes include Lake Malawi, teeming with cichlids and other tropical fish, and Lake Tanganyika, known for its crocodiles,

hippos, and water cobras. But bigger than them all, lying to the west of the Rift Valley on the borders of Kenya and Uganda, is Lake Victoria, which extends for 24,324 square miles (62,998 sq km), making it the largest lake in Africa and the second biggest body of fresh water in the world. Beneath its surface cruise giant Nile perch, along with tulip and other fish that are preyed upon by fish eagles and spotted-necked otters.

Savanna Woodland

At the edges of the grasslands, true savanna woodland can be said to begin when tree shade covers more than 20

percent of the terrain. But as with animals, different plant communities thrive in different conditions, and factors such as water, climate, altitude, and soil type have helped to create a number of distinctive woodland habitats.

Some of Africa's most beautiful trees grow beside its greatest rivers, creating dense ribbons of shade for birds and other animals. At Mana Pools National Park in Zimbabwe, for example, airy glades of majestic old winterthorns grace the banks of the mighty Zambezi River. Here and along its tributaries, the Chobe River in Botswana and the Luangwa River in Zambia, fish eagles yelp from the lofty crowns of the sycamore fig and sausage trees, with their smooth gray bark and strange, yard-long, salami-shaped fruits. These riparian forests provide ideal resting places for leopards, while all kinds of creatures, from green

Eyes and ears (above) are widely spaced on the top of a hippo's skull, allowing it to assess danger without leaving its watery sanctuary.

Flamingos (left) gather at lakes, estuaries, and saline pans; flocks can number several thousand birds and often depart as quickly as they arrived.

Fast and agile, klipspringers (right) elude predators by leaping from boulder to boulder.

pigeons to baboons and porcupines, feast on the fig tree's annual harvest. On the banks below, Nile crocodiles bask in the sun with jaws agape; and all day long, from the deeper pools, come the cavernous belly-laughs of hippos.

Farther south, in Botswana's Okavango Delta, islands of riparian forest rise above the floodwaters. Characteristic species to be found here include wild date palm, mangosteen, and the lofty jackalberry, whose dark crowns are a favorite roost of the shy Pel's fishing owl. Of all Africa's wetlands, the Delta is the most beautiful – a magical oasis of islands, water lilies, and papyrus reeds threaded by crystal channels. Pursued by packs of African wild dogs, herds of red lechwe antelope plunge across its drowned floodplains, and the elusive sitatunga – another swamp-dwelling antelope – hides in the reed beds.

Southern Africa is the home of mopane (*mo-PAH-nee*) woodland, which flourishes on the clay pan soils of hot, low-lying areas such as Zambia's Luangwa Valley and Botswana's Moremi Game Reserve. The mopane is a deciduous tree whose drooping leaves fold like the wings of a butterfly during the heat of day to conserve moisture.

In the African winter, mopane leaves assume the autumn colors of an English beech forest before falling in

September and October. But even then they are rich in protein, hence the importance of these woodlands as a year-round food source for elephants and other browsers. Large tracts of stunted mopane woodland are regularly coppiced by hungry elephants, and when allowed to attain their full height of 19 feet (6m), the trees grow in graceful aisles sometimes called cathedral mopane. Animals of the cathedral mopane include tree squirrels and greater kudu, while Arnot's chat is the most typical bird species.

Large areas of southern Africa are also covered with miombo woodland. Here *Brachystegia, Julbernardia,* and *Isoberlinia* are the dominant trees, opened up in places by sunny glades and shallow *dambos* – grassy depressions that fill with water during the rains. Typical

Miombo animals include roan and sable, two of Africa's most magnificent antelopes.

On the Rocks

Adding a sense of drama to the landscape, weathered granite inselbergs known in Africa as kopjes (an Afrikaans word pronounced *koppies*) create their own unique habitat. Worlds within worlds, these islands in the bush are home to rock-dwelling animals such as klipspringers (tiny antelope) and rock hyrax (like an overgrown guinea pig, but actually the nearest living relative to the elephant). They serve as a stony refuge for blue-and-orange agama lizards, lookout posts for cheetahs, and hiding places

The bright color of a poisonous tomato frog warns predators to stay away.

A baby ring-tailed lemur (right) rides on its mother's back; lemurs are endemic to Madagascar.

for lion cubs. These granite outcroppings occur all over Africa, but are best viewed in Zimbabwe's Matobo Hills National Park, a breeding stronghold for black eagles.

In South Africa, a combination of broadleaved and thorn trees create the bushveld habitat best typified by Kruger National Park; and in Zimbabwe yet another vegetation change takes place. This time it is teak forest, which thrives with wild syringa and other deciduous trees on the Kalahari sandveld soils of the Zambezi Valley.

In Kenya, mangrove forests tiptoe on spidery roots into the salty creeks of Dodori National Reserve. In the Arabuko Sokoke Forest Reserve near Malindi, 15 different kinds of owls and more than 80 forest butterflies find refuge in East Africa's largest surviving coastal tropical forest. Elsewhere on Kenya's Coral Coast, the marine parks of Watamu, Kisite, and Mpunguti reflect Africa's extraordinary diversity, pro-

Spitting cobras use their venom to blind and disable both predators and prey.

tecting miles of reefs and coral gardens, rare sea turtles, and more than 250 species of fish, including the giant groupers of Tewa Caves.

Forest Life

In the heart of East Africa, cloud forest clothes the lower slopes of great massifs such as Kilimanjaro, Mount Kenya, and the Rwenzoris. One of the best introductions to this montane forest habitat is the drive up to the rim of Ngorongoro Crater from the Lodware park gate. As the road climbs higher into the forest, you begin to see the first giant *Albizias* with their lacy spreading canopies. Red-thorn acacias cling to the ridges, draped with living hawsers of ruby vine. Out of the gullies, straight as ships' masts, rise the pale trunks of pillar-wood trees;

and finally, as you approach the Crater rim, these lesser trees give way to ancient groves of Nuxias, their gnarled limbs festooned with bearded lichens.

But a forest is more than just the sum of its trees. Beneath its evergreen canopy the air is damp and still, a twilight world that echoes to the bell-like calls of forest birds and the dawn chorus of black-and-white colobus monkeys, an unearthly, roaring *ra-ra-ra* that can be heard more than a mile away. Swallowtail butterflies with gorgeous green-and-black velvet wings flip through the filtered sunlight, and columns of voracious siafu (safari ants) pour like black treacle across forest paths.

All kinds of shy and secretive animals find refuge in Africa's tropical forests, from diminutive duikers scarcely bigger than a hare to the giant forest hog. The forests of Madagascar are home to scores of endemic species, from the charmingly friendly lemurs to giant cockroaches. In the lowland rain forest of the Congo Basin lives the forest elephant, a distinct subspecies with straight, slender tusks, and the extraordinary okapi, among the rarest of antelopes, with its giraffelike neck and zebra-striped flanks.

Another of Africa's rarest animals, the mountain gorilla, can be seen in Uganda's Bwindi Impenetrable Forest – so-called because of its dense undergrowth of vines and other vegetation. Bwindi is now home to more than 300 of these critically endangered primates, almost half the world population of this species. Elsewhere in Uganda, chimpanzees clamber through the Rabongo Forest in Murchison Falls National Park and a number of other areas, including Kibale Forest National Park and the Maramagambo Forest in Rwenzori Mountains National Park.

On the higher slopes of Mount Kenya and Aberdare National Parks in Kenya, montane forest trees such as juniper and coniferous *Podocarpus* give way to belts of bamboo forest. Beyond the bamboos grow giant tree heathers, and at an elevation of about 10,000 feet (3,000m)

comes the dramatic sight of the alpine moorlands, where altitude plays strange tricks with the mountain vegetation. Tussock grasses sprout shoulder high, and normally modest plants such as lobelias and groundsels become 20-foot (6-m) giants.

Islands in the equatorial skies, these lonely moorlands are the haunt of creatures that have evolved in isolation from their lowland relatives. Melanistic serval cats are common in the Aberdares,

and on Mount Kenya you may see scarlet-tufted malachite sunbirds sipping nectar from the lobelia flowers, or a Mackinder's eagle owl perched on a boulder. But above 14,700 feet (4,500m), there is nothing but rock and ice. By the time you reach the snows of Africa's highest mountain, Kilimanjaro, you will have completed a journey through a pyramid of habitats, the vertical equivalent of traveling from the Equator to the Arctic.

Endangered by habitat loss, wild chimps (right) are found in only a handful of forests in Tanzania and Uganda.

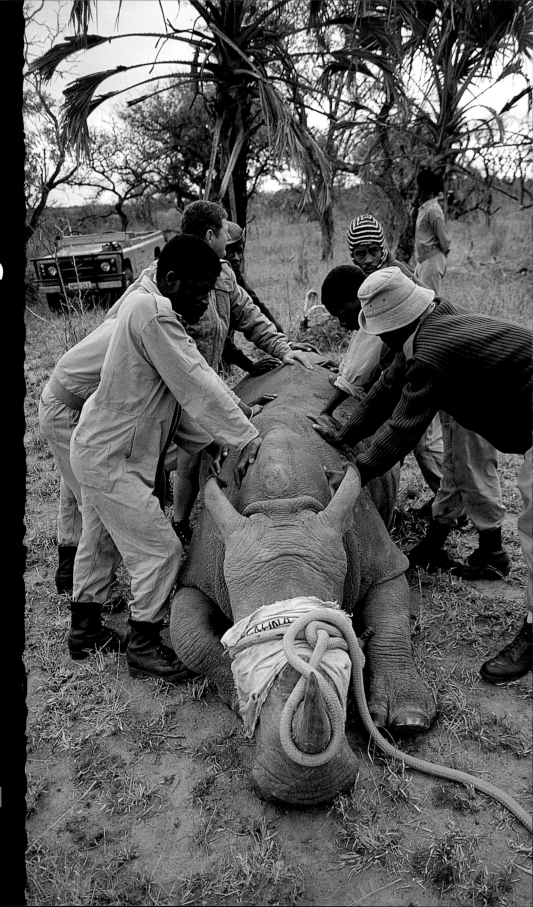

Standing on the vast grasslands of the Serengeti, surrounded by thousands of lowing wildebeests, it may be hard to understand how any African animal could be endangered. In fact, thousands of African species face extinction, and human beings are the root cause. ◆ The list of endangered species is too long to enumerate, but even a cursory examination of some of the best-known examples illustrates both the extent of the problem and some measures that are being employed to stem the decline. While the white rhinoceros is under threat, its cousin, the black rhino, is critically endangered, with only about 2,550 left in the wild. It is found in appreciable numbers only in Kenya, Namibia, South Africa, and Zimbabwe, though Tanzania's Ngorongoro Crater affords the best opportunity for daytime sightings. ◆ The black rhino was hunted heavily for sport throughout much of the 20th century, and its horn has long been considered a potent aphrodisiac

Poaching, agriculture, logging, and disease – all contribute to the downward spiral of African game populations.

in Asian medicine, though no scientific evidence supports this belief. But its most precipitous decline started in the 1970s, when rhinoceros-horn handles became the vogue for Yemeni daggers. Within a decade, prices for the horns soared by a factor of 20 or higher. Images of rhino carcasses with their horns hacked off became a staple in the press. ◆ Today, the dagger-handle market for rhino horn is in decline due to the increasing popularity of agate handles, although the market in traditional Asian medicine is still thriving. In many preserves, game scouts briefly capture rhinos and cut off their horns as a preventive measure. In some circumstances, rhinos are also moved into areas where they can be easily protected by scouts and wardens.

A tranquilized white rhino is moved to a new home where it will be safe from poachers. A cloth protects its eyes against damage.

An antipoaching patrol (left) discovers a snare in Rwanda's Virunga Mountains; snares are intended for bushbuck but often kill gorillas.

they are often killed in snares by hunters and poachers.

The situation has been exacerbated by years of horrific warfare in the Congo and Rwanda and by recent terrorist attacks in Uganda. Rangers can no longer patrol the mountain gorilla sanctuaries, and poaching is increasing. The International Gorilla Conservation Program is campaigning for funds in an attempt to re-establish ranger patrols and tourism in the gorilla territories.

Highland Wolves and Painted Dogs

Extinction also threatens the Simien wolf, a wild canid reviled by herdsmen for livestock predation. It's a bum rap: this shy predator prefers wild hares when given a chance. The wolf also competes for food with domestic dogs and cross-breeds with them. Such hybridization could eventually extirpate the wolf as a true, distinct species. Scientists are now monitoring wolf populations and eliminating hybrids, and have set up a captive breeding program. Efforts are also under way to bolster funding and regulation enforcement at the Ethiopian park in which they are found.

Another endangered canid is the African wild dog, also known as the painted wolf. No more than 5,000 of these beautiful, piebald predators

Breeding is also being facilitated in some reserves by removing calves and hand-rearing them, thus making the cows come into estrus more frequently.

Our Closest Relatives

Chimpanzees share the rhino's plight. Chimps are highly valued for medical research, since they share most of our genome. Poachers usually obtain young animals for the medical trade by killing their mothers, a double tragedy. The implacable destruction of their forest habitat by loggers and farmers has also contributed to the decline of chimpanzees, as has the insatiable appetite for "bush meat." There are thought to be fewer than 200,000 chimps living in the

wild, many in some of Africa's poorest countries, where the temptation to poach wildlife is particularly acute. In response to the crisis, an international organization known as the Committee for the Conservation and Care of Chimpanzees is producing action plans for every country in the chimp's range to facilitate preservation work.

Gorillas are also in dire trouble. While the two species of lowland gorilla number about 126,000, the mountain gorilla is on the brink of extinction; only about 630 animals survive in the rugged mountains at the borders of Rwanda, the Congo, and Uganda. The forest habitat of these gentle giants is shrinking rapidly in response to agricultural demands, and are left in the wild. Like the Simien wolf, this wide-ranging hunter is heavily persecuted by farmers whenever it leaves the game parks; it was even routinely shot inside the reserves as late as the 1970s. Wild dogs are good hunters, but they suffer when they have to compete with larger, more aggressive predators such as lions. They are also less than adept at dealing with traffic, and many wind up as road kill. But the biggest threat facing them is disease from domestic animals. Wild dogs have little natural resistance to the diseases routinely shrugged off by domestic dogs. The close social behavior of wild dogs assures that a malady will spread rapidly once an infectious agent enters a pack. Aggressive measures are under way to protect and augment wild dog populations, including captive breeding and reintroduction programs, road signs to warn motorists of their presence, and education campaigns to encourage greater tolerance by farmers.

There is one threat that affects virtually all of Africa's larger wildlife species: poaching. It is also particularly resistant to a solution, given the utter poverty afflicting most of the continent. A wild animal represents meat for a protein-starved family, and it is also a convenient source of profit. While the trade in animal contraband has slowed, it has by no means ceased. If Africa's wildlife is to survive well into the new millennium, poaching must be addressed. Most experts favor a holistic approach. Education programs help, but they must be accompanied by economic incentives so that wildlife becomes more valuable alive than dead. For many areas, ecotourism holds the greatest hope. Game farming is another approach rapidly gaining favor. Here, certain game species are "farmed" and harvested in natural habitats. This mode of agriculture protects habitat for a wide array of animals in addition to the commercially valuable species, and allows locals to have their wildlife and eat it too.

Efforts are also under way to establish corridors between preserves, providing the opportunity to resurrect some of the great game migrations of the past. Such corridors will reduce the periodic culling needed in some parks to reduce overpopulation by particularly fecund species.

Deadly Trade

Ivory has been highly valued for millennia, but only in the past century has demand for it threatened the survival of its primary source: the African elephant. The slaughter was under way in earnest by the early 20th century. Frederick Selous, a renowned white hunter of the period, sometimes killed six or more bull elephants a day; thousands of crates of tusks streamed out of Africa to Europe, where they were turned into billiard balls, piano keys, and personal adornments.

The establishment of Africa's great national parks in mid-century helped slow the killing, but poaching surged tremendously in the 1970s, fueled by an increased demand in Asia for ivory products. At the peak of the butchery, more than 100,000 elephants were shot a year. Between 1979 and 1987, Africa lost half of its elephant population. Global pressure to address the carnage compelled the Convention on International Trade in Endangered Species (CITES) to outlaw the sale of ivory. It quickly became unfashionable to display ivory trinkets in the West, and the price of ivory fell precipitously. The trade died, and the elephants prospered.

But there isn't necessarily a happy ending to the story. In 1997, Botswana, Namibia, and Zimbabwe petitioned CITES to allow a limited ivory trade with Japan. The three countries have burgeoning elephant populations and large ivory stockpiles; liquidation of the ivory, they argued, could be used to support further conservation. But it is possible that even a tightly regulated trade will stimulate poaching. If that happens, Africa's elephants may again find themselves teetering on the brink.

A pyre (right) of confiscated tusks, burned in 1987, demonstrated Kenya's commitment to stamp out poaching, but as long as there's a market for ivory, elephants will continue to die.

◆

Safari Destinations

◆

From the fertile grasslands of the Serengeti and the constantly changing waterways of the Okavango Delta to the ever-shifting sands of the Namib Desert, Africa's parks and reserves teem with an astonishing variety of wildlife.

Zululand Reserves
South Africa

CHAPTER 5

iewed from the safety of a rustic wooden hide, **Nsumo Pan**, a seasonal lakebed, is the very picture of serenity. Set against a backdrop of low hills, the tall stands of yellow fever trees that encircle the pan's shallow water radiate an eerie, almost translucent beauty as their jaundiced bark catches the afternoon sun. The hypnotic *piet-my-vrou* call of a red-chested cuckoo is accompanied by the gentle burbling of emerald-spotted doves, both drowned periodically by hadeda ibises exchanging their harsh cackles. ◆ In the center of the pan, a flotilla of pink-backed pelicans sails with disdainful pomp through a pod of equally unimpressed hippopotamuses. Yellow-billed storks and spoonbills pick methodically through the shallows, while sand plovers scurry in circles around the shore. Only visible **With coastal dunes, reed-fringed** through binoculars, a malachite kingfisher **lagoons, rustling scrub, and** hawks patiently from a low reed, an **golden grassland, Zululand** iridescent blue and orange jewel in the midst **is a virtual Eden, motherland** of a sea of green and brown. ◆ On the muddy **of all white rhinos.** verge, a family of warthogs terminates a satisfying wallow to bustle off, tails held comically erect, like hyperactive shoppers weaving determinedly through a busy supermarket. A shaggy male nyala antelope emerges from deep in the bush, its richly textured black coat glistening as it treads warily toward the water's edge, every sense alive to the possible presence of a hungry crocodile or leopard. Ponderous rather than cautious, a pair of white rhinos lumbers into view, following not their noses but their perpetually masticating mouths on a convoluted path that will, in good rhino time, lead them to the pan. ◆ Nsumo Pan is the centerpiece of **Mkuzi Game Reserve,**

Leopards, the most graceful of all the big cats, are notoriously elusive; finding them takes patience and skill.

Preceding pages: Namibia's sand dunes are the largest in the world and change hue with the desert light.

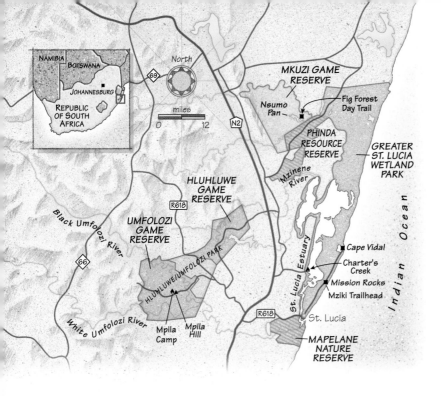

with good reason. The 237,216-acre (95,998-hectare) **Hluhluwe–Umfolozi** region harbors a quarter of the world's remaining 6,000 white (or square-lipped) rhinos. Africa's second-largest terrestrial mammal, the white rhino is an undeniably fearsome apparition, with its thick gray hide and long nasal horn. Fortunately, it is placid by nature, and as the largest exclusive grazer on Earth is generally too preoccupied with satisfying its insatiable appetite to pay much attention to human intruders. A white rhino making its way slowly through the grassland, head seemingly glued to the ground, is rather like an armor-plated lawn mower.

Hluhluwe-Umfolozi harbors elephants, lions, leopards, and buffalo, along with substantial herds of giraffes, zebras, and various antelope, most prolifically nyalas, impalas, and greater kudu. It is, however, the large number of rhinos that is most moving, only serving as a reminder that they have long been absent elsewhere in Africa. While visitors can be confident of encountering white rhinos on any given game drive, the reserve's 400 black (or hook-lipped) rhinos are altogether more elusive. This notoriously temperamental denizen of dense thicket is smaller than the white rhino, from which it can be distinguished not by coloration but by its hooked upper lip (the black and white misnomers stem from a mistranslation of the Dutch word *weit* – wide – a reference to the white rhino's squarish mouth).

Anything can – and often does – pass through the unfenced **Mpila Camp** at the heart of Umfolozi. Spotted hyenas habitually skulk around the chalets at night in search of post-barbecue scraps, and a cheetah once

one small gem in the patchwork of game reserves interspersed among the sugarcane plantations along the humid northern coastal belt of South Africa's KwaZulu-Natal province. We are in Zululand, as it's known, one of the wildest and most exciting parts of South Africa, a region of immense natural beauty and mind-boggling environmental diversity.

At the core of the Zululand Reserves lies **Greater St. Lucia Wetland Park**, Africa's largest estuarine system, a vast mangrove-lined body of saline water that was proclaimed a World Heritage Site in November 1999. To the northwest of these wetlands, Mkuzi Game Reserve and the contiguous, privately owned **Phinda Resource Reserve** protect tracts of classic African bush, teeming with big game and colorful birds. A short drive west of the estuary mouth lie the green hills of **Hluhluwe** and **Umfolozi**, two of Africa's oldest game reserves, founded in 1897 to protect the country's then-dwindling rhino population and managed as one unit following the creation of a corridor reserve in 1989.

Rhinos All Around

It is rhinos that have put the Zululand reserves on South Africa's tourist map, and

Nyala (left), members of the antelope family, usually have a single calf, and the maternal bond is strong.

The red bishop (opposite) likes reed beds and grasslands; males are often heard calling *zikzikzik zayzayzay*.

Mansiva Stream (below), in Hluhluwe–Umfolozi Game Reserve, is a lifeline for game during the dry season. When it rains, the crossing becomes impassable.

famously hurtled past in pursuit of an antelope, only to collapse panting next to the gas pump as if waiting to be refueled. All of which adds a certain spice to the short self-guided trail that runs uphill to the top of Mpila Hill, from where a vista of rolling green hills leads the eye toward the confluence of the **Black** and **White Umfolozi Rivers**. Walkers may bump into a herd of zebras or nyalas along the trail while cocking an eye skyward for a hovering black-shouldered kite, or a flock of vultures riding the thermals.

Forest, Lagoon, Dunes

Traditionally the preserve of dedicated anglers, the western shore of the **St. Lucia Estuary**, along the Indian Ocean coast between Maputo and Durban, sidesteps Zululand's nascent tourist circuit. Especially rewarding are the footpaths that run through the thick coastal forest at **Charter's Creek**. Here, the shy red duiker, one of South Africa's smallest and most attractive antelope, is often seen tiptoeing furtively through the campsite, while deeper in the forest

A Nile crocodile (right), fresh from three months in its egg, starts a new life at St. Lucia Estuary.

Cheetahs (below) rest through the heat of the day, hidden in the tall grass of Phinda.

one may encounter a warthog scuffling among the roots, a male nyala standing proudly in the shadows, or a troop of vervet monkeys clucking and squabbling in the canopy.

Zululand's bird life is legendary, and one of the joys of this coastal forest is the multitude of birdcalls. Sight yields to sound as tambourine doves call softly and mournfully from high in the thickets, and the brilliant blue-and-orange Natal robin emits a medley of clear melodies from deep within the undergrowth. But the most striking of Zululand's forest birds is

the trumpeter hornbill: a rooster-sized Dr. Seuss creation famed for its comically oversized bill and distressing cat-in-a-mangle wail. Charter's Creek is a good place to view local specialties such as Rudd's apalis and gray waxbill, both endemic to a small region of northern Zululand and southern Mozambique.

Altogether different in character, the eastern shore of St. Lucia is best explored from a rutted 20-mile (32-km) road that runs through the sliver of sandy land dividing the estuary from the ocean. Beginning at the town of **St. Lucia**, on the mouth of the estuary, and terminating at the heavenly beach at **Cape Vidal**, this is a lovely drive, passing through the world's tallest forested dune field and a variety of habitats, ranging from dense forest to reedy marshes. At **Mission Rocks**, a short footpath leads to

White Rhinos of Umfolozi

First observed by a Westerner, William Burchill, in 1817, the white rhinoceros was hunted so extensively that as few as 30 individuals survived in southern Africa by 1897, when the Umfolozi Game Reserve was established to protect its last stronghold.

Ever since, the rangers at Umfolozi fought a long, solitary battle to ensure the survival of this gentle giant, culminating in the 1960s with the first rhino translocation from Umfolozi to elsewhere in southern Africa. It is estimated that 6,000 white rhinos survive in the wild, practically all of them in southern Africa. It is doubtful that there's even one surviving white rhino which isn't descended from the Umfolozi herd. Elsewhere, an estimated 20 white rhinos cling precariously to life in the **Garamba Game Reserve**, deep in the Democratic Republic of the Congo, all that stands between the discrete northern race of white rhino and total extinction.

Young rhinos (above) aren't weaned until two years old and take five to seven years to reach maturity.

A tourist (below) uses binoculars to scan the shore during a bird-watching cruise of St. Lucia Estuary.

the top of a dune overlooking the rocky shores and turquoise waters of the Indian Ocean to the east and the vast St. Lucia Estuary to the west. A little farther down the road, a 20-minute walk leads to a pair of hides overlooking two small lakes populated by hippos, birds, and a steady stream of greater kudu, bushbucks, and reedbucks that come here to drink. Boat trips regularly explore the banks of the lagoonlike estuary, where crocodiles and river sharks wait patiently together for scraps from a careless fisherman or pelican.

Exclusive Animals

Tourist development in Zululand is generally low-key, making it an ideal area to explore over a few days in a private vehicle. The exception to this is Phinda Resource Reserve, a private conservancy abutting Mkuzi Game Reserve. Part neglected farmland, part hunting concession before it was bought by the Conservation Corporation in 1991, the new reserve was immediately subjected to a cleanup operation in which 15 tons of scrap metal were removed. The small number of skittish animals then resident in the 34,594-acre (14,000-hectare) reserve was boosted by an ambitious program of reintroductions, including lions, cheetahs, elephants, white rhinos, and most recently buffalo. Today, Phinda offers an upmarket safari experience

comparable to any in Africa, while its finely honed conservation program has already resulted in such an increase in the numbers of lions and cheetahs that more have been translocated from the reserve than were originally reintroduced there in 1992.

Four superlative luxury lodges scattered around the property make Phinda special, but the foremost attraction here is the game. Open vehicles with expert guides approach to within yards of lions and cheetahs in this carefully managed tract of bush. Another delight is the boat trips

along the **Mzinene River**, where crocodiles, antelope, and a huge variety of birds are likely to be observed. Two of the most sought-after birds in southern Africa, the white-backed night heron and African finfoot, are regularly spotted here. The river also supports a few breeding pairs of thick-billed weavers, which construct neat, basketlike nests.

The common waterbuck (left) rarely strays far from water. Its oily fur adds an unpleasant taste to its flesh but doesn't deter hungry lions, its principal predators.

A young giraffe (right) is cleaned by its mother.

Phinda's Rock Lodge (below) offers air-conditioned luxury in the heart of the bush.

Joining the Patches

Zululand today is in a state of transition, but the merging of Hluhluwe and Umfolozi in 1989 is pointing the way forward. Greater St. Lucia Wetland Park is a recent creation, forged from a number of previously disjointed small reserves. The eventual removal of the fence between Phinda and Mkuzi also seems a certainty, a step that would allow large animals such as lions – currently absent from Mkuzi – an extra 98,800 acres (40,000 hectares) in which to expand their territory.

For many conservationists working in the area, the dream is that one day the entire complex of Zululand reserves will be inter-linked, restoring the animals' freedom to migrate seasonally within the broader ecosystem and enriching the genetic stock of species currently pocketed into numerous small enclaves. If this dream can be realized without affecting the livelihood of the sub-sistence farmers who eke out an existence in the areas between the reserves, elephants may once again range freely between the green hills of the Zululand interior and the shores of the Indian Ocean – cause for rejoicing, indeed.

DETAILS

When to Go

Every season in Zululand has its advantages. During the wet summer months (November–April), birding is at its best and the scenery is verdant. But then there's the heat (85°–95°F/ 20°–35°C at midday) and humidity, and the increased risk of contracting malaria. The scenery is not as captivating during the dry winter months, but game is more visible once the foliage recedes, and temperatures are more bearable, with highs between 70°F and 80°F (21°–27°C).

Getting There

Enter South Africa via Cape Town or Johannesburg. SAA runs regular flights from both cities to Durban, which has the nearest major airport to Zululand. The roads are good, and cars can be rented in Durban. Most coach tours pass through Zululand, generally limiting their exploration to a game drive in Hluhluwe-Umfolozi and a visit to a Zulu cultural lodge. Phinda Resource Reserve offers upmarket fly-in packages from Johannesburg or Durban. The popular Baz Bus (8 Rosedene Road, Sea Point, Cape Town 8001; tel: +27-21-439 2323; web: www.bazbus.com) connects many sights in South Africa.

Trails have been marked in several reserves, notably the three-night Mziki Trail in Greater St. Lucia Wetland Park. Guided wilderness trails in Umfolozi offer the opportunity to stalk rhinos on foot. The guided Fig Forest Day Trail in Mkuzi is a must for birders. Day walks and night drives can be arranged on the spot; overnight hiking trails and guided wilderness trails should be booked in advance through KwaZulu-Natal Nature Conservation Service. Hotels and agencies in the town of St. Lucia offer boat trips on the estuary and game drives in nearby reserves; arrange these as you go.

INFORMATION

KwaZulu-Natal Nature Conservation Service

P.O. Box 13069, Cascades 3202, Pietermaritzburg, South Africa; tel: +27-331-845 1000; fax: +27-331-845 1001.

South Africa Embassies

United Kingdom: South Africa House, Trafalgar Square, London WC2N 8DP; tel: +44-20-7451 7299; fax: +44-20-930 1510; web: www.southafricahouse.com

United States: 3051 Massachusetts Avenue, N.W., Washington, DC 20008; tel: 202-232-4400; fax: 202-265-1607.

South Africa Tourist Board

P Bag X164, Pretoria, South Africa 0001; tel: +27-12-482 6200; fax: +27-12-347 8753; web: www.satour.co.uk

United Kingdom: 5–6 Alt Grove, Wimbledon, London SW19 4DZ; tel: +44-20-8944 8080; fax: +44-20-8944 6705; e-mail: satour@satbuk.demon.co.uk

United States: 500 Fifth Avenue, 20th Floor, Suite 2040, New York, NY 10110; tel: 212-730-2929; fax: 212-764-1980; e-mail: satourny@aol.com

Tourism Kwazulu-Natal

Station Building, 160 Pine Street, Durban, South Africa; tel: 031-304 7144; fax: 031-305 6693; e-mail: tkzn@iafrica.com; web: www.tourism-kzn.org.za

CAMPING

KwaZulu-Natal Nature Conservation Service

P.O. Box 13069, Cascades 3202, Pietermaritzburg, South Africa; tel: +27-331-845 1000; fax: +27-331-845 1001.

With the exception of Hluhluwe-Umfolozi, there are good campsites in most of the Zululand reserves. The Nature Conservation Service handles bookings. $

LODGING

PRICE GUIDE – double occupancy

$ = under $100 $$ = $100–$200
$$$ = $200–$300 $$$$ = $300+

Hilltop Camp

KwaZulu-Natal Nature Conservation Service, P.O. Box 13069, Cascades 3202, Pietermaritzburg, South Africa; tel: +27-331-845 1000; fax: +27-331-845 1001.

Perched on a hill in Hluhluwe Game Reserve, this camp has chalets that are luxurious by Conservation Service standards. It has a restaurant and a well-stocked shop. $$

Isinkwe Backpackers

P.O. Box 473, Hluhluwe, South Africa; tel/fax: +27-35-562 2258; e-mail: isinkwe@saol.com

This small hostel is in a patch of bush 10 miles (16 km) from the town of Hluhluwe. Inexpensive game drives to Hluhluwe and Mkuzi Game Reserves are offered in open vehicles. $

Mpila Camp

KwaZulu-Natal Nature Conservation Service, P.O. Box 13069, Cascades 3202, Pietermaritzburg, South Africa; tel: +27-331-845 1000; fax: +27-331-845 1001.

This unfenced self-catering camp in Umfolozi Game Reserve has new "safari units" that offer tented accommodations similar to those of a private game reserve. The store sells a few basics. $

Ndumo Wilderness Camp

United Kingdom: Outposts, Narracott, Drewsteignton, Exeter, Devon EX6 6PU; tel: +44-164-728 1665; fax: +44-164-728 1288;

e-mail: outposts@usa.net

United States: Tim Farrell and Associates, P.O. Box 7300, Wilton, CT 06897-7300; tel: 203-762-8050; fax: 203-762-7323; e-mail: SafariTim@aol.com

This tented camp in Ndumo Game Reserve has a rustic bush atmosphere. This is a great birding spot. $$$.

Phinda Resource Reserve

CCAfrica, P Bag X27, Benmore 2010, South Africa; tel: +27-11-809 4300; fax: +27-11-809 4400; e-mail: bookings@ccafrica.com; web:www.ccafrica.com

Four world-class lodges within a private reserve feature knowledgeable rangers, superb game viewing, and impeccable service and food. The Forest and Mountain Lodges are larger and relatively more affordable than the more intimate Vlei and Rock Lodges. $$$$

TOUR OPERATORS

Maputaland Tours

P.O. Box 221, St. Lucia 3936, South Africa; tel/fax: +27-35-590 1041; e-mail: maputaland@futurenet.co.za; web: www.zululand.co.za/maputaland

Tour guides based in St. Lucia lead day trips to most of the reserves in the surrounding area.

Tekwini Tours

Postnet Suite 150, P Bag X504, Northway 4065, South Africa; tel: +27-31-303 1199; e-mail: tekwini@global.co.za; web: www.tekwiniecotours.co.za

Three-day tours designed for backpackers explore Hluhluwe-Umfolozi and Greater St. Lucia Wetland Park.

Zulu Safaris

P.O. Box 802, Hilton 3245, South Africa; tel: +27-33-234 4466; e-mail: zulusaf@iafrica.com

All tours are guided by former conservation service rangers and can cater to special interests such as birding or coastal wildlife.

Excursions

The Drakensberg

KwaZulu-Natal Nature Conservation Service, P.O. Box 13069, Cascades 3202, Pietermaritzburg, South Africa; tel: +27-331-845 1000; fax: +27-331-845 1001.

The extent of South Africa's highest mountain range, at the southern tip of the Great Rift Valley, is only truly appreciated when one realizes that Lesotho, on the western slopes, is the only country in the world entirely above 6,300 feet (1,920m) in elevation. Enough footpaths cross the eastern South African slopes to keep an enthusiastic hiker busy for months. Giants Castle is recommended for superb prehistoric rock art and relatively dense concentrations of game. Royal Natal Park is in the most spectacular part of the range, dominated by a vast rock wall called the Amphitheatre.

Eshowe

Tourism Kwazulu-Natal, Station Building, 160 Pine Street, Durban; tel: 031-304 7144; fax: 031-305 6693; e-mail: tkzn@iafrica.com; web: www.tourism-kzn.org.za

The core of the original Zulu Empire, between Eshowe and Ulundi, is home to a clutch of Zulu cultural villages. The most famous, Shakaland, built as the set for the television series Shaka Zulu, is perhaps a little too slick. Altogether earthier, Simunye Zulu Lodge is reached by ox-drawn wagon, allowing overnight visitors to slow down to the pace of rural African life. The little colonial town of Eshowe has an old fort from the Anglo-Zulu War, and a small patch of mist-belt forest that offers great birding.

Maputaland Reserves

KwaZulu-Natal Nature Conservation Service, P.O. Box 13069, Cascades 3202, Pietermaritzburg, South Africa; tel: +27-331-845 1000; fax: +27-331-845 1001.

This cluster of reserves along the Mozambican border offers a variety of attractions. Tiny Ndumo Game Reserve has a healthy population of white and black rhinos and is routinely cited as the top birding spot in South Africa, with more than 400 bird species. The rich coral reefs of Sodwana Bay attract divers. Lake Sibaya is the largest natural freshwater body in South Africa, and Tembe Game Reserve has large herds of elephants.

Kruger
National Park
South Africa

CHAPTER **6**

The main road to the rest-camp at **Satara** winds through thorn-tree country: flat yellow savanna, splotched with venerable, weather-beaten anthills. A young lion, sated and panting, lies heart-stoppingly close to the roadside, his prey – a half-eaten giraffe – sprawled beside him. "Ja, this is a new thing the lions have learned," whispers the veteran South African visitor in the vehicle alongside your own. "Hooves slip on tarmac when the animals run fast. So the lions chase them onto the roads, then close in for the kill." ◆ Like its lions, **Kruger National Park** – South Africa's largest and most famous conservation area – is learning to adapt. Ever since apartheid ended and a new government came to power in 1994, the rationale behind its very existence has been the subject of heated debate. ◆ From its inception in 1899, black South Africans were denied access to the park except as poorly rewarded labor. Now there have been claims for land compensation from the impoverished rural communities living on its borders,

Seasoned travelers may prefer a more remote destination, but Kruger is perfect for first-timers, with superb game-viewing, easy access, and comfortable accommodations.

even calls for Kruger to be completely redistributed and given over to subsistence farming. ◆ Haunted though it is by a history of enforced exclusions, one thing is clear: this is indisputably one of the world's great wildlife sanctuaries. Stretching for some 7,520 square miles (19,480 sq km) along South Africa's northeastern border, this magnificent slice of wild lowveld (low country) is only slightly smaller than Israel. It has many moods and faces, thanks to more than a dozen different ecozones – from mountain bushveld and dense bushwillow woodlands to lush riverine systems and

Cheetah cubs remain with their mother for as long as two years. Hunting lessons begin at about six months, when the mother brings small game for the cubs to practice capturing and killing.

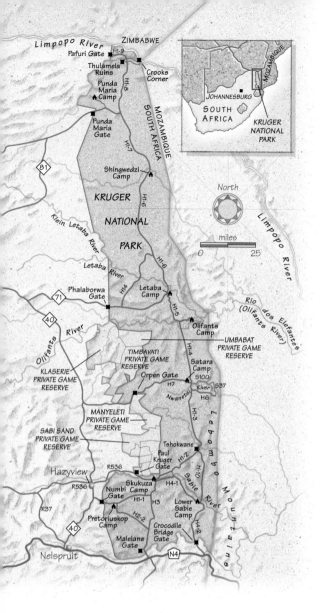

supermarket, filling station, and restaurant, Kruger is modeled along much the same lines as the big American national parks. Consequently, some safari purists turn up their noses, complaining that the infrastructure is simply too developed for a true wilderness experience.

In some areas (and especially during school holidays in summer), you do run the risk of sharing your sightings with a jam of up to 30 cars and even the occasional tour bus, everyone craning for a better look. Nor can you simply put your foot down on the accelerator and hurtle across the grassy savanna to any game you spot. You must stick to the roads and stay inside your vehicle.

But for those who prefer the do-it-yourself approach, this is one of the easiest parks in Africa for self-guided tours. The sheer variety of wildlife is astonishing, and most of the animals are so used to the presence of humans that they don't run away when vehicles stop. What's more, it offers productive game viewing year-round, and there are camps at prices affordable to almost everyone, a sadly rare commodity across Africa these days.

Southern Tip

Southern Kruger has both the widest range of landscapes and the greatest concentrations of big game – and tourists. Busiest of all is **Skukuza**, the park's administrative center, reached via **Paul Kruger Gate** some 26 miles (42km) east of **Hazyview** on the R536.

Toward the end of winter, when the veldt, or savanna, is at its driest, animals tend to congregate at dams and rivers to wait for the rains. The road from park headquarters to beautiful **Lower Sabie Camp** winds southeast alongside the **Sabie River**, where half-submerged hippos gaze lugubriously at the buffalo snorting and stamping around the water's edge, kicking up great clouds of orange dust. A crocodile curls on a rock like a question mark, while giraffes regally splay their legs and stretch their endless necks down to drink. A family of warthogs –

thorny savanna. And it's home to more animal species than any other park in Africa, including a staggering 507 bird, 147 mammal, 118 reptile, and 34 amphibian species.

The People's Park

With an extensive web of tarmac and gravel roads linking rest-camps, each with its own

tufted tails erect – trot briskly toward a mud slick for a communal wallow.

Visit between November and March, though, and you'll find the reed-fringed riverbanks abuzz with the raucous chatter of the black-and-yellow masked weaver birds busily putting the finishing touches to round basket-nests that dangle precariously above the water. Indeed, summer is when all of Kruger's resident birds don their bright breeding plumage and many of the large mammal species have their young.

The flat country northwest of **Malelane Gate** in the park's southern section is one place you might see the rangy, brindled African wild dog. Consider yourself lucky if you do; this is one of Kruger's most elusive and endangered species. As recently as the 1970s, wild dogs were considered vicious pests and were even shot in the park by rangers. Now there are fewer than

A masked weaver (left) builds a dangling nest of reeds and shoots.

Hippo fights (opposite, bottom) are common between rival males; their stubby teeth and powerful jaws can cause fatal wounds.

Wild dogs (below) are Africa's most efficient hunters but have become the most endangered of all carnivores due to habitat loss.

5,000 left across Africa, and Kruger has more than 360 of them.

Farther north lies the park's wettest and most mountainous region. Bustling **Pretoriuskop**, the main rest-camp in this area (and the park's oldest), is another easy drive from Hazyview – just 17 miles (27km) via **Numbi Gate**. Sable antelope, kudu, and zebras forage in the surrounding bush-willow woodlands, and this is also a good place to spot bulky white rhinos, trotting between thorn trees on incongruously dainty hooves and tearing at the withered grass with their great shovel-shaped lips.

Lion Heart

South of the **Olifants River**, great swaths of stunted knob-thorn and marula-tree savanna spread east as far as the foot-hills of Mozambique's Lebombo Mountains. These hot, scrubby plains are the grazing grounds of zebras, wildebeests, and impalas, as well as their hungry predators: leopards, cheetahs, wild dogs, and lions. In fact, central Kruger is home to one of the largest concentrations of lions in the world, so the odds of sighting one are good.

Busy Satara is second only to Skukuza in size, and like that camp suffers from a rather regimented design and impersonal atmosphere. Birders love it, though: the tall mahogany and sausage trees that shade the grounds are a magnet for buffalo weavers and glossy starlings (if you settle for a pic-nic lunch outside your chalet, keep a sharp eye on your fries).

The road that winds through the open country east of Satara hugs the **Nwanetsi River** for some 19 miles (41km); this is an outstand-ing game drive, good for sighting not just the browsers and grazers drawn to the water but the big cats who prey on them. **Tshokwane** picnic site, about 25 miles (40km) from camp on the road south to Skukuza, is another hot spot for lions, but it sees a lot traffic as a result.

The predators provide plenty of high drama but be alert for interesting subplots – dainty, ballerina-like klipspringer antelope, for example, are often spotted on the boulder-speckled hills just north of **Olifants Camp**. Look out, too, for the baby pangolin hitching a ride on its mother's back as she scuttles across the dusty road, or the bateleur eagle careening down from a dark blue sky on black-and-white wings, its fierce eyes glinting in the sun.

Spread along a bend in the river from which it takes its name, **Letaba** is one of the park's prettiest camps, although, inexplicably, very few huts were built with river views. This is good elephant country: you may find yourself warily edging your vehicle into reverse as a solitary bull strolls across the road, supremely con-fident of his right of way. The most civilized vantage point is the camp restaurant's long

The Big Five

The idea of a Big Five dates from the mid-19th century, when safaris were led by "Great White Hunters" intent on shooting wild animals for trophies. Inevitably, some creatures were more prized than others, thanks to the skill it took to track them, the risk involved in confronting them, and the quality of the trophy retrieved.

Based on these criteria, the five animals that every hunter wanted to bag were the elephant, lion, leopard, rhino, and buffalo. The sport decimated game populations, yet remained fashionable. Indeed, when the Sabie Game Reserve (Kruger's oldest section) was established in 1899, the initial intention was to create a reserve of breeding stock to supply the future needs of hunters.

Today, of course, hunting is strictly controlled, but for modern safari visitors armed with nothing more lethal than a long lens or a video camera, the Big Five retain their cachet.

A secretary bird (above) hunts on foot and is fond of snakes, though it also eats lizards and mice. It's named after its crest, which is said to resemble quill pens behind the ear of a secretary.

A male lion (left), his face bloodied by a fresh kill, has a short and violent life in the wild, using his great strength and stamina in continual fights for supremacy against rival males.

veranda. It overlooks the **Letaba River**, and guests can join the elephants for a sundown drink – a pint glass for the people, a noisy gallon per trunkful for the elephants.

To the Limpopo

Few visitors ever stray into the northern Kruger, and it's true that these arid brown plains dusted with giant, twisted baobabs lack the concentration and variety of game found in the south. Yet its fans swear by the stark beauty of the landscape and the game-spotting challenges it presents. This is where you'll see larger antelope such as sable, tsessebe, and the elusive nyala, along with lovely birds like the Cape parrot and tropical boubou. It's also fine country for elephants.

Shingwedzi is the largest of the three northern rest-camps, but remote **Punda Maria**, with its quaint 1930s huts set amid tall jackalberry and nyala trees, is one of the most appealing in the park.

Unashamed Luxury

Much of Kruger's western boundary is fringed by a series of private reserves, which together make up the famous wilderness areas of **Sabi Sand** and **Timbavati**, along with the less-well-known **Klaserie**, **Umbabat**, and **Manyeleti**. Over the past few years, a string of upmarket lodges offering a five-star safari experience has opened here. In 1993, all fences between them were pulled down, so wildlife from Kruger can move unimpeded across the region and sometimes right through the camps, with elephants and hippos among the regular visitors.

Here, with people paying hundreds of dollars a day, nothing is left to chance and Big Five sightings are almost guaranteed. Small, exclusive lodges, none housing more than 24 guests, are set along rivers and

Hikers (top) survey the landscape from a granite outcropping. Guided hikes sell out well in advance; make reservations early.

Sure-footed klipspringers (left) are often seen perched on boulders.

A warthog's tusks (left) are formidable weapons used primarily for defense.

Zebra stripes (below) are designed to disorient predators in the heat of the chase.

waterholes, and guests can view game from their private quarters. Escorted from luxury chalet to open Jeep, visitors plunge into deep bush, halting only a claw's length away from wildlife scouted out by trackers a few hours before. The vehicles stay in contact by radio so no rare sightings are missed.

Facing the Future

This competition has belatedly spurred Kruger into an image change. Gone are the days when surly wardens kept tourists waiting in the broiling sun outside locked rest-camp gates while they took a lunch break. Now, the gates stay open all day, as do the gas stations and stores. Some of the stricter rules – such as the one prohibiting the sale of alcohol in camp supermarkets – have been relaxed.

Along with an ever-widening choice of accommodations, there is an adventurous package of outdoor activities to sign up for, including escorted game drives and long-distance walks in the wild. Many of Kruger's more elusive inhabitants – from leopards to spotted hyenas – are best spotted on organized night drives offered by the larger camps.

Management has also begun to acknowledge that Kruger has a cultural history as well as splendid natural assets; in fact, research has revealed it to be something of an archaeological treasure-house. Visitors can now take guided tours of **Thulamela**, the ruins of a major Iron Age settlement recently unearthed on a mountain near the park's Zimbabwean border.

Ranger Training

Kruger puts all its new field rangers through an intensive training program. Recruits, who must be at least 18 and have a high school diploma, are given a six-week grounding in such basics as the history and geology of the park, spoor identification and tracking, map reading and first aid, and the astronomy of the southern skies. Flora and fauna identification and animal behavior all play a key part in practical field exercises.

In recent years the threat posed by poaching has taken center stage. Recruits are also trained in paramilitary and counterinsurgency techniques so that they can defend themselves against modern-day poachers armed with automatic weapons. The park's eastern boundary forms South Africa's border with Mozambique, so Kruger's rangers must also learn to act as impromptu border guards. Tourists looking for something extra can participate in a few days of ranger training at **Sabi Sabi**, one of the exclusive lodges on the edge of Kruger.

Exploring on foot (above) is the best way to learn the secrets of the bush.

A praying mantis (below) is easily mistaken for a twig. It creeps along slowly before seizing its prey.

Perhaps the most ambitious project in the pipeline is a proposal to pull down the fences along Kruger's Mozambican and Zimbabwean borders, nearly doubling the protected area and establishing the world's largest national park. Such a hugely extended Kruger would not only encompass complete ecosystems but allow the resumption of the traditional east-west migration of species such as zebras, wildebeests, and elephants (at the moment, Kruger's elephants have to be culled or translocated to other parks on a regular basis in order to maintain their numbers at a manageable 7,000).

Of course, this would make Kruger an even greater tourist draw and an important source of foreign currency (sizable cuts in the park's government subsidy have caused accommodation rates to soar, turning vacations here into a luxury few South Africans can afford). And in the "new" South Africa, this fine vision may come to nothing without community support. "We have to foster a sense of responsibility toward the place among all the stakeholders here," says environmental education manager Gert Erasmus. "If local people don't benefit from the park, naturally there will be hostility."

Staff now meet local leaders on a regular basis to discuss how the border villages can benefit from Kruger's resources – everything from access to water and firewood to jobs in tourism. An accessible environmental education program is under way, too, attracting busloads of schoolchildren and community groups on investigative day trips.

Small steps, perhaps, but important ones, for they underline a paradox. South Africa's flagship conservation area is no natural wilderness. If Kruger National Park is to survive its next hundred years, it will have to manage the world outside its borders as well as the wildlife within.

DETAILS

When to Go

Kruger is rewarding year-round, but best seen during the dry winter season, from April to August, when daytime temperatures average 70°F (21°C) to 80°F (27°C). Nights, however, can be very cold, and rest-camp rondavels, or basic chalets, are unheated. The rainy season, from November to March, is humid and hot, with daytime temperatures reaching 100°F (38°C). In summer, Kruger is malarial and prone to thunderstorms, but midsummer (December to February) is when many birds and large mammals bear their young.

Getting There

Enter South Africa via Johannesburg International Airport. SAA runs regular flights from Johannesburg to the park's headquarters, Skukuza, where private lodges collect passengers. Other local airports are in Hoedspruit and Nelspruit. Car rentals are available at all, and Kruger is probably the most driver-friendly park in Africa.

By road, there are eight gates along the park's southern and western borders. From Johannesburg, it's about 255 miles (410km) along the N4 to Malelane Gate, in the far south, or via Hazyview to the Paul Kruger Gate near Skukuza. Gates and camps open at dawn and close at night, so allow plenty of time to reach your camp, or you could be fined for arriving late. Day and night game drives aboard an open vehicle, guided by an experienced ranger, are available from most park camps. They can be booked at the warden's office, or through private operators.

Kruger's long-distance walks in the wild are led by experienced, armed rangers. Three-night excursions operate out of seven base camps, with accommodations in rustic huts.

INFORMATION

Mpumalanga Tourism Authority

P.O. Box 679, Nelspruit 1200 (N4 Highway, Halls Getaway Building, Block F), South Africa; tel: +27-13-752 7001; fax: +27-13-759 5441; e-mail: mtanlpsa@cis.co.za; web: www.mpumalanga.com

South Africa Embassies

United Kingdom: South Africa House, Trafalgar Square, London WC2N 8DP; tel: +44-20-7451 7299; fax: +44-20-930 1510; web: www.southafricahouse.com

United States: 3051 Massachusetts Avenue, N.W., Washington, DC 20008; tel: 202-232-4400; fax: 202-265-1607.

South Africa National Parks

P.O. Box 787, 613 Leyds Street, Pretoria 0001, South Africa; tel: +27-12-343 1991, fax: +27-12-343 0905; e-mail: reservations@parks-sa.co.za; web: www.parks-sa.co.za

South Africa Tourist Board

P Bag X164, Pretoria 0001, South Africa; tel: +27-12-482 6200; fax: +27-12-347 8753; web: www.satour.co.uk

United Kingdom: 5–6 Alt Grove, Wimbledon, London SW19 4DZ; tel: +44-20-8944 8080; fax: +44-20-8944 6705; e-mail: satour@satbuk.demon.co.uk

United States: 500 Fifth Avenue, 20th Floor, Suite 2040, New York, NY 10110; tel: 212-730-2929; fax: 212-764-1980; e-mail: satourny@aol.com

CAMPING

Kruger National Park

South African National Parks, P.O. Box 787, 613 Leyds Street, Pretoria 0001, South Africa; tel: +27-12-343 1991, fax: +27-12-343 0905; e-mail: reservations@parks-sa.co.za; web: www.parks-sa.co.za

There are campgrounds at all rest-camps, at Balule bushveld camp, and at Malelane bush lodge. All have communal kitchens and washing facilities; cooking utensils, dishes, and silverware are not provided. A maximum of six people is permitted per site. $

LODGING

PRICE GUIDE – double occupancy

$ = under $100 $$ = $100–$200
$$$ = $200–$300 $$$$ = $300+

Kruger National Park

South African National Parks, P.O. Box 787, 613 Leyds Street, Pretoria 0001, South Africa; tel: +27-12-343 1991, fax: +27-12-343 0905; e-mail: reservations@parks-sa.co.za; web: www.parks-sa.co.za

Travelers wishing to stay in the park have several options. Each of the five secluded bush lodges must be booked as a whole. The biggest, Roodewal and Malelane, sleep up to 19 in cottages and bungalows; the smallest, Jock of the Bushveld, sleeps 12. Only Malelane has electricity. There are kitchen facilities, but bring all supplies except bedding.

Nine small, remote bushveld camps offer seclusion, with no shops or restaurants. Each has up to 10 self-catering cottages that sleep no fewer than four people. $

Each of Kruger's 10 rest-camps has electricity, a store, a restaurant, and communal cooking facilities. Self-catering accommodations range from cottages with private baths for six people to basic two-person huts with communal washing facilities. Pretoriuskop, Mopani, Shingwedzi, and Berg-en-dal camps have pools; Skukuza, a good-sized village, has a bank, post office, and golf course. $-$$

Londolozi and Ngala Lodges

CCAfrica, P Bag X27, Benmore 2010, South Africa; tel: +27-11-809 4300; fax: +27-11-809 4400; e-mail: bookings@ccafrica.com; web:www.ccafrica.com

Londolozi in the Sabi Sand Game Reserve just outside Kruger is famous for its big cats. Its three camps provide a romantic colonial atmosphere, including candlelit dinners under the stars. Ngala Lodge is in the central Timbavati area. $$$–$$$$

Mala Mala

Sabi Sand Game Reserve, P.O. Box 2575, Randburg 2125, South Africa; tel: +27-11-789 2677; fax: +27-11-886 4382; e-mail: jhb@malamala.com; web: www.malamala.com

Celebrities and the very rich flock to this luxurious private reserve, regarded as one of the world's finest. $$$$

Sabi Sabi

Sabi Sand Game Reserve, P.O. Box 52665, Saxonwold 2132, South Africa; tel: +27-11-483 3939; fax: +27-11-483 3799; e-mail: res@sabisabi.com; web: www.sabisabi.com

A long-standing private reserve, Sabi Sabi is in deep bush on the banks of the Sabie River. Selati is the most exclusive of three lodges, with eight colonial-style thatched suites lit by oil lamps. The larger Bush and River Lodges have more of a hotel atmosphere, but all three offer good food and service and first-class game drives. $$$–$$$$

TOUR OPERATORS

Welcome Tours

P.O. Box 1127, 582 Lepelaar Road, Hazyview 1242, South Africa; tel: +27-13-737 7945; fax: +27-13-737 6293; e-mail: rroux@welcome.co.za; web: www.welcome.co.za

Half- and full-day guided tours into the park leave from Numbi Gate daily at dawn. Meals and refreshments are not included.

Excursions

Blyde River Canyon

Mpumalanga Tourism Authority, P.O. Box 679, N4 Highway, Halls Getaway Building, Block F, Nelspruit 1200, South Africa; tel: +27-13-752 7001; fax: +27-13-759 5441; e-mail: mtanlpsa@cis.co.za; web: www.mpumalanga.com

A scenic nature reserve crisscrossed by walking trails encompasses 11-mile (18-km) Blyde Canyon, South Africa's answer to Arizona's Grand Canyon. Bird life includes a breeding colony of the rare bald ibis. The road south to Graskop leads along the canyon rim and Drakensberg escarpment past viewing sites such as God's Window, where cliff outposts frame breathtaking views of the lowveld.

Pilanesberg National Park

P.O. Box 1201, Mogwase 0305, South Africa; tel: +27-14-535 5355; web: www. tourismnorthwest.co.za

Thanks to a major relocation program, this extensive park is home to some 10,000 animals (including the Big Five) and more than 300 species of birds. The park is spread around a volcanic crater near Sun City in northwest South Africa. There are good roads and walking trails. Accommodations range from luxury lodges to self-catering, tented bushveld camps.

Swaziland

Ministry of Tourism, Environment, and Communications, P.O. Box 2652, Mbabane, Swaziland, tel: +268-4044 556; web: www.realnet.co.sz

This tiny, landlocked kingdom is an easy drive southeast of Kruger National Park. It has no less than five main parks and reserves of its own, all impressively well-stocked and maintained, with landscapes ranging from rain forest to misty highlands, towering mountains to subtropical bush. The pick of the bunch is Hlane Royal National Park, 65 miles (104km) northeast of the capital, Mbabane. Hlane has lions, elephants, hippos, and white rhinos. The local culture is fascinating, too, with royal ritual centers on Lobamba in the Ezulwini Valley.

Okavango Delta
Botswana

CHAPTER **7**

Forty million years ago, three powerful rivers – the Okavango, Kwando, and Zambezi – crashed down from the Benguela Highlands in what is now Angola. As they met the flatlands, all three spilled into a vast superlake estimated to cover some 30,000 square miles (78,000 sq km), an area the size of France. From here they journeyed eastward, joining the Gariep and Limpopo Rivers, eventually reaching the sea in Mozambique. Then the earth began to heave. At first, fault lines blocked off the Kwando and Zambezi, turning them east onto their modern paths and creating the first gorge of Victoria Falls. The Okavango, left on its own, was simply unable to sustain the superlake, and when the eastern Gumara and southern Thamalakane faults developed along its path, it gave up the unequal struggle and subsided, soggily, into the sand. The **Okavango Delta** was born. ◆ This magnificent wetland, astonishingly not yet included on the UNESCO World Heritage list, is one of the

Constantly shifting waterways flood and recede, nourishing a stunning diversity of flora and fauna.

greatest natural wonders in the world, an oasis on a vast scale, covering an area roughly the size of Massachusetts in northern Botswana. It floats on the world's largest sea of sand, the Kalahari, which covers a massive 970,000 square miles (2.5 million sq km) from South Africa to the Congo and is, in places, up to 1,000 feet (300m) deep. It is this cushion of sand which protects visitors to the delta from the ongoing seismic upheavals deep beneath their feet. Up to 40 earthquakes are recorded in the region each year. ◆ Above ground, however, it is water that rules. The only per-manent water is the sluggish **Okavango River**, which perpetually carves out new channels and oxbows as islets form and block its path. The rest is as

A dugout canoe, poled by a local guide, is the best way to explore the myriad waterways and glassy lagoons of the Okavango Delta.

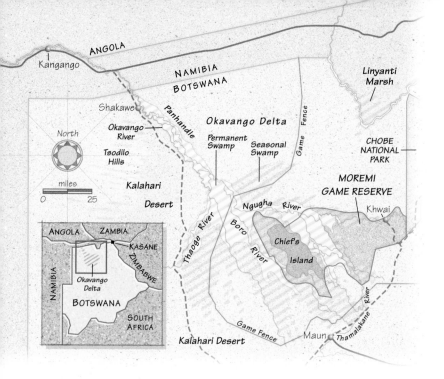

fragile wetlands hangs in the balance.

Humans have lived on the fringes of the delta for at least 100,000 years. Today, the area has a total population of only 40,000, 70 percent of whom live off the land and earn no salary. The first known inhabitants were the aboriginal Banoka (River Bushmen). Within the past 200 years they have been joined by the Bayei, the Hambukushu, Batawana, baKalahari, the ovaHerero and, most recently, refugees from war-torn Angola, who live in 13 settlements on the western edge.

The only protected area of the whole delta is **Moremi Game Reserve**, on the eastern edge; much of the rest is held under a series of huge private concessions with strict guidelines on usage and land management. A game fence, designed to stop the spread of foot-and-mouth disease, runs through the middle of the delta. There are some camps to the west of the fence, but most of the lodges are to the east, where the quality of game is much better.

This sparse scattering of exclusive camps has become the easiest way to navigate around the region – at least they remain in one place. With the watercourses shifting

fickle as the seasons. With the onset of the rains, brief but torrential summer storms fill outlying shallow pans, and once a year floodwater gushes down from the highlands to spill across the plains. In most years, the floods disappear as rapidly as they arrive. Around 90 percent of the delta's water is lost to the sand and evaporation and more is taken out upstream by thirsty people and industry. The delta is shrinking, 30 percent smaller now than 50 years ago, and only two percent of the original flow survives to continue southeast as the little **Thamalakane River**. With parched Namibia asking for a further eight percent of the water, the very survival of the

The yellow mongoose (above) resides in grasslands and savannas, and feeds mostly on insects.

Red lechwe (right) are adapted to life in the marshes; when threatened, they take to the water.

The Okavango River (right) meanders through northern Botswana, slowing and spreading towards the world's largest desert delta.

every season, there is no way to draw an accurate map, and the few poorly maintained supply roads are of little help. The lodges themselves are only realistically accessible by small plane from Maun, to the south, or Kasane, to the north. The flights are worth it, however, for it is only from above, as you hop from camp to camp, that you realize how big and flat and empty the delta really is. It is enough to make strong men agoraphobic.

Red, Gold, and Green

The passing of the seasons is only too obvious from the air. In October, at the end of the dry season, the red-gold Kalahari sand looks like an aging jigsaw puzzle, the baked, bare earth cracked into a million pieces by dried-up riverbeds, oxbow lakes, and salt-encrusted pans. The graying trees seem almost bare, their leaves withered under a relentless sun, and the danger is from bushfires as tinder-dry grass crackles under the restless hooves of animals searching out the last living shoots. Infrequently, a flash of intense sapphire marks the position of a permanent lagoon.

In March, at the height of the rainy season, the image could not be more different. The whole region, as far as the eye can see, is covered by an ocean of emerald grass and vermilion trees. Near the riverbanks, baboons squabble over the pendulous fruit of the sausage trees, for all the world like giant salamis, while elephants scuffle in the dust for marula berries. The plane faces new challenges. Ahead, a looming wall of charcoal clouds presages the arrival of a thunderous storm. In the center of the runway, one of the few totally dry areas in the vicinity, a family of warthogs is on its knees, digging for salt.

By July the scene has changed again. The rainwater pans have dried and with them has gone the grass. Once more the battle-scarred patchwork of old watercourses is on display, but the river is in full spate. Strong lines of gushing water, brown with silt, are fringed by luxuriant vegetation from jackalberry, ebony, and knobthorn trees to towering bulrushes and papyrus.

A Hand Across the Desert

The delta is roughly the shape of an out-stretched hand. In the northwest, the arm is formed by the **Panhandle**, a fault 9 miles (15km) wide that holds the river together. This area of deep water is less desirable for game viewing but wonderful for fishermen, with some 80 species of fish. The palm of the hand is made up of the inner, **permanent swamp**, a magnificent vista of pans and grasslands, water meadows in summer, and permanent lagoons and rivers all year round. There is plenty of game here; some 36 species of mammals and 200 species of birds have been recorded. However, it can prove hard to find and track the animals, who have a thousand sources of water and thick vegetation as perfect camouflage. Conveniently for the tourists, many of them have learned the rules of the road, padding along the dusty tracks to keep their feet dry. Red-billed francolins and helmeted guinea fowl scatter frantically as a rare safari vehicle approaches. An elephant stops for a snack, carefully knocking a tree across the road in his quest for the tender shoots. Great pug marks in the dust clearly mark the presence of a prowling lion. As dusk falls, the impalas move out onto the sun-warmed sand to sleep. The open road makes them feel safer at night. Nightjars flutter down for a dust bath, while spring hares, like tiny long-eared kangaroos, leap away from the approaching headlights.

In the water meadow, wildebeests and buffalo cannot resist the tender spring shoots, but only the red lechwe, the delta's signature antelope, seem truly at home in the water, their hunched backs, short front legs, and powerful back legs designed to spring across the floodplains.

Far more than the animals, however, it is the small things that make the delta special: the busy dung beetles, nature's sewage workers, carefully rolling away balls of elephant dung; the sideways slither of a rock python disappearing into the wild date palms; the cloud of brown-veined white butterflies that flutters across the path, bizarrely always moving in a northeasterly direction; the wheel-

Buffalo (top) stampede through the shallows.

A saddlebilled stork (above) makes a clean kill in the Okavango wetlands. These large and colorful birds eat mainly insects, reptiles, and frogs.

ing dance of the blue-cheeked bee-eaters as they swirl through the air hunting for tsetse flies.

Even the plants are fascinating – wild sage, used as a natural insecticide, the pale pink stalks of cat's tail, used as a cure for gonorrhea, and the jazzy red and yellow flame lily, highly toxic and of little use, except for decoration.

The water's edge is thick with birds – cormorants and darters, knob-billed ducks and great white egrets, African jacanas (lilytrotters) and spur-winged geese. Above them circles a black-shouldered kite, while on a nearby tree, in a symphony of black and white, a pied kingfisher and majestic African fish eagle survey the water.

Poling through Paradise

The only real way to see this secret world is by mokoro. Once laboriously carved from a single trunk of a giant hardwood tree, now more commonly made of fiberglass, the mokoro is a flat-bottomed canoe poled quietly through the narrow rivulets and channels of the delta like a punt. It slides with a whisper through a field of head-high grass – thick, sharp blades, flat-topped grasses with black seedheads like tiny helicopter blades, and

A pygmy goose (top) twitters gently in the still waters of the Delta, diving below the surface for food.

Tsetse flies (right) have a loud buzz and painful bite. Worse, they transmit sleeping sickness.

feathery fronds that release clouds of white and raspberry-pink pollen as you brush against them. From the surface, it is impossible to see that they are growing in a couple of feet of water.

To one side, a herd of lechwe cannons past in a rainbow shower of spray. A tiny mascarene grass frog clings desperately to a wildly swaying stalk, buffeted by their bow wave. Out of sight, a blacksmith plover calls squeakily as it pecks its way along the shore.

The grass gives way to elephant-high reeds, papyrus sedge, and bulrushes as the mokoro noses its way slowly into an open pool. At the far side, a flurry of coughing marks the progress of a hippo bull, who moves forward to confront the intruder, rearing and beating the water with his front feet, glistening pink jaws agape in challenge. From this level, the danger is all too obvious and the poler retreats quickly

Lurking Nasties

People shudder when they think of mosquitoes or the half-inch-long tsetse fly; farmers quake at the mere mention of foot-and-mouth disease – and with good reason. The anopheles mosquito is not only supremely irritating, it is the bearer of malaria, one of the world's most pernicious and potentially fatal diseases, which is also becoming immune to the various prophylaxes faster than people can invent new ones. The tsetse fly has a viciously painful bite, but more seriously it transmits trypanasomiases – sleeping sickness – a disaster for humans and cattle, while foot-and-mouth disease means instant slaughter for any herd of infected stock. Yet these three fearsome guardians have been responsible for the survival of much of Africa's wildlife. Only those areas unsuitable for settlement or farming have been left untamed, and with no other suitable use, many have been turned into game reserves and national parks.

There are constant efforts to reduce the threat, most of which have proved detrimental to the local wildlife. Spraying to kill mosquitoes has resulted in the deaths from chemical poisoning of many other species. Game fences hundreds of miles long, put up to keep wildebeests and buffalo out of areas used for cattle farming, impeded traditional migration routes and resulted in the deaths of hundreds of thousands of animals. Only the black-and-blue chemically saturated flags (the colors attract flies, so avoid wearing them while on safari) set up to attract and destroy tsetse flies have proven successful. But with the flies gone, the farmers are free to move in, and the area left to the game shrinks once again.

into a side channel thick with water lilies basking in the early-morning sun.

The Fingertips

The farther south and east you go, toward the fingertips of the **seasonal swamp**, the drier the land and the greater the intensity of the game clustered along the water's edge. Those looking for vast herds and guaranteed Big Five sightings, however, would generally still do better elsewhere. The rhinos have all been translocated for safekeeping, and locals are keen to point out that when visiting the Okavango, game viewing is only one aspect of the ultimate wilderness experience.

The best of the game is undoubtedly found in the 1,882-square-mile (4,874-sq-km) Moremi Game Reserve, made up of the large

tongue of dry land that licks into the far-eastern section of the delta and the 386-square-mile (1,000-sq-km) **Chief's Island** next door. Here you will find a wide range of vegetation, from reed beds along the lagoons to riverine forest, grasslands, and mopane scrub, punctuated by giant baobab trees. The range of animals and birds within a relatively small area is extraordinarily diverse, from elephants and impalas, giraffes, and zebras to predators such as lions and leopards. The northern tip of the tongue is famous for its storks and herons. Walking safaris are not allowed here, and the permanent water is too deep for mokoro trips, which can run only during a limited season.

But all that is forgotten as you sit on board a larger boat, sipping a gin and tonic while the sunset flames red-gold behind the bold silhouettes of a marching line of ilala (real fan) palms. Opposite, there is a long, thin island, created by centuries of silt backing up behind one of the area's spectacular termite mounds. Now curtained by wild date palms and crowned by mangosteen trees, it has become the roost for a colony of ungainly, balding marabou storks who perch precariously, their massive bodies threatening to overwhelm the narrow branches. With a grunt, a hippo hauls its gleaming black barrel body out of the water and stomps off through the reeds for a long night's grazing. A small crocodile slithers into the water, only his eyes and nostrils breaking the surface. There is a building clamor of bubbling, snoring, squeaking, and croaking. The frogs have started their nightly chorus.

Elephants (top) drink by filling their trunks with water and squirting it into their mouths.

A frog (left) perches on a water lily blossom.

Fruit bats (right) hang from trees during the day, wrapped in their membranous wings.

TRAVEL TIPS

DETAILS

When to Go

There are three seasons in the Delta. The dry season lasts from August to November. Temperatures are 70°F (21°C) to 80°F (27°C) in August and September, but regularly top 100°F (38°C) in October and November. Game viewing is good, with animals clustered around the channels. From December to March, Delta temperatures are still between 80°F (27°C) and 100°F (38°C), but it's also wet; the game is dispersed, but bird and plant life are at their best. Many lodges are closed. Probably the best time to visit is from April to August, when it's cooler and drier. The channels are high, but the rainwater pans are dry, and game clusters around the rivers.

Getting There

The easiest access is through Johannesburg in South Africa. From there, fly to Maun in central Botswana. Alternatively, fly to Victoria Falls in Zimbabwe and cross the border to Kasane. Delta Air (P.O. Box 39, Maun, Botswana; tel: +267-660 044; fax: +267-661 703; e-mail: synergy@info.bw) is one of several charter companies operating air taxis to lodges from Maun and Kasane. Moremi National Park is accessible by road with four-wheel-drive vehicles, but it is a long, bumpy drive. Game viewing is by four-wheel-drive vehicle, mokoro, or tour boat.

INFORMATION

Botswana Embassies

United Kingdom: 6 Stratford Place, London W1N 9AE; tel: +44-20-7499 0031; fax: +44-20-7409 7382.

United States: 1531–1533 New Hampshire Avenue, N.W., Washington, DC 20036; tel: 202-244-4990; fax: 202-244-4164.

Department of Tourism

P Bag 0047, Gaborone, Botswana; tel: +267-353 024; fax: +267-308 675; e-mail: botswanatourism@gov.bw; web: www.botswana-tourism.gov.bw.

Department of Wildlife and National Parks

P.O. Box 131, Gaborone, Botswana; tel: +267-661 265; fax: +267-661 264; e-mail: dwnpbot@global.bw

CAMPING

Department of Wildlife and National Parks

P.O. Box 131, Gaborone, Botswana; tel: +267-661 265; fax: +267-661 264; e-mail: dwnpbot@global.bw.

Facilities range from very basic campsites in Moremi to luxury mobile safaris that come with a full staff. For basic accommodations, plan to bring all your provisions, including fuel and drinking water. $–$$$

LODGING

PRICE GUIDE – double occupancy

$ = under $100 $$ = $100–$200
$$$ = $200–$300 $$$$ = $300 +

Eagle Island Camp

Gametrackers, P.O. Box 786432, Sandton 2146, South Africa; tel: +27-11-481 6052; fax: +27-11-481 6065; e-mail: gtres@iafrica.com; web: www.orient-express.com

This luxurious lodge in Xaxaba, at the heart of the Delta, is made up of 12 thatch-shaded tents on a wooded island. There are animals, but the focus is on the water and bird life. The same company operates the tented Khwai River Lodge on the border of Moremi Game Reserve. $$$$

Kwetsani

United Kingdom: c/o Outposts, Narracott, Drewsteignton, Exeter, Devon EX6 6PU; tel: +44-164-728 1665; fax: +44-164-728 1288; e-mail: outposts@usa.net

United States: c/o Tim Farrell and Associates, P.O. Box 7300, Wilton, CT 06897-7300; tel: 203-762-8050; fax: 203-762-7323; e-mail: SafariTim@aol.com

Kwetsani is on an island in the central Delta, with thatched canvas tree houses linked by wooden walkways. Activities include day and night game drives, mokoro trips, and walks. $$$$

Sandibe

CCAfrica, P Bag X27, Benmore 2010, South Africa; tel: +27-11-809 4300; fax: +27-11-809 4400; e-mail: bookings@ccafrica.com; web:www.ccafrica.com

Eight thatched chalets overlook the Santandibe River near the border of Moremi Game Reserve. The walls and electricity help the less adventurous feel secure, but, like all camps in the Delta, animals are free to wander in. Activities include drives, walks, and mokoro trips. Access is by air only. $$$$

Xakanaxa Camp

Moremi Tours and Safaris, P.O. Box 2757, Cramerview 2060, South Africa; tel: +27-11-465 3842/3; fax: +27-11-465 3779; e-mail: moremi@sprintlink.co.za.

A San name meaning "place of water," Xakanaxa is a relaxed camp with tents sprawled along a reed-fringed riverbank in Moremi Game Reserve. Game viewing by land is excellent. Boat trips are offered, but because the camp is within the national park, there are no game walks or night drives. $$$$

TOUR OPERATORS

Afro Ventures

P Bag X27, Benmore 2010, South Africa; tel: +27-11-809 4300; fax: +27-11-809 4514; e-mail: jnb@afroventures.com; web: www.afroventures.com

Mobile safaris explore the Delta.

Ker and Downey
P.O. Box 27, Maun, Botswana; tel: +267-660 375; fax: +267-661 282; e-mail: safari@kerdowney.bw; web: www.kerdowney.com

United States: 2825 Wilcrest Drive, Suite 600, Houston, TX 77042-6007; tel: 800-423-4236; fax: 713-917-0123; e-mail: info@kerdowney.com; web: kerdowney.com

This tour operator runs several camps and mobile safaris in the Delta.

Moremi Tours and Safaris
P.O. Box 2757, Cramerview 2060, South Africa; tel: +27-11-465 3842; fax: +27-11-465 3779; e-mail: moremi@sprintlink.co.za

This small tour operator with a lodge in the Delta offers tours throughout Botswana.

Okavango Tours and Safaris
Marlborough House, 298 Regents Park Road, London N3 2TJ, UK; tel: +44-20-8343 3283; fax: +44-20-8343 3287; e-mail: info@okavango.com; web: www.okavango.com

This company started in the Delta and specializes in the area, running tours and camps.

Wilderness Safaris
United Kingdom: c/o Outposts, Narracott, Drewsteignton, Exeter, Devon EX6 6PU; tel: +44-164-728 1665; fax: +44-164-728 1288; e-mail: outposts@usa.net

United States: c/o Tim Farrell and Associates, P.O. Box 7300, Wilton, CT 06897-7300; tel: 203-762-8050; fax: 203-762-7323; e-mail: SafariTim@aol.com

The company owns more than a dozen exclusive lodges in Botswana and runs scheduled and customized tours and mobile safaris throughout southern Africa.

Excursions

Abu Camp
Elephant Back Safaris, P Bag 332, Maun, Botswana; tel: +267-661 260; fax: +267-661 005; e-mail: info@elephantbacksafaris.com; web: www.elephantbacksafaris.com

This lodge, on the western side of Okavango Delta and 30 minutes by air from Maun, is something special – and very expensive. It was on this 500,000-acre (200,000-hectare) concession that the American Randall Moore reintroduced three circus-trained African elephants and began the idea of elephant-back safaris. There are now 15 elephants – six adults and nine youngsters – and guests can help look after them, do half- and full-day safaris, game drives, walks, and mokoro trips. The camp sleeps 10 guests for six-day stays.

Central Kalahari Game Reserve
Department of Wildlife and National Parks, P.O. Box 131, Gaborone, Botswana; tel: +267-661 265; fax: +267-661 264; e-mail: dwnpbot@global.bw

Covering 20,400 square miles (53,000 sq km) of central Botswana, this virtually unexplored reserve was set up as a refuge both for animals and the country's few remaining San people. The terrain is quite varied, with open plains, salt pans, sand dunes, and mopane scrub in the north (which also has the best game viewing); bushveld in the center; and woodland in the south. To the east of the reserve, the Khama Rhino Sanctuary protects Botswana's entire rhino population.

Kgalagadi Transfrontier Park
Department of Wildlife and National Parks, P.O. Box 131, Gaborone, Botswana; tel: +267-661 265; fax: +267-661 264; e-mail: dwnpbot@global.bw

Formerly known as the Kalahari Gemsbok Reserve, this remote park covers 3,400 square miles (9,000 sq km) of the Kalahari Desert across the dry Nossob River, Botswana's southern border with South Africa. It was estab-lished to protect the beautiful desert-dwelling gemsbok. Access routes have opened in Botswana for four-wheel-drive vehicles. There are no facilities, so visitors must carry all the supplies they'll need. An entry permit is a must.

Chobe
National Park
Botswana

CHAPTER 8

t's the end of a long day's grazing. As the sun begins to cool, an old bull elephant tugs at a last clump of grass and, chewing thoughtfully, ambles into the river. The water gets deeper and the flow stronger until, partway across, he is forced to use his trunk as a snorkel. Near the far shore, a boat full of breathless tourists waits to see where he will emerge … just a few feet away from them. He pauses to check them out, beady black eyes just above the surface, then heaves himself in a cascade of muddy water onto a narrow strip of sand, scattering a slaty egret, three sandpipers, and a squacco heron ahead of his soft, round feet.　◆　The muddy path up the bank is a well-worn track. At the top, he stops, and, with a sigh fast approaching ecstasy, leans into the polished trunk of an old acacia tree. He rubs one flank, then the other, lifts up each foot in turn and, hooking his trunk over a high branch, even scratches under his chin. For about 10 minutes, all that can be heard is the rasping of skin against bark and the

The Chobe River meanders through parched savanna and woodland, attracting elephants, buffalo, and hippos to its life-sustaining waters.

occasional flatulent gurgle of a well-fed elephant. Then, massage over, he disappears into the bush.　◆　The bull spent the day, as he does most days, on a small, flat island in the middle of the **Chobe River**. Each year, as the floodwaters gush down from the highlands, it vanishes completely. Yet this undistinguished island became the subject of a bitter seven-year court battle between Botswana and neighboring Namibia. In January 2000, sovereignty was eventually awarded to a jubilant Botswana, leaving everyone else wondering what all the fuss was about.

Aardwolves, relatives of the hyena, feed on termites and insect larvae, with an occasional feast of rodents or eggs. When scared, they puff up their manes – then run away.

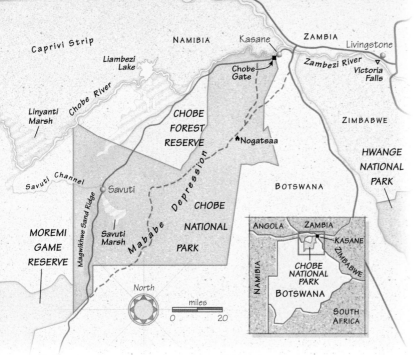

patchwork of forest reserves and private concessions connects Chobe to nearby **Hwange National Park** in Zimbabwe, and the two great reserves effectively act as one ecosystem, the wildlife wandering freely between them. In spite of its vast size, however, relatively little of the park is used by tourists, few of whom ever stray more than about 12 miles (19km) inland from the narrow strip of riverine forest and grasslands along the Chobe River.

At Chobe, they knew. The south bank of the Chobe River is the most game-rich stretch of **Chobe National Park**. The north bank, in Namibia's troubled Caprivi strip, is unprotected. The island is a favorite grazing area for elephants and buffalo who cross each day to crop the river-sweet grass. Without protection, the trusting wildlife, brought up within the safety of a national park, would be fair game to hunters. The court decision has guaranteed their safety – and an unforgettable spectacle for tourists.

The Chobe River

Founded in 1968, Chobe National Park covers a massive 4,081 square miles (10,570 sq km) in the northeastern corner of Botswana. A

The river begins life as the Kwando in the Benguela Highlands of Angola, then becomes the Linyanti before a final stretch as the Chobe. For millions of years, it fed south into the same superlake as the Okavango, until a series of earthquakes abruptly altered its course, carrying the torrent due east, to join the Zambezi. Life along its banks is never dull. Boat trips offer spectacular game viewing as you thread your way cautiously between submerged pods of snorting hippos. On one grassy bank, a young crocodile and a mature water monitor face off like bookends in a contest of wills over a small but infinitely desirable patch of sunlight. The lizard wins, but if he tries the same trick in a few years' time, he will be lunch. For now, the croc

curved horns as dangerous as scimitars. In the dappled shade of the jackalberry trees, a tiny, yellow-and-brown giraffe, a couple of months old and not yet weaned, stretches skyward in envious imitation of his mother. Downwind, from the broad branch of an ancient teak tree, unblinking gold eyes watch the young giraffe's feeble efforts – a leopard, dappled black and gold, planning what to have for supper and waiting for the little one to stray from the herd.

Because animals migrate freely to Hwange, it is virtually impossible to count them accurately; authorities place the number of elephants in Chobe anywhere from 45,000 to 90,000. Whatever the figure, there is no doubt that this is the single greatest concentration of these prehistoric pachyderms on the planet. In the dry winter season, the riverbank shudders under the feet of thunderous herds of several hundred elephants or tens of thousands of buffalo and wildebeests that trample the riverine vegetation. Northern Chobe is also the one place in Botswana

backs away, heading downstream to lurk furtively underwater like a floating log, in hopes an inattentive bird will try to perch.

As the floodplain broadens out, the animals queue for their turn at the water's edge. A goliath heron poses, statue-still, beside a clump of reeds, blinking as a malachite kingfisher swoops past in a flash of turquoise light. A 100-strong herd of buffalo pushes its way through to the front like a gang of Viking hooligans, horned helmets slipping low over bony brows. A small, skittish herd of puku, a central African antelope similar in size and color to an impala, moves hastily aside. Behind, in stately procession, comes a magnificent column of sable antelope. The sun gleams on their coats of burnished dark chocolate, noses and underbellies dipped in cream, and soaring, backward

Lions (left) spend most of their time at leisure, hunting only every few days.

Double-decker boats (top) are the classic way for visitors to explore the Chobe River.

Ostrich chicks (right) follow their mother's lead. Though flightless, mature ostriches are fast runners.

Elephants

The largest land mammals on the planet, adult elephants stand up to 10 feet (3m) tall and weigh up to 6½ tons. Elephant calves remain dependent on their mothers for up to five years and reach sexual maturity by 13. During the terrible teens, the males gradually move off to join a bachelor herd, while the females become more involved in child care. Females normally start breeding at 18, producing a calf every two and a half to four years until the age of 50. Males spend about three months of every year in a sexually active condition known as musth and live until about 70.

Elephants are remarkably social animals, living in family groups of up to 20, with the eldest female acting as matriarch. Their rumbling infrasound communications, too low for the human ear, can reach across an area of 40 square miles (100 sq km). They have excellent memories and are known to express a wide range of emotions – joy, tenderness, grief, and anger.

An elephant's tusks, actually its upper incisors, grow as much as 9 inches (23cm) a year throughout its life. They are vital equipment, used for digging, ripping bark, foraging, wresting tree trunks, and as weapons. Most elephants are either right or left tusked (look for which is shortest, through wear). Their most essential tool, however, is their trunk, an extraordinary piece of biotechnology, with up to 100,000 muscle units in six main groups. A combination upper lip and nose, it is used to rub eyes, scratch, threaten, and carry objects, and as a snorkel, a drinking straw, shower (capable of scooping up nearly a gallon of water), and for smelling. At the end are two delicate "fingers," which allow them to pick up the tiniest objects. If the trunk is injured and unusable, the animal inevitably dies.

Elephants (left) form stable family groups and gather at the Chobe River in herds of several hundred.

long as the water lasts. Twelve pumped water holes have been set up in the **Nogatsaa** area, about 40 miles (65km) due south of Chobe Gate, to provide year-round water to the southern and central areas. Several have hides overlooking the water which can be booked for spartan camping; developed campgrounds are on the drawing board.

Savuti and Linyanti

On the far western edge of the park, the **Linyanti Marsh** is found around the fault line that caused the river to turn in its tracks. Like the Chobe riverfront, the marsh offers superb game viewing in the dry season when the animals cluster along the water's edge. A little to the south, the **Savuti** area marks the far northern extent of the ancient superlake, a long-dry sea of sand punctuated here by rocky kopjes that are a favorite retreat of leopards and baboons. The vegetation is sparse, a scattering of baobabs, acacias, mopane, and seasonal grasses knitting together the floor of the old lake bed, known here as the **Mababe Depression**. Above it, the gently rolling **Magwikhwe Sand Ridge** is part of the original shoreline. Here you will find a very different set of trees – white seringa, a mass of flowers in spring and russet leaves in autumn, the white paperbark false-thorn, the false sourplum, and carrot tree. All that remains of the

where game viewing is relatively cheap and accessible; tourists come by the thousands, and every lion is ringed by safari vehicles. Strong efforts are being made to ease the congestion by moving people and animals inland.

Nogatsaa

The hot, dry interior of the park is a patchwork of mopane woodland and flat Kalahari sandveld; there are simply no permanent water sources. Wooed by the summer rains, the grass grows tall, scrubby gray bushes burst into vivid life, the flat-topped umbrella acacias cloak their wicked thorns with a soft covering of feathery leaves, the shallow pans fill with water, and the animals disperse deep into the bush. But they stay only as

water is the sorry marsh of the **Savuti Channel**, which appears to flood and dry according to whims of its own that have nothing to do with prevailing conditions in the surrounding area, leaving forests of dead trees like abandoned candelabra.

Now bone dry for much of the year, Savuti truly comes into its own only in summer, when the grasslands are alive with wildflowers and the plains animals move south, accompanied as ever by an honor guard of predators. Great herds of zebras, wildebeests, and impalas roam comfortably close to the lolling heaps of lions as they lie in shady corners licking the blood from their whiskers and digesting last night's warthog. Across the vlei, squabbling lappetfaced vultures dart bald, pink heads in between the bones, and a black-backed jackal prowls around the throng hoping to slink in between the beating wings and seize a mouthful of stringy flesh. A flash of purple iridescence marks the flight of a plum-

Southern carmine bee-eaters (left) like to nest in exposed riverbanks.

Impalas (below) bound away from danger; powerful jumpers, they can leap 10 feet (3m) into the air and travel 30 feet (9m) in a single bound.

colored starling; a family of ostriches lurches past – father black, mother brown, the cappuccino-colored brood hidden by the grass. An old acacia is hung with carefully woven balls of twig, and the whole crown flutters yellow with the frenzy of masked weavers trying to fill the ever-gaping mouths of their chicks. An old male chacma baboon sits upright on a rocky outcrop; it is his turn to act as sentry, while tiny wizened babies frolic in the dust and the females of the troop lie languidly in the shade, picking fleas from each others' heads. Should those lions stand up, his bark of alarm will scatter the animals into the safety of the trees. But for now, there is only the hot, drowsy buzz of an afternoon in the bush.

TRAVEL TIPS

DETAILS

When to Go

Winter (June to September) is the best time to visit Chobe, when skies are clear, average midday temperatures are 70°F (21°C) to 80°F (27°C), and massive herds of elephants and other animals crowd the riverbank in search of water. The animals are still there in October, but by then the temperature soars to 100°F (38°C). Mid-November to April is the rainy season, with midday temperatures around 90°F (32°C), heavy storms, thick mud, and mosquitoes. Animals scatter into the bush, but vegetation is lush and bird life abundant.

Getting There

Northern Chobe is one of the most accessible wilderness areas in Africa. The nearest major international airports are in Johannesburg, South Africa, and Harare, Zimbabwe. The nearest airport to Chobe is in Kasane, but flights are more frequent to Victoria Falls, across the Zimbabwe border. Cars can be rented in both towns, but if you're renting in Zimbabwe, verify that you can take the vehicle across the border. Most Kasane hotels and tour operators will arrange airport transfers from Victoria Falls. Most people visiting the southern lodges fly in on charter planes from Kasane or Maun, on the Okavango Delta.

Small lodges arrange game drives, walks, and boat trips for their guests. Larger hotels will book organized activities. Passenger vehicles are suitable along the northern strip in the dry season, but a four-wheel-drive vehicle is essential during the rains or on any trip into the central and southern areas of the park. Provisions are unavailable within the park; visitors must bring fuel, food, water, and equipment.

INFORMATION

Botswana Embassies

United Kingdom: 6 Stratford Place, London W1N 9AE; tel: +44-20-7499 0031; fax: +44-20-7409 7382.

United States: 1531–1533 New Hampshire Avenue, N.W., Washington, DC 20036; tel: 202-244-4990; fax: 202-244-4164.

Department of Tourism

P Bag 0047, Gaborone, Botswana; tel:+267-353 024; fax: +267-308 675; e-mail: botswana-tourism@gov.bw; web: www.botswana-tourism.gov.bw

Department of Wildlife and National Parks

P.O. Box 131, Gaborone, Botswana; tel: +267-661 265; fax: +267-661 264; e-mail: dwnpbot@global.bw.

CAMPING

Chobe National Park

Botswana Parks and Reserves Reservations Office, Maun, Botswana; tel: +267-661 265; fax: +267-661 264.

Public campgrounds within the park are limited, but plans are under way to upgrade existing facilities and add more. Campsites will remain basic, however, requiring visitors to provide their own supplies. On the riverfront in the north, a new campground at Ihaha has flush toilets and showers; some have hot water. In the south, Linyanti has limited flush toilets and showers with hot water, while Savuti has pit latrines and a protected water standpipe, but no showers.

LODGING

DumaTau

United Kingdom: c/o Outposts, Narracott, Drewsteignton, Exeter, Devon EX6 6PU; tel: +44-164-728 1665; fax: +44-164-728 1288; e-mail: outposts@usa.net

United States: c/o Tim Farrell and Associates, P.O. Box 7300, Wilton, CT 06897-7300; tel: 203-762-8050; fax: 203-762-7323; e-mail: SafariTim@aol.com

Eight canvas chalets under thatch roofs edge the Savuti Channel. This is one of four small luxury camps that share Wilderness Safaris' private concession at Linyanti, on the western border of Chobe. The others are Linyanti, Savuti, and the slightly larger King's Pool. $$$$

Jack's Camp

Uncharted Africa Safari, P.O. Box 173, Francistown, Botswana; tel: +267-212 277; fax: +267-213 458; e-mail: bianca@unchartedafrica.co.za; web: www.onsafari.com

Activities at this 1940s-style tented safari camp in the Makgadikgadi Pans include game viewing, walks with San trackers, archaeological expeditions, and, after the rains, encounters with some of the world's largest flocks of flamingos. $$$$

Kwando

P.O. Box 1264, Parklands 2121, South Africa; tel: +27-11-880 6138; fax: +27-11-880 1393; e-mail: kwandojnb@global.co.za; web: www.kwando.com

This 890-square-mile (2,305-sq-km) private concession on the Kwando River, to the west of Chobe, is made up of riverine forest, a dried floodplain, and mopane woodland. There are two small, tented camps: Lebala, facing the plains, and Lagoon, on the waterfront. The price includes all meals, activities, and air transfers. $$$$

Mowana Safari Lodge

c/o Summit Hotels and Resorts; tel: +44-20-8490 5791; fax: +44-20-8994 6475; e-mail: deborah.stow@utell.com

This large, hotel-style lodge on the banks of the Chobe is within easy reach of the park gates. Stores and a travel agency are on the premises. The price excludes game-watching activities and park fees. $$$

Savuti Elephant Camp

Gametrackers, P.O. Box 786432, Sandton 2146, South Africa; tel: +27-11-481 6052; fax: +27-11-481 6065; e-mail: gtres@iafrica.com

This 12-tent camp in the Savuti region of Chobe has excellent game viewing, birding, and San rock paintings. Because the camp is inside the national park, there are no walks or night drives. $$$$

TOUR OPERATORS

Afro Ventures

P Bag X27, Benmore 2010, South Africa; tel: +27-11-809 4300; fax: +27-11-809 4514; e-mail: jnb@afroventures.com; web: www.afroventures.com

Mobile safaris explore Chobe National Park.

Okavango Tours and Safaris

Marlborough House, 298 Regents Park Road, London N3 2TJ, UK; tel: +44-20-8343 3283; fax: +44-20-8343 3287; e-mail: info@okavango.com; web: www.okavango.com

This company, which started in the Okavango Delta, specializes in trips throughout Botswana.

Wilderness Safaris

United Kingdom: c/o Outposts, Narracott, Drewsteignton, Exeter, Devon EX6 6PU; tel: +44-164-728 1665; fax: +44-164-728 1288; e-mail: outposts@usa.net

United States: c/o Tim Farrell and Associates, P.O. Box 7300, Wilton, CT 06897-7300; tel: 203-762-8050; fax: 203-762-7323; e-mail: SafariTim@aol.com

The company owns exclusive lodges in Botswana and runs scheduled and customized tours and mobile safaris throughout southern Africa.

Excursions

Makgadikgadi and Nxai Pans

Department of Wildlife and National Parks, P.O. Box 131, Gaborone, Botswana; tel: +267-661 265; fax: +267-661 264; e-mail: dwnpbot@global.bw

Ancient salt pans cover an eerily desolate area of central Botswana the size of Portugal. Islands of grass, palms, and baobabs support huge populations of zebras, wildebeests, and predators. Around them stretch gleaming white plains of salty sand that transform in the rainy season into broad, shallow lakes that attract flamingos. Part of the largest pan, Makgadikgadi, is a 1,600-square-mile (4,100-sq-km) national park; much of the rest is carved into huge private concessions. To the north, Nxai National Park encompasses the smaller Nxai and Kgama-Kgama Pans.

Tsodilo Hills

Department of Tourism, Ministry of Commerce and Industry, P Bag 0047, Gaborone, Botswana; tel: +267-353 024; fax: +267-308 675; e-mail: botswana-tourism@gov.bw; web: www.botswana-tourism.gov.bw

These rose-colored granite ridges in northeast Botswana are sacred to the San people, and the archaeological record in the area is superb. Along the cliff faces are at least 2,000 rock paintings, the earliest created some 4,000 years ago, the most recent in the 20th century. The region is remote; visitors need four-wheel-drive vehicles and their own supplies, including food, fuel, and water.

Tuli Block

Department of Tourism, Ministry of Commerce and Industry, P Bag 0047, Gaborone, Botswana; tel: +267-353 024; fax: +267-308 675; e-mail: botswanatourism@gov.bw; web: www.botswanatourism.gov.bw

A growing collection of private reserves and lodges surrounds the small Tuli Reserve in far eastern Botswana. Now linked with similar reserves across the border in Zimbabwe, the Tuli Block is destined to become one of the first segments of a new peace park along the Limpopo River, linking Botswana, Zimbabwe, South Africa, and Mozambique. In the meantime, the game viewing is good, if not magnificent, and the prices are generally lower than those in the Okavango or Chobe regions.

Namib–Naukluft National Park

Namibia

CHAPTER **9**

Rise before dawn and watch in awe as sinuous, deep apricot dunes glow against pockets of black-velvet shadows. As the sky brightens, the shadows blur and the colors fade to a delicate white-gold. It is only in these early hours, when the sand is cool and compacted by dew, that it's possible to reach the tops of what are, at 1,000 feet (300m), among the highest dunes in the world. Below the dunes, white clay pans known as vleis shimmer in the heat. ◆ The name **Namib–Naukluft** hardly trips off the tongue and is barely known outside Namibia, but the towering, sensuously rounded dunes at **Sossusvlei** appear on calendars the world over. Sossusvlei itself lies at the end of the seasonal **Tsauchab River**, which flows from the mountains to the east but never reaches the sea, its course blocked by a great dam of dunes. Only about once every 10 years is there sufficient water to reach Sossusvlei, causing the river to back up and create a series of large pools. These

Explore the planet's oldest desert, a stark, beautiful, ever-changing sculpture of sand and rock.

evaporate quickly, leaving behind a thin layer of cracked mud, curled at the edges and tracked with the footprints of the lucky few who witnessed the spectacle at its most dramatic. Water can stay in the pan for several months, and with it comes flocks of birds. Visitors sometimes spot avocets stalking the fringes of the pan, Cape teal swimming in the pools, or the somewhat surreal sight of a white stork loafing on a sand dune in an otherwise empty desert. ◆ Namib–Naukluft is one of the largest national parks in Africa, encompassing 19,210 square miles (49,754 sq km) and stretching from **Luderitz** in the south to **Swakopmund** in the north. At its widest, it links the **Naukluft Mountains** and the **Great Western Escarpment**

Blown by the wind, Namibia's dunes march across the landscape, engulfing everything in their path. Even wildlife finely attuned to the desert environment eventually succumbs to thirst or predation.

Ever-vigilant meerkats, or suricates (right), stand guard at their communal burrow.

Gemsbok (below) trudge through the wastes of the Namib–Naukluft Desert. Specially adapted blood vessels cool their brains in the heat of the day.

via a corridor of land purchased in 1979 to give free passage to migrating species such as the rare Hartmann's mountain zebra and gemsbok. Much of this great desert wilderness is virtually impenetrable; the road along the Tsauchab River to Sossusvlei offers one of the best opportunities to get deep into the park. Whether you travel through the wasted landscape to Sossusvlei

or merely catch a sunset at Elim Dune near the entrance gate, take time to appreciate the desert. It rarely gives instant gratification; instead, an appreciation of its subtle beauty deepens with every moment you spend here.

Precious Moisture

The desert is far from empty. The river valley and some of the accompanying vleis contain sufficient groundwater to support vegetation such as nara melons and camel thorns. These, in turn, provide shade, shelter, and food for any number of creatures large and small. Strong winds and stinging sand may annoy visitors but are vital for both the Namib and its inhabitants. This desert is a living organism in its own right, constantly rolling north until it reaches an insuperable barrier such as a river that sweeps the sand out to sea.

At the same time, the wind picks up detritus – seeds, bits of grass, other organic matter – and deposits it on the slipface of the dunes where it is pounced upon by detritus feeders such as the tenebrionid beetles or "toktokkies," hardy insects highly adapted to desert life. Among their number are some of the only white beetles in the world, which scoot over the dunes at high speed on long legs, in hot pursuit of a blown seed or a reluctant female.

While rain is practically nonexistent, the Benguela Current sweeps north from the Southern Ocean, bringing frigid air to Namibia's west coast. As the cold, moist air rolls off the sea, it mixes with the desert heat, generating the thick fog that caused so many ships to founder

and earned the region its ominous name, the Skeleton Coast. In the desert, however, the fog is life-giving as it condenses on cool surfaces like the back of one species of beetle, which stands with its tail raised to encourage the collected moisture to run down to its mouth.

In turn the beetle provides sustenance for lizards, chameleons, and golden moles, which tunnel through the sand in search of insect larvae. These species are then preyed upon by jackals, raptors, and sidewinder snakes, among others. Larger animals such as oryx and springbok also survive here, having adapted to sucking the small amounts of moisture they need from the arid brush they browse. They may look odd standing on the crest of a dune in the full glare of the sun, but they are making use of even the slightest drafts to keep cool during the hottest part of the day.

Water Canyon

The one place where there is almost always water is **Sesriem Canyon**, a narrow cleft carved through the bed of the Tsauchab River. It is well worth the descent to the canyon floor, where there is shade at all but the hottest time of day. Mats of twigs and sticks snagged in pockets high on the walls are a dramatic reminder of the floods that sometimes pour through the gorge. The ragged walls are used for nesting and roosting by rock pigeons, which, in turn, are preyed upon by raptors.

There is almost always a pool of water at the bottom, topped off when the river floods during the annual rains. This was once a well-known watering hole used by ox wagons. Six (*ses*) lengths of reins (*riems*) had to be knotted together in order to lower a bucket from the canyon rim to the pool below – hence the name.

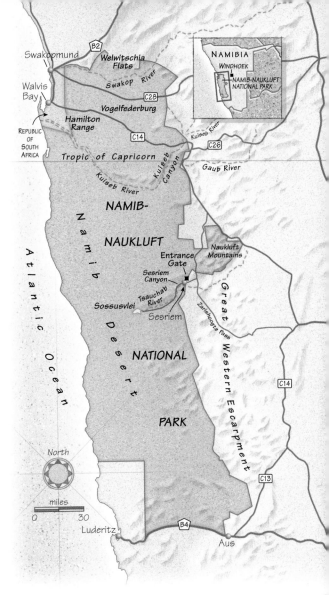

Multicolored Moonscape

The dunes at Sossusvlei are only one of many desert landscapes. Travel north and then west from here along the road to Swakopmund and you pass through some of the most empty and contorted land-

Web-footed geckos (top) draw moisture from the cold Atlantic fogs that settle across Namibia's coastal desert.

The side-winding adder (right), a member of the viper family, sinks into the sand at the first sign of danger.

Desert Plants

Extreme conditions demand extreme adaptations, and it is hard to think of a tougher place to live than the Namib Desert, whose plants have devised a number of extraordinary survival strategies.

Lithops, stone or pebble plants, are succulents that escape the attention of hungry herbivores by growing in the protective cracks of rocks and looking for all the world like stones. When the rains come, they burst briefly into bloom before resuming their former low-key existence. In contrast, a large welwitschia, which can live for more than 1,000 years, sprawls like a sea monster across the desert sand, its two leaves ripped into thin, tendril-like threads by the wind. These plants put off browsers by being distasteful and fibrous.

Even more ingenious are window algae, which grow under white quartz. The plants subsist on sunlight that passes through the translucent stone and water droplets that condense on the surface and drip down the sides.

Welwitschia plants (left) can live for more than 1,000 years.

The baked earth of Sossusvlei (right) is one of the harshest environments on the planet.

Condensation (below) is the only reliable source of moisture for this desert-dwelling katydid.

---

scapes in Africa. In one area, metamorphosed black shale and schist glint in the sun, standing on edge beside the road like ghoulish teeth. In another, rocks in the green, pink, and vanilla shades of Neapolitan ice cream rear up beyond a plain of rippling, parchment-colored grass. Just after crossing the **Tropic of Capricorn**, the road winds down into two dry riverbeds, first the **Gaub** and then the **Kuiseb**. These deep gulches, lined with trees and scrub living on groundwater, are a haven for some 50 species of birds.

From the Kuiseb, the road follows an almost straight route across the park to **Walvis Bay**. These gravel plains seem endless and are much flatter and less interesting visually than the dune fields farther south, but there are a few landmarks. Almost

cheek by jowl with the low limestone hills of the **Hamilton Range** is the granite batholith of the **Vogelfederburg**, which receives more precipitation than the plains. Small pools scattered around its wind-sculpted mass are home to fairy shrimps and other small creatures that lay eggs capable of withstanding drought, waiting only for enough water to hatch.

Not far from here, in the northernmost area of the park, are **Welwitschia Flats**, sometimes visited on a half-day excursion from nearby Swakopmund. The area is known for the ancient, creeping welwitschia plants endemic to the Namib (and thought to be one of the oldest plants in the world), as well as for some spectacular landforms. The mounds and craters of the usually dry **Swakop** riverbed, for example, bring to mind a lunar landscape. Visit when the light is low and shadows turn the swirls and ripples of rock into a vast abstract sculpture. There are also fascinating dolerite dikes created by the injection of molten rock into cracks in the granite. The softer granite eventually eroded away, leaving ridges topped with dark-gray dolerite fins protruding like bony plates atop a dinosaur's back. It's a particularly apt image in this ancient desert, where a fascinating variety of specialized plants and animals, some endemic to this area, have eked out a living for untold millennia.

TRAVEL TIPS

DETAILS

When to Go

The temperature on Namibia's coast varies greatly from day to day and is often cold with dreary fog and drizzle, even in high summer. Be prepared with long trousers, a fleece pullover, and a waterproof jacket at any time of year. Summer (December to January) is busy and typically hot, with midday temperatures between 70°F (21°C) and 90°F (32°C). Expect some stormy afternoons between December and March, but the rains rarely make roads impassable. In May and June, temperatures are 60°F (16°C) to 75°F (24°C) at midday; it can be cold at night in July and August. From April to May and late July to early September the area is busy with local residents on vacation, and advance reservations are essential.

Getting There

Namibia's main international airport is in Windhoek, but intercontinental services are limited. A common alternative is to connect via Johannesburg, South Africa. In Namibia, there are fly-in safaris from Windhoek and Swakopmund to Sossusvlei. The luxurious Desert Express train (P Bag 13204, Windhoek, Namibia; tel: +264-61-298 2600; fax: +264-61-298 2601; web: www.transnamib.com.na/dx) is a fine way to reach the coast.

Most tours cover Namib–Naukluft National Park, Sossusvlei, Swakopmund, and Cape Cross. Longer itineraries take in Fish River Canyon. Good roads and sparse traffic make driving easy. A standard vehicle will take you to within 3 miles (5km) of Sossusvlei; consider a guided tour to get deep into the desert.

INFORMATION

Directorate of Environmental Affairs

Ministry of Environment and Tourism, P Bag 13306, Windhoek, Namibia; tel: +264-61-284 2366; fax: +264-61-224 900.

Namibia Embassies

United Kingdom: 6 Chandos Street, London W1M 0LQ; tel: +44-20-7636 6244; fax: +44-20-7637 5694; e-mail: namibia-highcom@btconnect.com

United States: 1605 New Hampshire Avenue, N.W., Washington, DC 20009; tel: 202-986-0540; fax: 202-986-0443.

Namibia Tourism

P Bag 13346, Windhoek, Namibia; tel: +264-61-284 2360; fax: +264-61-284-2364; e-mail: tourism@iwwn.com.na; web: www.tourism.com.na

United Kingdom: 6 Chandos Street, London W1M 0LQ; tel: +44-20-7636 2924; fax: +44-20-7636 2969; e-mail: namibia@globalnet.co.uk

United States: c/o Kartagener Associates, 12 West 37th Street, New York, NY 10018; tel: 212-465-0619; fax: 212-868-1654.

Namibia Wildlife Resorts

P Bag 13378, Windhoek, Namibia; tel: +264-61-236 975 or +27-21-419 3190; fax: +264-61-224 900 or +27-21-421 5840; e-mail: nwr@iwwn.com.na

CAMPING

Sesriem Camp

Namibia Wildlife Resorts, P Bag 13378, Windhoek, Namibia; tel: +264-61-236 975 or +27-21-419 3190; fax: +264-61-224 900 or +27-21-421 5840; e-mail: nwr@iwwn.com.na

Twenty campsites, each with its own braai (barbecue) site, lie in the shade of ancient camel thorn trees. $

LODGING

PRICE GUIDE – double occupancy

$ = under $100 $$ = $100–$200
$$$ = $200–$300 $$$$ = $300+

Kulala Desert Lodge

P.O. Box 40584, Windhoek, Namibia; tel: +264-63-293 234; fax: +264-63-293 235; e-mail: kulala@iwwn.com.na

This desert lodge, 18 miles (29km) from Sesriem, has thatched tents connected to flat-roofed buildings with bathroom facilities. Outside steps enable the occupants to enjoy the view and sleep on the roof. Activities cost extra. $$

Mövenpick Sossusvlei Lodge

P.O. Box 6900, Ausspannplatz, Namibia; tel/fax: +264-61-248 338; e-mail: info@movenpick.co.na; web: www.movenpick-hotels.com

Close to the park gates, this lodge, painted in desert colors, consists of scattered canvas bedrooms with private bathrooms, a small pool, and a buffet-style barbecue that offers a chance to try game meat. Activities cost extra. $$

Sossusvlei Mountain Lodge

CCAfrica, P Bag X27, Benmore 2010, South Africa; tel: +27-11-809 4300; fax: +27-11-809 4400; e-mail: bookings@ccafrica.com; web:www.ccafrica.com

This new lodge, about 250 miles (400km) southwest of Windhoek, is in 445,000-acre (180,000-hectare) Namib Rand Nature Reserve, bordering the national park. Ten air-conditioned chalets with private baths overlook a grass plain and red sand dunes. A pool is on the property. $$$

Swakopmund Hotel

Bahnhof Street, P.O. Box 616, Swakopmund, Namibia; tel: +264-64-400 800; fax: +264-64-400 801; e-mail: shec@iafrica.com.na

This impressive colonial station building has been converted to a hotel with 90 bedrooms, a fine restaurant, pool, and casino. $$

Wilderness Sossusvlei Camp

Namib Travel Shop, P.O. Box 6850, Windhoek, Namibia; tel: +264-61-225 178; fax: +264-61-239 455; e-mail: iaind@nts.com.na

United States: Tim Farrell and Associates, P.O. Box 7300, Wilton, CT 06897-7300; tel: 203-762-8050; fax: 203-762-7323; e-mail: SafariTim@aol.com

In this lodge, built around a kopje, each room has a private bath and its own plunge pool. Rooms are linked to the dining room and bar by a wooden walkway. $$$

TOUR OPERATORS

Charly's Desert Tours

11 Kaiser Wilhelm Street, P.O. Box 1400, Swakopmund, Namibia; tel: +264-64-404 341; fax: +264-64-404 821; e-mail: charlydt@iwwn.com.na

Day trips from Swakopmund explore the northern part of the desert and Welwitschia Flats.

Namib Sky Adventure Safaris

P.O. Box 5197, Windhoek, Namibia; tel: +264-63-293 233; fax: +264-63-293 241; e-mail: namibsky@iwwn.com.na

Book in advance for early-morning hot-air-balloon flights from several private lodges in the area.

O. C. Ventures

P.O. Box 784, Windhoek, Namibia; tel: +264-61-236 692; fax: +264-61-236 693; e-mail: ocv@mweb.co.na

Knowledgeable guides lead custom tours for small groups.

Oryx Tours

P.O. Box 2058, Windhoek, Namibia; tel: +264-61-217 454; fax: +264-61-263 417; e-mail: oryx@oryxtours.com.na

This local tour operator offers a wide variety of scheduled and customized tours, from day trips on the dunes to two-week safaris.

Excursions

Fish River Canyon

Directorate of Environmental Affairs, Ministry of Environment and Tourism, P Bag 13306, Windhoek, Namibia; tel: +264-61-284 2366; fax: +264-61-224 900.

Fish River Canyon in southern Namibia is the second-largest canyon in the world. Best viewed in low light, when its cliffs of banded rock disappear dramatically into the distance, visitors will hardly see another soul. To hike the canyon, book well in advance with the Ministry of Environment and Tourism office in Windhoek. The small spa at Ai-Ais hot springs is set in the canyon's southern end.

National West Coast Tourist Recreational Area

Namibia Wildlife Resorts, P Bag 13378, Windhoek, Namibia; tel: +264-61-236 975; fax: +264-61-224 900; e-mail: nwr@iwwn.com.na

For much of the year, this coastal strip between Swakopmund and the Ugab River is empty – of people, animals, even plant life. This is desert terrain. In high summer, however, Namibians flock here by the thousands to escape the heat and to fish. There are large campsites along the C34 at Mile 14, Jakkalsputz, Mile 72, and Mile 108. Desert tours and boat trips can be arranged, but the highlight is undoubtedly the Cape Cross fur seal colony, home of 300,000 animals.

Walvis Bay

Mola Mola Safaris, 122 Sam Nukoma Avenue, P.O. Box 980, Walvis Bay, Namibia; tel: +264-64-205 500; fax: +264-64-207 593; e-mail: mola-mola@iafrica.com.na

Sandwiched between the desert and the sea, Walvis Bay is

a haven for wildlife. Hundreds of waders, herons, egrets, ducks, gulls, and terns live in reedy pools at the bird sanctuary. The lagoon is edged with vast colonies of flamingos and pelicans. Dolphins play around the bows of boats heading out to the huge seal colonies.

Etosha
National Park
Namibia

CHAPTER **10**

The overriding color of **Etosha**, the "Place of Emptiness," is white – white rocks, white dust, and a white shimmering pan some 72 miles (116km) long and 42 miles (68km) wide that occupies nearly a quarter of the park. It is a vast, gleaming dinner plate across which dance distant mirages; an occasional springbok or ostrich meanders past like a black speck on a white page. ◆ The **Etosha Pan** was once an inland sea. A San legend claims that it was formed by the tears of a Heiqum woman who wept as she cradled her dead child. When the tears dried, all that remained was glittering, white salt. Water still enters the pan in the rainy season via the **Ekuma** and **Oshigambo Rivers**, though water levels of any considerable depth are rare. Some water usually remains in the main pan close to **Namutoni** near the park's eastern entrance, and it is in this area, particularly in the adjacent **Fisher's Pan**, where you may spot flamingos and other waterbirds after a good rain. ◆ Etosha is one of Africa's **Water holes along the edge of a dry, ancient seabed attract a fascinating array of wildlife, including cheetahs and rare black rhinos.** largest parks despite being reduced to less than a third of its original size by various governments over the years. Its 8,600 square miles (22,270 sq km) stretch far beyond Etosha Pan, though the best game viewing is at the water holes scattered along the main road, which skirts the southern border of the pan and connects that park's three rest-camps: Namutoni, **Halali**, and **Okaukuejo**. ◆ Few people bother to do game drives in the park. It is far better to wait beside a water hole and let the animals come to you. Pinstriped zebras line up at water's edge, small groups of stately, curly-horned kudu wander out from behind the brush, and springbok and black-faced

Black rhino horns are not made of bone but of a tissue similar to hair and nails. Though generally placid, rhinos are unpredictable and will charge if annoyed or threatened.

impalas come down in large herds with red hartebeests. Oryx and plumed ostriches prefer water holes in drier areas. Male oryx spend much of their time sparring with each other, their rapier-like horns coming dangerously close to spearing their opponents. The horns often become locked as one male tries to force another to its knees. At last the weaker animal breaks free and runs off, pursued briefly by the victor. Ostriches watch the battles between sips, their heads bobbing up and down like the synchronized motions of oil pumps.

Giraffes are among the most cautious drinkers, checking the area thoroughly before daring to splay their front legs and drop their heads to the water, an awkward and vulnerable position. Watch them carefully for they often reveal the presence of a predator – all suddenly turning in the same direction to peer down their noses at an approaching leopard.

Big Cats

Lions are often spotted near the water holes. Although they usually lie in the shade under low vegetation a little way back from the pools, they occasionally indulge in "beachfront" sunbathing. That's when large herds of thirsty antelope hang back, patiently waiting until the cats leave before drinking, or inching toward the water only to bolt away at the slightest rustle of a leaf.

The Etosha lions are said to be larger than those elsewhere in Africa, and many have black manes. One of the best ways to locate them is to keep a lookout for their saucer-sized paw prints in the dust. Like many other game-park animals, they have adapted to modern conveniences and frequently use the park roads to get from place to place. Other, smaller cats like the African wildcat, which resembles a household tabby from a distance, turn up from time to time and are most active just before dark. Etosha also has one of the largest resident cheetah populations in Africa. The cats are normally found in a belt of grassy plains along the southern edge of the pan, where they can use their speed to best advantage when hunting.

Elephant herds are commonly sighted at such water holes as **Goas** near Halali. From mid-morning onward, family groups make their way through the mopane and combretum scrub, and as one family leaves the water hole, the next rolls out of the bush in single file. The young elephants are particularly exuberant. As they approach the pool, they can hold back no longer and break into a brisk trot, trunks flailing as they make for the cool water. After drinking their fill, the

Drinking is a challenge for giraffes (left), who have only seven vertebrae in their long necks and need to splay their legs to reach the water.

Gemsbok (top) duel for supremacy in the dust of an Etosha pan.

Built for speed, a cheetah (right) sprints after its prey; the cats can achieve bursts of speed in excess of 60 miles (100km) per hour.

Cheetahs on the Run

Cheetahs are best known for being the fastest land mammals, capable of achieving speeds in excess of 60 miles (100km) per hour over short distances. Their life, however, is difficult: lions and other large predators dispossess these lightweight sprinters of their kill, and overenthusiastic game watchers in national parks often drive them from their prey.

Cheetahs prefer to hunt in open country, and Namibia's farmland areas suit them perfectly, especially as there are few lions. As a consequence, Namibia has become the world cheetah stronghold. Unfortunately, local farmers persecute them in the belief that they take large numbers of livestock. The International Cheetah Research and Education Centre has stepped in on the cheetahs' behalf. The organization not only rehabilitates and releases injured cats but provides farmers with guard dogs for their livestock and helps educate them about conserving this beautiful and increasingly scarce animal.

A flock of quelea birds (right) gathers at a water hole; the birds can strip trees and crops in seconds.

Stripes (below) on Burchell's zebras are as individual as fingerprints; no two are exactly alike.

juveniles lie down to bathe while their mothers suck up water or lumps of semiliquid mud and spray it over their backs, flanks, and bellies. Having had their turn, the now-black and gleaming elephants exit, and the next dusty group, almost white in comparison, tramps in through the entrance.

Like its lions, Etosha's elephants are said to be larger than those elsewhere, though it may merely be easier to grasp their full size in this wide-open landscape. Certainly their tusks rarely achieve any appreciable length. Even the old bulls that often monopolize the water hole at Okaukuejo have thick tusks that are kept short by the harsh, stony environment. Another large herbivore, the black rhino, is a special feature of Etosha. These rare creatures are particularly common at the Okaukuejo water hole, where floodlights enable guests at nearby bungalows to watch game around the clock. It's not unusual for several rhinos to turn up in a single evening or for observers to see them interact with each other or with elephants and lions.

Birds in Abundance

Okaukuejo is also excellent for bird-watching, as is Halali, situated near the midpoint of the main park road in Etosha's only hilly area. Nightjars turn up at both camps, wheeling through the night sky in pursuit of insects that swarm around the floodlights. Fork-tailed drongos and pale-winged starlings, although diurnal birds, join in too. A great many wading and waterbirds are attracted to the water holes during the day, and the grounds of the rest-camps are worth exploring for the owls that often roost there.

In general, birds in the area of the rest-camps are accustomed to the presence of people and tolerate being approached fairly closely. Okaukuejo is noted for its hornbills and African hoopoes. Other birds to watch out for in the park are kori bustards, the largest flying birds in the world, and some 35 raptor species ranging from the tiny pygmy falcon to the martial eagle.

Traveling beyond the main tourist tracks along the southern edge of the pan is rough going, and there are few places elsewhere in Etosha that are truly worth visiting for their own sake. In any case, the entire western flank of the park is closed to the public. Restless travelers may want to investigate a small patch of rather knobbly moringa trees west of Okaukuejo known as either the Haunted or Fairy Tale Forest. Otherwise, they can visit the converted, "Beau Geste" fort, now a national monument, at Namutoni. Originally built in 1906, it was destroyed by a force of

Desert Survivors

"Nasty, brutish, and short" is how English philosopher Thomas Hobbes summed up the life of man in a "state of nature." It's been assumed ever since that so-called primitive people are engaged in a constant struggle for survival, while we civilized folk lead lives of ease and affluence.

In the 1960s, Harvard anthropologist Richard Lee put that notion to the test in his study of the San people of southern Namibia and southwestern Botswana. A linguistically distinct group with a tenure of some 70,000 years in southern Africa, the San had long been forced into the harsh environment of the Kalahari Desert by the incursion and outright persecution of Bantu and European pastoralists. Here they lived lightly on the land, gathering scores of edible plants, felling game with poisoned arrowheads, and extracting moisture from water-bearing roots and melons during the dry season. Nomadic and egalitarian, they possessed only what they could carry and shared scarce resources.

Surprisingly, Lee discovered that the San had to work only about 20 hours per week to provide themselves a balanced and varied diet. The rest of their time was devoted to leisure. What's more, their diet conformed to modern ideas of good nutrition – low in fat, salt, and sugar, and high in fiber, vitamins, and polyunsaturated oils. Although their technology was simple and their needs were few, it was clearly wrong to say that they struggled to survive.

Unfortunately, the San haven't fared well in recent decades. Of the 50,000 that remain, few pursue a traditional hunter-gatherer lifestyle, and those that eke out a living in the "modern" world have been plagued by the distinctly modern afflictions of poverty and hunger.

Owambos, and faithfully reconstructed in 1956. The Namibian flag is lowered at sunset every evening from the top of the main turret, where the views of the "Place of Emptiness" are among the best in the park.

The weathered face of a San elder (top) tells a story of survival in an unforgiving land.

San hunters (above) search for desert game.

Night falls over a former German fort (left) now used as a safari lodge.

DETAILS

When to Go

You can visit Namibia at any time. December and January are likely to be both busy and hot, with midday temperatures up to 90°F (32°C) and some stormy afternoons from December to March. However, the rains rarely make roads impassable or pose serious inconveniences. From April to May and late July to early September, Etosha is busy with local residents on vacation, and advance reservations are essential. May, June, and September have midday temperatures of 70°F (21°C) to 75°F (24°C); it can be cold at night in July and August. September and October are the best months for game viewing, with the water sources shrinking and wildlife more visible. It can be uncomfortably hot in October and November, with high temperatures up to 100°F (38°C).

Because of political unrest in nearby Angola, it is recommended that you check with your embassy for travel advisories before making plans.

Getting There

Windhoek is Namibia's main international airport, but intercontinental services are limited. The common alternative is to connect via Johannesburg, where SAA and Air Namibia offer regular service.

Once in Namibia, there are fly-in safaris from Windhoek, some exclusively to Etosha, others including Etosha in a longer itinerary visiting other parts of the country. These tend to be expensive but are good if your time is limited. Most people opt to drive themselves or take a guided safari in a minibus or four-wheel-drive

vehicle. Roads in Namibia are generally very good, especially by African standards, and traffic is light. From Windhoek it is a little more than 260 miles (420km) to Okaukuejo and 320 miles (510km) to Namutoni.

A standard vehicle will handle all of the roads in Etosha that are open to visitors, but vehicles with high clearance give you better views of wildlife.

INFORMATION

Directorate of Environmental Affairs

Ministry of Environment and Tourism, P Bag 13306, Windhoek, Namibia; tel: +264-61-284 2366; fax: +264-61-224 900.

Namibia Embassies

United Kingdom: 6 Chandos Street, London W1M 0LQ; tel: +44-20-7636 6244; fax: +44-20-7637 5694; e-mail: namibia-highcom@btconnect.com

United States: 1605 New Hampshire Avenue, N.W., Washington, DC 20009; tel: 202-986-0540; fax: 202-986-0443.

Namibia Tourism

P Bag 13346, Windhoek, Namibia; tel: +264-61-284 2360; fax: +264-61-284 2364; e-mail: tourism@iwwn.com.na; web: www.tourism.com.na

United Kingdom: 6 Chandos Street, London W1M 0LQ; tel: +44-20-7636 2924; fax: +44-20-7636 2969; e-mail: namibia@globalnet.co.uk

United States: c/o Kartagener Associates, 12 West 37th Street, New York, NY 10018; tel: 212-465-0619; fax: 212-868-1654.

Namibia Wildlife Resorts

P Bag 13378, Windhoek, Namibia; tel: +264-61-236 975 or +27-21-419 3190; fax: +264-61-224 900 or +27-21-421 5840; e-mail: nwr@iwwn.com.na

CAMPING

Government Rest-Camps

Namibia Wildlife Resorts, P. Bag 13378, Windhoek, Namibia; tel: +264-61-236 975 or +27-21-419 3190; fax: +264-61-224 900 or +27-21-421 5840; e-mail: nwr@iwwn.com.na

Etosha has three government rest-camps, at Okaukuejo, Halali, and Namutoni. All offer camp-sites or a choice of bungalows, some with private baths. The camps have floodlit water holes and instant access to the national park. Facilities include a park office, store, restaurant, filling station, pool, and post office. $

LODGING

PRICE GUIDE – double occupancy

$ = under $100 $$ = $100–$200
$$$ = $200–$300 $$$$ = $300+

Etosha Aoba Lodge

Fisher's Pan Game Farm, P.O. Box 469, Tsumeb, Namibia; tel: +264-67-229 100; fax: +264-67-229 101; e-mail: aoba@tsu.namib.com; web: www.natron.net/tour/etoaoba/main.html

This small lodge is set deep in the bush, about half an hour from the Von Lindequist Gate near Namutoni. It sleeps up to 20 people. $$

Mokuti Lodge

P.O. Box 403, Tsumeb, Namibia; tel: +264-67-229 084; fax: +264-67-229 091; e-mail: mokuti@tsumeb.namib.com; web: www.mokuti.namib.com

This large private lodge beside Namutoni's Von Lindequist Gate has small bungalows scattered around the grounds. Short trails afford views of white-faced bontebok, among other game. $$

Mushara Lodge

P.O. Box 90538, 135 Krupp Street, Windhoek, Namibia; tel: +264-

61-253 992; fax: +264-61-221 919;
e-mail: discover@iafrica.com.na

Thatched chalets with private baths, a restaurant, and a pool are features of this lodge, about six miles (10km) from Namutoni's Von Lindequist Gate. $$$

Ongava Lodge

Wilderness Safaris, c/o Namib Travel Shop, P.O. Box 6850, Windhoek, Namibia; tel: +264-61-225 178; fax: +264-61-239 455; e-mail: iaind@nts.com.na

United Kingdom: Wilderness Safaris, c/o Outposts, Narracott, Drewsteignton, Exeter, Devon EX6 6PU; tel: +44-164-728 1665; fax: +44-164-728 1288; e-mail: outposts@usa.net

United States: Wilderness Safaris, c/o Tim Farrell and Associates, P.O. Box 7300, Wilton, CT 06897-7300; tel: 203-762-8050; fax: 203-762-7323; e-mail: SafariTim@aol.com

Close to Andersson Gate near Okaukuejo, this lodge accommodates up to 20 guests on an 86,500-acre (35,000-hectare) concession area bordering Etosha. Activities include walks and day and night game drives. $$$.

TOUR OPERATORS

Oryx Tours

P.O. Box 2058, Windhoek, Namibia; tel: +264-61-217 454; fax: +264-61-263 417; e-mail: oryx@oryxtours.com.na

This local tour operator offers a wide variety of scheduled and customized tours.

O. C. Ventures

P.O. Box 784, Windhoek, Namibia; tel: +264-61-236 692; fax: +264-61-236 693; e-mail: ocv@mweb.com.na

Guides with detailed knowledge provide personal, mainly customized, tours for families and small groups.

Excursions

Caprivi Strip

Namibia Tourism, P Bag 13346, Windhoek, Namibia; tel: +264-61-284 2360; fax: +264-61-284 2364; e-mail: tourism@iwwn.com.na; web: www.tourism.com.na

The lush, green panhandle of northeast Namibia, watered by the giant Zambezi, Chobe, and Okavango Rivers, is rich with wildlife, including hippos, crocodiles, waterbuck, buffalo, reedbuck, red lechwe, and sitatunga. There are three national parks along the Caprivi Game Reserve: Mahango, the farthest west, borders the Okavango River; Mamili and Mudumu, two new national parks, lie farther east. Mamili is mainly marshland, while Mudumu is riverine forest habitat.

Damaraland

Namibia Tourism, P Bag 13346, Windhoek, Namibia; tel: +264-61-284 2360; fax: +264-61-284 2364; e-mail: tourism@iwwn.com.na; web: www.tourism.com.na

Damaraland has wonderful mountain scenery and many cave paintings, some sadly vandalized. The rocks at Twyfelfontein have been engraved with patterns and pictures of animals dating back to the Stone Age. These, like the nearby dolerite columns of Burnt Mountain and the Organ Pipes, are best seen in low light. All three sites are about 60 miles (100km) south of Khorixas. Nearby, the Petrified Forest is well known for its desert-adapted elephants and rare Hartmann's mountain zebras. Spend a couple of nights at Damaraland Camp or Palmwag to increase your chances of seeing them.

Skeleton Coast National Park

Namibia Tourism, P Bag 13346, Windhoek, Namibia; tel: +264-61-284 2360; fax: +264-61-284 2364; e-mail: tourism@iwwn.com.na; web: www.tourism.com.na

Frequently shrouded in fog by the cold Benguela Current and battered by the South Atlantic, this uninhabited, uncompromising shore has caused numerous wrecks – hence its name. Along with its skeletal ships, the coast is known for colonies of Cape fur seals and visiting whales. Brown hyenas and even lions plunder the strand. Much of the stony desert is remarkably delicate, with brown lichen fields, like rusty steel wool, which can be transformed by infrequent water. Vehicle tracks on the dunes can last for decades.

Hwange
National Park
Zimbabwe

C H A P T E R **11**

Few places on earth so vividly illustrate the life-giving properties of water as **Hwange National Park**. In April or May, as summer draws to a close, the last rains of the season fall over this arid tract of Zimbabwean bush, roughly the size of Belgium yet practically bereft of natural sources of perennial water. Over the months that follow, every hint of moisture is sucked from the earth by the scorching African sun, except in the few places where humans intervene. ◆ Come August or September, with the ground baked hard and the grass a dull, dead brown, all life converges on a series of pumped water holes. Large herds of grazers arrive, attracted from the distant thirstlands of Botswana by the sweet smell of standing water. And then there are the elephants, nearly 35,000 of the massive creatures, a pachydermal phenomenon of staggering proportions. By late October, the bush vibrates incessantly with the sound of trumpeting bulls. ◆ Aficionados of Hwange

Man-made water holes have transformed this once-neglected region into a world-class game reserve.

regard long game drives during the dry season as an unnecessary expense of energy. Far better, they say, to wait beside a water hole and watch the drama unfold. Rival herds of elephants jostle for drinking space, while mixed groups of wildebeests and zebras mill between their legs, and legions of buffalo arrive in a cloud of dust to wallow in the shallow pans. Every so often, lions and spotted hyenas slink onto the stage to slake their thirst – and to hunt. In the dry season, Hwange is unique in the extent to which young elephants form a substantial portion of the diet of Africa's two largest predators.

Young baboons rely on their mothers for nutrition and safety and, after about six weeks old, are often seen riding on their mothers' backs.

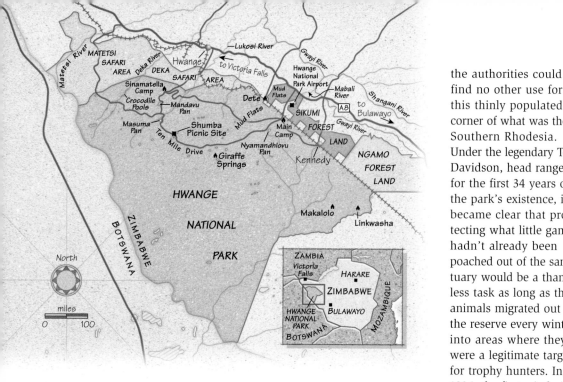

 the authorities could find no other use for this thinly populated corner of what was then Southern Rhodesia. Under the legendary Ted Davidson, head ranger for the first 34 years of the park's existence, it became clear that protecting what little game hadn't already been poached out of the sanctuary would be a thankless task as long as the animals migrated out of the reserve every winter into areas where they were a legitimate target for trophy hunters. In 1936, the first windmills were erected to pump water all year into a few select pans; today, diesel pumps are used for the same purpose at 60 pans.

Useless Land

Situated in northwest Zimbabwe along the Botswana border, Zimbabwe's largest park, founded in 1928, protects a huge 5,612-square-mile (14,535-sq-km) tract of savanna interspersed with thick stands of acacia, teak and mopane woodland. In ecological terms, it is essentially an extension of the Kalahari sandveld ecosystem that dominates neighboring Botswana, forming the eastern extent of the range of such dry-country endemics as Bradfield's hornbill and red-billed francolin.

Hwange was originally set aside as a game sanctuary for the simple reason that

Ten Mile Drive

Main Camp, which lies close to the Bulawayo–Victoria Falls trunk road, is the most accessible point of entry to Hwange. It is also the starting point for the superb **Ten Mile Drive**, a loop that wears heavily on brake and clutch with another exciting animal encounter every 500 yards. Literally and figuratively, the high point of this loop is the stilted viewing platform overlooking **Nyamandhlovu Pan**, visited by a virtually endless stream of wildlife – the ubiquitous elephant herds; lofty giraffes demonstrating their undignified drinking stance; shy, majestic greater kudu; families of highly

Spotted hyenas (above) are capable predators but often band together to steal game brought down by big cats.

Game-viewing platforms (right) make it easy to observe wildlife without disturbing it.

Elephants (right) disperse into the bush during the November rains; an adult can consume more than 300 pounds (136kg) of vegetation a day.

strung warthogs; and squabbling baboons.

For most day-trippers, Ten Mile Drive *is* Hwange, and while this loop does offer arguably the most consistent game viewing in the public sector of the park, it is also the one area that tends to be marred by vehicle congestion.

Adventurous travelers should explore deeper into the park, following the nominally tarred road that leads westward to **Sinamatella Camp**. Perched on one of the few sizeable hills found in this predominantly flat reserve, Sinamatella offers views of up to 30 miles (50km) across the surrounding mopane woodland, while the nearby **Mandavu** and **Masuma Pans** are among the largest and most productive bodies of water in the park. Sinamatella is also noteworthy for regular nocturnal raids by honey-badgers, small but pugnacious predators that have, reportedly, been known to run between the legs of male buffalo and bite off their testicles.

Humans, Keep Out

Only a tiny portion of Hwange, essentially the far north, is traversed by public roads, a product of the long-standing policy confining tourist development to the reserve's periphery. Much of the southern part of the park remains wilderness, entirely closed to visitors, while the remainder has been chopped up into three exclusive concessions that function in most respects as private reserves. Visitors

to **Makalolo**, **Linkwasha**, and **Giraffe Springs**, each of which hosts one small upmarket bush lodge, have the privilege of experiencing the African bush at its most untrammeled, a rare haven where one can still drive for hours without seeing another vehicle, evoking the atmosphere of safaris before the advent of package tours.

Rigid gate-closing times are applied in the public part of the park, but game drives in the remote southern concessions continue long after the setting sun has transformed the sky from daylight blue, through golden

The lilac-breasted roller (right), one of Africa's most colorful birds, favors mopane woodland. Crowned cranes (far right) flock in grasses and marshes.

Alert and active, a black-backed jackal (below) relies on cunning to survive in the bush. Principally a scavenger, it also hunts small animals.

Under Cloudy Skies

The common wisdom that Hwange is essentially a dry-season park is likely to be repeated only by somebody who hasn't been there during the rains. While it's true that after late November the vast herds of elephants disperse beyond the park boundaries leaving only semiresident bulls and small

red and deep purple, to the star-spangled nights typical of wild Africa. During the magical hours following sunset, lucky visitors may encounter leopards and spotted hyenas, smaller predators such as African wildcats (the progenitor of the domestic cat) and genets, as well as nocturnal birds such as nightjars, owls, and coursers. Every now and then, the spotlight picks out what appears to be a pair of disembodied eyes bouncing up and down in the dark. This is a spring hare, an unusual rabbit-sized rodent particularly common on the sandy soils of Hwange, and the only African mammal whose mode of locomotion resembles that of a kangaroo.

matriarchal herds, other wildlife is still plentiful and the lush summer scenery is magnificent – an almost surreal landscape of tall grass and swaying *ilala* palms over-hung by blue skies and fluffy white clouds.

Hwange is an impressive birding destination at any time of year. Particularly notable are the gigantic kori bustards, decidedly campy ground hornbills (check out the eye-lashes!), and dazzling lilac-breasted rollers. Avian activity reaches fever pitch during the rains, when the myriad shallow depressions that dot the park become seasonal water pans, and the parched plains are transformed into grassy swamps. The proliferation of standing water provokes an eruption of

The Upside-Down Tree

Distinguished by its bulbous trunk, ghostly bark, and bare branches that reach for the sky like upturned roots, the baobab tree is found throughout much of tropical Africa in hot, dry, relatively low-lying areas. As a result of its distinctive shape, the baobab lies at the center of numerous legends, perhaps none more pervasive than the notion that it was turned upside down as a punishment for annoying the Almighty. The Masai around Tanzania's Tarangire National Park believe that these ancient trees, thought to live more than 1,000 years, provide sanctuary for the spirits of revered ancestors.

The baobab is Africa's largest tree. Its massive, spongy trunk becomes hollow as it grows old and fat and provides homes for a legion of small animals and birds. The pith surrounding the seeds in the hard gourdlike fruit can be eaten; it has a slightly sour, floury texture, not unlike cream of tartar.

Steeped in legend, Africa's baobab trees (below) tower over their arid homelands.

Leopard spots (bottom) blend perfectly with the speckled light of their treetop haunts.

insects and amphibians, which in turn attracts a huge influx of migrant and nomadic birds. Storks and waders haunt the fringes of the swamps, pairs of crowned cranes prance decorously through the tall grass, and Palaearctic eagles and hawks flock eagerly around emerging flying-ant colonies.

It is during the rains, too, that many of the region's most colorful birds come into breeding plumage: paradise and shaft-tailed wydahs with their absurdly proportioned tails, bright yellow weavers, and the gold-and-scarlet bishops that float like oversized bumblebees above patches of swampy grass. Most memorable of all are the migrant flocks of red-and-blue carmine bee-eaters that swoop and dive around safari vehicles, gulping down insects that fly up in the car's wake.

Big Five

For first-time visitors to Africa, Hwange is superb Big Five country: lions, elephants, and buffalo can be taken more or less for granted, while more elusive black rhinoceroses and leopards are present in significant numbers. Yet there is so much more to Hwange than lions and elephants. It is, for instance, one of the few reserves that harbors the full hand of Africa's "big five" antelope – eland, roan, sable, greater kudu, and gemsbok. An estimated 300 to 400 Cape hunting dogs represent nearly 10 percent of the global population, and tiny but endearing bat-eared foxes, a dry-country specialty, often emerge from their burrows in the late afternoon to feed on small birds and rodents.

Of the 107 mammal and 420 bird species recorded in Hwange, none are more meaningful than elephants. Poached close to extinction in this part of Zimbabwe prior to 1928 and devastated by ivory poachers in the 1980s, the great number of elephants who migrate through Hwange represent a triumph of survival over wholesale slaughter. To drive out of camp on a crisp winter morning and come across a herd of a hundred or more elephants at a water hole drinking and playing, snorting and trumpeting, is a sensation beyond rational description. Raise a cup of steaming coffee in the direction of these social and intelligent creatures. It would be an immeasurably poorer world without them.

TRAVEL TIPS

DETAILS

When to Go

For wall-to-wall elephants, winter (June to September) is the time to visit Hwange. The large herds start to move into the reserve in June and July, and the population density peaks from September through early November. Winter is also marginally better for seeing predators. The summer months (mid-November to early May) aren't quite as good in terms of game viewing, but the scenery is stunning, and the birding superlative – and there is still plenty of wildlife around. Winter months are clear and dry with an average high temperature of 70°F (21°C); October is dry but extremely hot (about 95°F/35°C). The rains fall in summer, when the temperature is around 90°F (32°C).

Getting There

Zimbabwe's main international airport is in Harare, but many visitors to Hwange fly to Johannesburg, where SAA and Air Zimbabwe have regular flights to Victoria Falls, the nearest full-service airport to the park (under two hours' drive). A local flight connects Hwange's small airport with Harare, Kariba, Victoria Falls, and Bulawayo. Daily charter flights from Victoria Falls link the southern concessions. For drivers, Main Camp lies about 10 miles (16km) west of the trunk road between Bulawayo and Victoria Falls and can be reached in an ordinary car. With care, most of the roads within the reserve are passable in any car, though it would be wise to confirm this after heavy rain. Vehicles can be rented in Harare, Bulawayo, or Victoria Falls. Tour operators in Victoria Falls offer a selection of organized packages ranging from day trips to four-day safaris.

Travel Advisory: Due to political unrest in Zimbabwe, visitors are urged to consult their embassies for the latest travel advisories before making their plans.

INFORMATION

Zimbabwe Embassies

United Kingdom: Zimbabwe House, 429 The Strand, London WC2R 0SA; tel: +44-20-7836 7755; fax: +44-20-7379 1167.

United States: 1608 New Hampshire Avenue, N.W., Washington, DC 20009; tel: 202-332-7100; fax: 202-483-9326.

Zimbabwe National Parks Board

Central Booking Office, P.O. Box CY862, Harare, Zimbabwe; tel: +263-4-739 8330.

Bulawayo Booking Office, P.O. Box 2283, Bulawayo, Zimbabwe; tel: +263-9-63646.

Zimbabwe Tourist Board

United Kingdom: Zimbabwe House, 429 The Strand, London WC2R 0SA; tel: +44-20-7836 7755; fax: +44-20-7379 1167; web: www.mother.com/zimweb

United States: Rockefeller Center, 1270 Avenue of the Americas, Suite 1905, New York, NY 10020; tel: 212-332-1090; fax: 212-332-1093.

CAMPING

Hwange National Park

Zimbabwe National Parks Board, Central Booking Office, P.O. Box CY862, Harare, Zimbabwe; tel: +263-4-792 782.

Bulawayo Booking Office, P.O. Box 2283, Bulawayo, Zimbabwe; tel: +263-9-63646.

Advance booking is essential for public camps within Hwange. Large and accessible Main Camp has affordable chalets with equipped kitchens and plenty of camping space. A small store stocks basic foods and drinks, and there's a restaurant and bar. Guided walks visit a nearby water hole, and game drives can be arranged using private four-wheel-drive vehicles that wait outside the restaurant. Sinamatella is the best of Hwange's public camps, situated on a solitary hill deep within the park. Accommodations are similar in price and standard to Main Camp. The store stocks nothing more substantial than cookies, but the restaurant is excellent. There are similar facilities in the small, somewhat remote Robins Camp in the far northwest of the park, the best area for seeing large predators.

Several of Hwange's fenced picnic sites can be booked as private campsites. Most overlook water holes, which can make for a genuinely exciting night. Mandavu, Kennedy I, Masuma, and Ngwethla are particularly recommended.

LODGING

Matetsi

CCAfrica, P Bag X27, Benmore 2010, South Africa; tel: +27-11-809 4300; fax: +27-11-809 4400; e-mail: bookings@ccafrica.com; web:www.ccafrica.com

Two luxury lodges are in the private Matetsi Game Reserve that links Hwange and Victoria Falls. Safari Lodge has scattered air-conditioned chalets overlooking a game-rich floodplain; Water Lodge overlooks the Zambezi River. Prices include all meals, game viewing, and a shuttle into Victoria Falls. $$$

Victoria Falls Hotel

P.O. Box 10, Victoria Falls, Zimbabwe; tel: +263-13-4203; fax: +263-13-4586; e-mail: zimsun@zimsun.co.zw

Expanded since it first opened in 1905, this classic hotel has retained a distinctly sepia-tinged, Edwardian mood with stately interiors and landscaped grounds overlooking the waterfall. $$$

Wilderness Lodges

United Kingdom: Outposts, Narracott, Drewsteignton, Exeter, Devon EX6 6PU; tel: +44-164-728 1665; fax: +44-164-728 1288; e-mail: outposts@usa.net

United States: Tim Farrell and Associates, P.O. Box 7300, Wilton, CT 06897-7300; tel: 203-762-8050; fax: 203-762-7323; e-mail: SafariTim@aol.com

Wilderness Safaris runs all three of the private concessions in the remote southern section of the national park. The game drives – with qualified rangers – are consistently exciting with lions, cheetahs, hyenas, elephants, and hippos regularly sighted. The service, food, and accommodations meet the highest standard. Makalolo Plains Lodge is a stilted camp overlooking a grassy floodplain. Linkwasha Camp, also set next to a floodplain, offers the highest probability of sighting eland, sable, and greater kudu. The most isolated of the three, Giraffe Springs is in the best part of the park for birding and for sightings of unusual mammals. $$$

TOUR OPERATORS

Dingane Tours

P.O. Box 107, Victoria Falls, Zimbabwe; tel: +263-13-4554; fax: +263-13-4217; e-mail: elewalk@africaonline.co.zw

Based in Victoria Falls, this small but reputable company offers a variety of short tours to Hwange and elsewhere in the region, and can arrange rafting, canoeing, helicopter trips, and other excursions aimed at upscale tourists.

Shearwater

P.O. Box 125, Victoria Falls, Zimbabwe; tel: +263-13-4531; fax: +263-13-4341; e-mail: shearadv@zol.co.zw

Popular with backpackers, this company based in central Victoria Falls runs daily rafting and canoeing trips on the Zambezi River and can arrange other activities upon request.

Excursions

Great Zimbabwe

Zimbabwe Tourist Board, Rockefeller Center, 1270 Avenue of the Americas, Suite 1905, New York, NY 10020; tel: 212-332-1090; fax: 212-332-1093.

These extensive and immensely atmospheric stone ruins are the remains of an indigenous city, capital of the massive Empire of the Mwene Mutapa, which flourished between the 8th and 15th centuries. Great Zimbabwe is a revelation, proof positive that Africa had a long and glorious history long before European colonists reached the continent.

Matobo National Park

Zimbabwe National Parks Board, Central Booking Office, P.O. Box CY862, Harare, Zimbabwe; tel: +263-4-792 782.

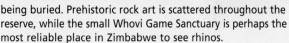

A short drive south of Bulawayo, the immense granite boulders and precarious balancing rock formations of the Matobo Hills are a hiker's paradise, with plenty of small game such as klipspringer, rock hyraxes, black eagles, and colorful agama lizards. The peculiar rock elephant shrew is easy to see at the park's most famous viewpoint, Rhodes' Grave, the rocky summit where Cecil John Rhodes insisted on being buried. Prehistoric rock art is scattered throughout the reserve, while the small Whovi Game Sanctuary is perhaps the most reliable place in Zimbabwe to see rhinos.

Victoria Falls

Victoria Falls Publicity Association, P.O. Box 97, Victoria Falls, Zimbabwe; tel: +263-13-4202.

It's a rare tourist who visits Hwange and doesn't continue to nearby Victoria Falls. This mile-wide waterfall, wreathed in rainbows, is one of Africa's most impressive natural landmarks and certainly the most famous. In recent years the town of Victoria Falls has set itself up as the adventure capital of southern Africa, with whitewater rafting in the Zambezi Gorge, the world's highest commercial bungee jump from a bridge in the no-man's-land between Zimbabwe and Zambia, microlight flights over the falls, even elephant-back safaris. Fortunately, the waterfall itself remains untainted by the frenzied commercialism that surrounds it.

Mana Pools
National Park
Zimbabwe

CHAPTER **12**

n Mana Pools the Zambezi River splits and splays, wide and languid, folding around islands and spreading off to feed side channels, flowing in a stream more than a mile wide. Fresh from the tumult of Victoria Falls and not completely tamed by the vast artificial Lake Kariba, in wet years it still washes life into floodplains baked hard over the dry season and fills countless depressions and natural canals. Around them, parklike stands of acacia, ebony, Natal mahogany, and fig trees, browsed high by dusty armies of buffalo and huge herds of elephants, are interspersed with grassland and riparian forest. Over the eons the river has altered course countless times, scooping long lakes into the valley floor until a lattice of oxbow lakes and waterways spreads across a wide valley of fertile alluvial soil. Some, such as **Chine** and **Long Pools**, retain water year-round. ◆ **Mana**

Drift with the current among hippos and crocodiles in a remote Zambezi waterland.

Pools National Park stretches 30 miles (50km) along the south bank of the Zambezi River at the Zimbabwe–Zambia border and extends 20 miles (32km) south to where the Zambezi Escarpment rises from the floodplain as a natural barrier. Across the water, Zambia's **Lower Zambezi National Park** preserves an area twice as large, rising into hills of broadleaf woodland. It is a natural haven for wildlife and, in the dry season, attracts the greatest concentration of game in southern Africa – reason enough for UNESCO to grant it World Heritage status. ◆ It's not just the density of game that makes Mana Pools so special. It is its sheer remoteness, and how close visitors can get to the natural world. Access to the park is only by plane to private airstrips at **Chikwenya** and **Rukomechi**, or on land by a dirt road leading from the main Harare–Chirundu Road to the park offices at **Nyamepi**.

Elephants gather at a lake near the Zambezi River. Highly social, they communicate with a complex language of sounds, many inaudible to humans, that is only now beginning to be understood.

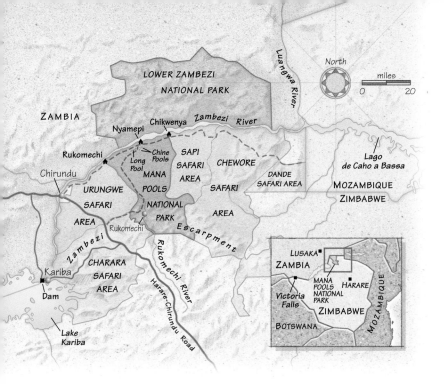

Urungwe Safari Area.
From here, it is a three-day canoe journey to the **Rukomechi River**, which marks the boundary of Mana Pools National Park. Along these shores, the wildlife extravaganza starts to build, but the most rewarding and game-crowded stretch of all is from Rukomechi to Chikwenya, 35 miles (56km) downstream at the eastern border of the park. By canoe this takes four days; longer, if you stop to walk among the game.

It is also possible to follow the river as it flows east, down as far as the Luangwa Valley. However, while on the north bank the wildlife is still protected in Zambia's Lower Zambezi National Park, to the south are the Zimbabwean hunting safari areas of **Sapi**, **Chewore**, and **Dande**.

Travel within the park, impossible in the wet season, is never easy. As a matter of policy, park authorities restrict vehicle numbers, and you won't find crowds of minivans here. Some lodges and permanent tented camps provide open Land Rovers with tiered seats, but even these are relatively uncommon.

Paddling for Africa

The famous 19th-century explorer David Livingstone called the Zambezi "God's Highway," and the water still provides the easiest – and most atmospheric – way to travel through the park. Most visitors experience Mana Pools by drifting with the current in two-person fiberglass canoes.

Some canoe safaris start in the shade of massive Kariba Dam, though the first three days, shadowed within a rocky, steep-sided gorge, are not terribly interesting. Most launch at **Chirundu**, upstream of the park's western border but already thick with game, selectively protected in the

Into the Hippo's Jaws

On any stretch of the Zambezi, encounters with wildlife can cause a frisson of fear. The slender chains of Canadian-style canoes on river safaris frequently pass straight through the bedrooms of snorting, honking hippos. Statistics say these are the most dangerous animals in Africa. A two-ton hippo snoozing in the shallows will panic in its efforts to reach deep water if it feels threatened, breezing straight through any canoe that might be in its way. At the first sight of telltale eyes glaring over the river surface paddlers slow, approaching nervously, banging their paddles lightly on their gunwales, herding the grumbling hippo to midstream safety before gliding past quickly in the shallows. Even so, mock charges, great open-jawed threatening surges, are common. A seriously annoyed hippo could charge underwater, rising at the last minute with a canoe-crunching bite.

If a pod of hippos means caution, this is nothing compared to the sheer terror caused by an elephant splashing calmly across the river on a collision course as the canoe drifts inexorably with the river current. Adding spice to the venture is the estimate that there's a resident crocodile, on average, for every 50 yards of riverbank. In case of hippo attack, the advice is to swim for the shore, while with a croc it's best to cling to your canoe. Take your pick and cross your fingers. Fortunately, encounters that turn into real adventures are rare. Most canoe safaris avoid such excitement, and the meetings with animals are intimate but pass with mutual respect.

A yawning hippo (left) displays its mighty jaws and tusklike lower teeth.

A lone male buffalo (below) can be extremely dangerous, attacking out of insecurity or simple bad temper. Swinging horns and trampling hooves often prove fatal.

A yellow-billed stork (opposite) feeds on the move, constantly probing marshes for insects and grubs.

Back on Shore

If river travel is too terrifying – and it can be – take to the land. Zimbabwean guides are the best trained in Africa, and, armed with their advice and the comforting presence of their guns, walking safaris stalk heart-stoppingly close to Africa's largest mammals.

Black rhinos were once common here. Their numbers have been decimated by poachers, but solitary animals can still be found, tucking sharp thorn trees into their hook-lipped mouths and funneling huge ears to listen for danger. When disturbed, they are apt to explode into an unpredictable charge – sometimes toward the threat, often in the other direction.

If rhinos are rare, other game is in plentiful supply. Buffalo gather into dusty armies

Missionary Explorer

Born in 1813 in Blantyre, Scotland, to poor but pious parents, David Livingstone was working in the cotton mills by age 10, studying at night to qualify as a doctor. In 1841 he traveled to Africa to work at Kuruman mission, 700 miles (1,130km) north of Cape Town. From there, he restlessly traveled farther, looking for suitable mission sites, fighting disease, hostile tribespeople, and wild animals. While recovering from a lion attack that left his left arm useless, he married Mary Moffat, daughter of a fellow missionary.

At 39, he embarked on his first great journey: blazing a trail from the heart of southern Africa to the west coast. With 27 men, he spent 17 months traveling 1,500 miles (2,400km) to arrive, exhausted, at Luanda in Angola. Next he determined to carve a route through to the eastern seaboard, navigating the Zambezi to arrive 19 months later at Quilimane, in Mozambique. For the first time, Africa had been spanned.

Next, the British government equipped a lavish expedition for the now famous explorer, and he discovered Lake Nyasa, the Shire River, and the Kongone entrance to the Zambezi. But illness took its toll on his helpers, wrecking the missions he tried to leave behind and, in 1862, taking the life of his wife. His tireless campaign against the slave trade brought him into conflict with the Portuguese, who persuaded the British to cut his funding.

Alone and broke, he eventually set off into Tanzania and over the next four years discovered Lakes Tanganyika, Moero, and Bangweolo, arriving exhausted at Ujiji, the headquarters of the trade in ivory and slaves, from where he mounted expeditions into the upper Congo. It was here, in 1871, that the journalist Henry Stanley found him, close to death, meeting with the famous words "Dr. Livingstone, I presume?" Livingstone died in 1873.

David Livingstone (left) is commemorated in a statue overlooking his celebrated "discovery," Victoria Falls.

Canoeists (right) pause to observe carmine bee-eaters (opposite, middle) nesting in the eroded banks of the Zambezi River.

A female waterbuck (opposite, bottom) grazes in the shallows; waterbuck travel in small herds and are often found in reeds and tall grasses near water.

Pools, so the highest growth is left for the elephants who can be seen straining upward on their hind legs to reach choice branches, or shaking the trees and vacuuming up seeds from the ground. Their notoriously inefficient digestive system extracts barely 40 percent of the seeds' valuable nutrients, allowing other animals to benefit a few hours down the line.

Smaller antelope are present in huge numbers, with impalas herding in bachelor groups and breeding harems. Shaggy waterbuck with a target ring on their bottoms, pop-art zebras, and pale-striped kudu move in smaller groups, splashing shoulder-deep from riverbank to island. Shy nyala antelope, similar to kudu but smaller and more chestnut colored, lurk within the dense riverine undergrowth. To make sure none of these herbivores goes to waste, lions, leopards, and hyenas are plentiful and always nearby, with cheetahs occasionally spotted and several packs of African painted dogs passing through on fast, effective hunting runs.

up to 2,000 strong and, in the dry season, more than 10,000 elephants crowd into this narrow corridor of land.

They don't just come for the water. Another prime attraction is the winterthorn tree, growing in tall umbrellas on open sandy ground. Its foliage sprouts through the dry season, providing forage for chattering baboons and browsing wildlife as well as shade from the burning sun. Later, when food is at its scarcest, each tree drops up to 880 pounds (400kg) of protein-rich seed pods. In the season of need, these can mean the difference between life and death. Giraffes are strangely absent from Mana

Soaring Skyward

The range of habitats attracts a huge variety of bird life, with 350 species identified. Fish eagles circle overhead, and the banks are lined with waders and waterfowl. Flocks of quelea swarm the woodlands, dense as locusts and almost as voracious. Rarer specialties include the trumpeter hornbill, Lilian's lovebird, and the red-winged pratincole, sometimes rising in great, wheeling columns. Fishermen can cast their lines for tigerfish, bream, and vundu, a type of catfish that can weigh up to 110 pounds (50kg).

As the light fails, canoes are pulled up on islands, tents are erected, and safari chairs set up in vantage points overlooking the river. A new cast of wildlife strolls onto the stage. Fruit bats flap heavily across the fiery sky, and hippos surge from the water for their nightly graze. Elephants wander close, checking on the new human arrivals on their territory, and then drift silently away into the bush. A spotted hyena skulks from its den wafting a powerful scent of carnivore, and a honey badger scurries between the tents. In a timeless land beyond the reach of electricity there are no lights in sight. But above the dark of the bush the sky is lit with the countless pinpricks of stars, brightening into a tapestry that sheds a ghostly glow on the agonized thorns of acacia and the dangling seeds of the sausage tree. Phantom shadows hint at nightly predators and the air shivers with the roar of lions. Their calls carry for miles, but always sound far closer. Time to retreat to the safety of your tent.

TRAVEL TIPS

DETAILS

When to Go

The best time of year for game viewing is in the dry months of August through October, when the waters of the Zambezi River and Mana Pools attract huge herds of buffalo, kudu, eland, zebras, waterbuck, and elephants. In October, however, high temperatures reach 100°F (38°C), and occasionally a hot wind can blow you upstream. From April through June, the bush is green, the bird life prolific, and the skies clear and dry with an average midday temperature of 75°F (24°C), but the game may be harder to find. The Mana Pools are closed through the rainy season (mid-November through April). Malaria is a risk year-round.

Getting There

Travelers fly into Harare or Victoria Falls (major regional operators include Air Zimbabwe, SAA, and British Airways-Com Air), then take a commuter flight to Kariba. From there it is a two-hour drive to Chirundu, and an hour by fast boat – or three days by canoe – to Rukomechi. A new air service run by Sefofane Zimbabwe Air Service (P.O. Box CT442, Victoria Falls; tel: +263-13-4576) flies daily from Kariba to Rukomechi and Chikwenya airstrips, bringing the Mana Pools into easy reach for the first time. A rough dirt road is passable only with a four-wheel-drive vehicle, even in the dry season.

Canoe safaris last from one to seven nights, reaching ever farther into Mana Pools. A fully catered safari from Rukomechi to Chikwenya, traversing the entire length of the national park, takes four days. Participation safaris, on which clients assist with the practicalities of camping and cooking, are much less expensive. Although canoe safaris offered on the Zambian side of the river are often cheaper, safety regulations are not always as stringent as those in Zimbabwe, and groups are often larger.

Travel advisory: Due to political unrest in Zimbabwe, visitors are urged to consult their embassies for the latest travel advisories before making their plans.

INFORMATION

Zimbabwe Embassies

United Kingdom: Zimbabwe House, 429 The Strand, London WC2R 0SA; tel: +44-20-7836 7755; fax: +44-20-7379 1167.

United States: 1608 New Hampshire Avenue, N.W., Washington, DC 20009; tel: 202-332-7100; fax: 202-483-9326.

Zimbabwe National Parks Board

Central Booking Office, P.O. Box CY862, Harare, Zimbabwe; tel: +263-4-739 8330.

Bulawayo Booking Office, P.O. Box 2283, Bulawayo, Zimbabwe; tel: +263-9-63646.

Zimbabwe Tourist Board

United Kingdom: Zimbabwe House, 429 The Strand, London WC2R 0SA; tel: +44-20-7836 7755; fax: +44-20-7379 1167; web: www.mother.com/zimweb

United States: Rockefeller Center, 1270 Avenue of the Americas, Suite 1905, New York, NY 10020; tel: 212-332-1090; fax 212-332-1093.

CAMPING

Mana Pools National Park

Zimbabwe National Parks Board, Central Booking Office, P.O. Box CY862, Harare, Zimbabwe; tel: +263-4-792 782.

Bulawayo Booking Office, P.O. Box 2283, Bulawayo, Zimbabwe; tel: +263-9-63646.

Inexpensive but limited facilities, with self-catering campsites and two-bedroom lodges, are near the park's Nyamepi headquarters. $

LODGING

PRICE GUIDE – double occupancy

$ = under $100 $$ = $100–$200
$$$ = $200–$300 $$$$ = $300+

River Lodges of Africa

P Bag 7013, Chiredzi, Zimbabwe; tel: +263-31-3129; fax: +263-31-3179.

Four small luxury lodges, run by leading black-rhino conservationist Clive Stockhill, offer excellent game viewing. All meals and activities are included in the price. $$$$.

Rukomechi and Chikwenya Lodges

United Kingdom: Outposts, Narracott, Drewsteignton, Exeter, Devon EX6 6PU; tel: +44-164-728 1665; fax: +44-164-728 1288; e-mail: outposts@usa.net

United States: Tim Farrell and Associates, P.O. Box 7300, Wilton, CT 06897-7300; tel: 203-762-8050; fax: 203-762-7323; e-mail: SafariTim@aol.com

Wilderness Safaris runs Rukomechi and Chikwenya Lodges in Zimbabwe. Accommodations overlook the Zambezi and offer rustic luxury in thatched chalets set among riverine trees. Sixteen beds in each lodge ensure the experience is private. All meals and activities are included in the price. $$$$.

Vundu Camp

Ivan Carter Safaris, Box 211, Ruwa, Zimbabwe; tel: +263-73-22392; fax: +263-73-2301.

The only fully independent camp in the Mana Pools, Vundu is open from April 15 to November 15. Six walk-in tents, in rustic surroundings, each sleep two. All meals and activities are included in the price. $$$$

TOUR OPERATORS

Classic Africa Safaris

P.O. Box BW81, Borrowdale, Harare, Zimbabwe; tel/fax: +263-4-860 064; e-mail: classicafrica@zol.co.zw; web: www.classicafrica.co.zw

This upscale operator runs walking and canoeing safaris for small groups.

Goliath Safaris

Pool House, Bronte Hotel, 132 Baines Avenue, P.O. Box CH294, Chisipite, Harare, Zimbabwe; tel: +263-4-739 8336; fax: +263-4-708 843; e-mail: goliath@id.co.zw

Tour guides run participatory trips on the Zambezi River; transportation to Harare is included.

John Stevens Safaris

Bushlife Zimbabwe, P.O. Box GD305, Greendale, Harare, Zimbabwe; tel: +263-4-495 650 or +263-4-498 548; fax: +263-4-496 113; e-mail: bushlife@harare.iafrica.com

Run by one of the pioneering tour operators in this remote area, upscale, informed safaris offer comfortable travel with overnights in tented camps; facilities are plentiful, if sometimes rustic.

Karibu

P.O. Box 35196, Northway 4065, Durban, South Africa; tel: +27-31-563 9774; fax: +27-31-563 1957.

Guides lead canoeing and camping safaris throughout southern Africa, including the Mana Pools, with options to suit varied budgets. The outfit operates three lodges overlooking the Zambezi River in Zambia.

Shearwater Canoe Safaris

P.O. Box 229, Kariba, Zimbabwe; tel: +263-61-2265; fax: +263-61-2459; e-mail: cansaf@worldonline.co.za

Participation safaris depart frequently on four-day excursions in which clients sleep in tents.

Excursions

Chimanimani National Park

Zimbabwe National Parks Board, Central Booking Office, P.O. Box CY862, Harare, Zimbabwe; tel: +263-4-792 782.

On Zimbabwe's eastern border with Mozambique, the park contains some of the country's most dramatic scenery. The ragged blue ramparts of the Chimanimani Mountains, draped in cloud forest and teeming with birds, are a paradise for hikers, and the folded and faulted silvery schist landscape is completely different from the rest of the country. Access is easiest by car; accommodations can be found in Chimanimani village, and there is camping in the park.

Gonarezhou National Park

Zimbabwe National Parks Board, Central Booking Office, P.O. Box CY862, Harare, Zimbabwe; tel: +263-4-792 782.

Until recently off-limits due to the war in Mozambique, Gonarezhou is the second largest but least-known park in Zimbabwe, linked in 1999 to the Save Conservancy Area by a wildlife corridor. Years of poaching mean the elephants here are apt to run when they see humans, but the bird life is superb and game stocks are recovering. There are chalets and campsites, but the best places to stay are four lodges in the Save Conservancy.

Matusadona National Park

Zimbabwe National Parks Board, Central Booking Office, P.O. Box CY862, Harare, Zimbabwe; tel: +263-4-792 782.

The slender, bare branches of submerged teak trees fork dramatically against the mountain landscape on this southeastern shore of Lake Kariba. In the dry season, the water's edge is packed with animals, including buffalo, elephants, and

attendant predators, but the remote mountains provide satisfying game viewing year-round. Accommodations vary from basic but well-positioned campsites to luxurious private reserves bordering the park. Access is by air or boat from Kariba; the road is passable only by four-wheel-drive vehicle.

South Luangwa National Park

Zambia

CHAPTER 13

A pair of menacing golden eyes glows deep in the leafy canopy of an ebony tree. Behind them lurks the shadowy figure of a chunky male leopard. Oblivious to the spotlight illuminating the night, it grapples with an object wedged between the branches – the corpse of an antelope, killed the previous night and stowed out of reach of such rivals as lions and spotted hyenas.   ◆   At the base of the tree, a second leopard emerges, a subadult male, neither powerful nor bold enough to challenge its elder. A game scout suggests that it was this younger leopard who killed the antelope, only to have its dinner hijacked. Or perhaps the younger animal is hanging around in the hope that the other will move off once it has eaten its fill. Either way, this nocturnal encounter with the most elusive of Africa's large cats ranks as a definitive South Luangwa moment.   ◆   **South Luangwa**, the largest and most accessible of the four national parks in Zambia's **Luangwa Valley**, is widely regarded as *the* best place in Africa

A ribbon of water is a lifeline for wild animals in a land of climatic extremes.

to see leopards, though local experts are at a loss to explain why. While the leopard density is exceptional, double that of South Africa's Kruger National Park, the frequency of sightings may also have something to do with the fact that night safaris were pioneered here years before they took off else-where, giving leopards and other nocturnal predators more time to become habituated to spotlights.   ◆   Known locally as the Valley, this flat southern extension of Africa's Great Rift is dominated by the Luangwa River, a tributary of the Zambezi. The first serious attempt at conservation in the region began in 1904, when a short-lived game reserve was established to protect the Thornicroft's giraffe. It wasn't until the 1950s, however, that the

Oxpeckers groom a greater kudu, among the largest of the antelope. The male's spiral horns can measure more than 5 feet (1.5m) in length.

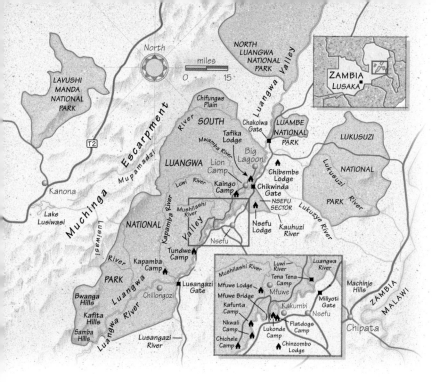

Flash Floods and Desperate Droughts

Every aspect of life at Luangwa is influenced by its seasonal ecology. For six months of the year, sometimes longer, not a drop of rain falls. Then, come November, the wind sweeps in a succession of brief but violent thunderstorms that seem to explode out of nowhere, lashing wildly against the trees and drenching the red earth, only to clear up as abruptly as they appeared.

Over the space of a few months, up to 50 inches (130cm) of rain soak the volcanic soil of the valley. The parched earth erupts into a lush green carpet, while the giant mahoganies and ebonies that line the river become heavy with fresh foliage. Seasonal watercourses are transformed from dry, sandy beds into angry torrents. The Luangwa itself might rise several meters overnight, ripping away at its own banks, redefining its tortuous course, and spilling into a flanking network of oxbow lakes and seasonal marshes.

This is Luangwa's season of plenty, when the animals disperse far and wide to take advantage of the bountiful water and grazing away from the river. Tourism, by contrast, grinds nearly to a halt, as game-viewing

visionary conservationist Norman Carr persuaded a local chief to set aside an area of tribal land as a game reserve and build a tourist lodge to raise proceeds for the community, thereby creating the blueprint for the modern practice of ecotourism.

Oddly, the creation of the four national parks in 1972 was followed by a period of intense poaching. Black rhinos, once numerous, were extirpated in the valley. The elephant population decreased from 100,000 in 1970 to 12,000 in 1990; it has since risen to 15,000, but the massive tuskers of old are an infrequent sight today.

A Jackson's chameleon (above) resembles a leaf as it moves slowly along a branch on pincerlike claws.

Visitors on a walking safari (right) encounter a herd of Cape buffalo; an armed guide is a sensible precaution.

vehicles are unable to navigate the park's saturated roads. Many tourist lodges close for the duration of the rains, and those that remain open cater mainly to birders, for whom South Luangwa is now at its most alluring. Yellow-billed storks form vast breeding colonies in the ebony trees; garishly adorned crowned cranes flock around the marshes; all manner of migrant waders and waterfowl join the resident herons and spoonbills at the river's edge; and the bush rattles with avian activity as smaller birds enter breeding mode. Experienced birders have been known to record more than 300 species in the course of a two- to three-night visit at this time of year.

The last rains generally fall in April. After that, the Luangwa River slowly recedes to a sluggish, shallow ribbon dwarfed by a wide, sandy floodplain. By August, the oxbow lakes shrink to shallow ponds – if they haven't dried up altogether – while the riotous green tones of January shrivel to a cover of yellowing grass. Ironically, it is now, when the landscape is at its harshest, that game-viewing is at its most rewarding. From August to October, innumerable herds of elephants, buffalo, and other plains animals congregate within walking distance of the Luangwa River, the only source of water for miles around.

A leopard (right) feeds on a warthog it has dragged up a tree to keep the meal safe from scavengers.

Within the river, pods of up to 100 hippos accumulate wherever the water is sufficiently deep for them to submerge. By October, wallowing space is at such a premium that older bulls are driven out by their younger, stronger peers, forced to retreat into the riverine woodland in search of sustenance and shade.

Changing Perspectives

Exploring the park usually starts at one of several camps or lodges. By day, game drives reveal prodigious herds of buffalo, elephants, zebras, and hippos. One can count on seeing

an experienced guide and armed ranger, the rumbling of the car engine is replaced by the seductive cooing of doves and the wind whistling gently through the yellow grass. The visitor is introduced to the minutiae of the bush: the flitting and chirruping of colorful small birds, a chameleon wobbling goggle-eyed along a branch, a malevolent-looking spider huddled expectantly in a corner of its web. This is the same Africa one sees from a vehicle, but on foot it seems fuller, richer, more immediate. Faced by the cold stare of a buffalo, one becomes painfully aware of the vulnerability of an intruder in the bush.

Night Life

It is at night, however, that South Luangwa

half a dozen antelope species, from the diminutive Sharpe's grysbok to the majestic greater kudu and a local specialty, the puku, a handsome kob-like antelope with a russet coat and lyre-shaped horns. Several races of widespread plains animals are unique to the valley. Crawshaw's zebra, for instance, lacks the shadow stripes found on other southern African zebras, while Thornicroft's giraffe, which numbers no more than 700 in the wild, can be distinguished by its pale lower legs and clean-edged markings.

On walking safaris in the company of

truly comes into its own. Night drives, if permitted at all, are often disappointing at other African reserves. Not so in South Luangwa, where it is unusual to go 10 minutes without picking out one of the elusive creatures that stalk the African bush beneath the stars. Those staunch safari favorites, the leopard and lion, can be taken for granted over the course of a couple of nights. The beautiful large-spotted genet might be seen half a dozen times on any given drive, while the closely related African civet is frequently observed trotting purposefully

through the bush and sniffing the ground ahead. Other specialties include the porcupine, a bundle of quills that rattle like cheap jewelry when it runs, and the four-toed elephant shrew, a bizarre rat-sized creature with an elongated and incessantly twitching snout and a kangaroo-like manner of bouncing along on its hind legs.

For yet another unique perspective on the park, consider viewing it from a microlight aircraft, perhaps the best way to grasp the relationship between the main river and the

A young buffalo (top) relies on its herd for protection against predators.

Crocodiles (right) snatch their prey in powerful jaws, then roll to inflict the killing injury; they can survive for several months without food.

Hippos (below) wallow together in pools and rivers; females often form "schools" with their young.

innumerable oxbow lakes that are scattered along its fickle course. Flights depart from Tafika Lodge, and the pilot provides the commentary as this go-cart-with-wings swoops over a panorama of elephant herds and crocodiles lazing on the riverbanks.

It's one of the experiences that confirms South Luangwa's place among Africa's finest reserves. Though the park may not have the same name recognition as the Serengeti or Kruger, it offers consistently good game viewing in an untrammeled, wild setting. Tellingly, few visitors are first-time travelers in Africa. This is a game reserve for the cognoscenti, one whose reputation has spread largely by word of mouth and which draws back the initiated again and again.

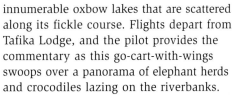

Hippos and Crocs

Found in all the great waterways and lakes of Africa, hippos and crocodiles are among the most impressive of Africa's large animals and arguably the most dangerous.

The Nile crocodile is the world's largest reptile, commonly measuring up to 15 feet (4.6m) long and reputed to live up to 100 years. It is a formidable predator, virtually invisible when submerged and surprisingly swift when it pounces on an antelope or other prey and drags it into the water. These days, the largest crocodiles are all but confined to conservation areas (unless protected, any croc big enough to kill an adult human is likely to be hunted by villagers), though fatal crocodile attacks are not unheard of along the inhabited shores of Africa's lakes and rivers. The farming of crocodiles for meat and skin is an increasingly common practice. Many farms double as tourist attractions, allowing visitors to get far closer to these enormous reptiles than is safe in the wild.

The hippo is entirely different. This enormous aquatic vegetarian spends most of the day submerged in rivers or lakes, emerging only at night to feed on land. Hippos regularly pass through riverside tourist lodges, treading quietly, but betraying their presence as they chomp noisily on the grass. Male hippos are viciously territorial among themselves – and most old males have the scars to prove it – but are generally docile otherwise so long as they are in water. On land, however, their instinct is to head for water at the slightest sign of danger, mowing down whatever is in their way, which is why hippos are responsible for killing more people than any other large African animal.

TRAVEL TIPS

DETAILS

When to Go

The dry season (May to October) is generally the best time to visit. Animal concentrations around the main game-viewing circuits increase as the dry season progresses, but so does the temperature, reaching unbearable highs by October (up to 110°F/43°C). The optimal month is August, when temperatures reach 90°F (32°C). The rainy season, from November to April, is excellent for birding. Many lodges close during the rains, and bush camps within the park are dismantled; lodges that stay open concentrate on birding expeditions.

Getting There

Fly-in visitors arrive first at the Zambian capital, Lusaka, served by several international carriers, including British Airways, KLM, Air France, and SAA (via Johannesburg). Zambian Airways (P.O. Box 310277, Lusaka; tel: +260-1-271066; e-mail: roanair@ zamnet.zm) flies daily between Lusaka and the all-weather airport at Mfuwe, roughly 18 miles (30km) from the park entrance. Most of the larger tourist lodges lie scattered along the river within a few miles of the park entrance gate at Mfuwe Bridge.

For those who want to drive in, Mfuwe is 450 miles (750km) on a rough road from Lusaka, with only one relatively large town, Chipata, en route. Buses between Lusaka and Chipata take the better part of a day. From there, a rather hit-and-miss local minibus service connects Chipata to Mfuwe, dropping travelers at Flatdogs Campsite. Most lodges at South Luangwa offer packages that include game drives, walks, and night drives. Visitors who drive themselves can explore the park independently by day, but must use a licensed operator for night tours. Flatdogs Campsite is the best place to organize activities.

INFORMATION

Zambian Embassies

United Kingdom: 2 Palace Gate, London W8 5NG; tel: +44-20-7589 6655.

United States: 2419 Massachusetts Avenue, N.W., Washington, DC 20008; tel: 202-265-9717; fax: 202-332-0826.

Zambia Tourist Offices

P.O. Box 30017, Lusaka, Zambia; tel: +260-1-229 087; fax: +260-1-225 174; e-mail: zntb@zamnet.zm; web: africa-insites.com/zambia

United Kingdom: c/o High Commission, 2 Palace Gate, London W8 5NG; tel: +44-20-7589 6655; e-mail: zntb@aol.com

United States: 800 Second Avenue, Ninth Floor, New York, NY 10017; tel: 212-949-0133; fax: 212-979-0134.

CAMPING

Camping is permitted at public campsites only.

LODGING

PRICE GUIDE – double occupancy

$ = under $100 $$ = $100–$200
$$$ = $200–$300 $$$$ = $300+

Flatdogs Camp

P.O. Box 100, Mfuwe, Zambia; tel: +260-62-45068; fax: +260-62-45025; e-mail: moondog@super-hub.com

Situated on the riverbank close to Mfuwe Bridge, Flatdogs is the obvious base for budget visits to South Luangwa, offering inexpensive accommodations, game drives, and walking safaris. $

Kapani Safari Lodge

P.O. Box 100, Mfuwe, Zambia; tel: +260-62-45015; fax: +260-62-45025; e-mail: kapani@zamnet.zm

Founded by Norman Carr, the doyen of Luangwa conservationists, this lodge overlooks a lagoon about two miles (3km) south of Mfuwe Bridge. The lodge acts as a base for three seasonal bush camps: Luwi, Nsolo, and Kakuli. The main lodge is open all year, catering to birders during the rains. $$$$

Lufupa Camp

P.O. Box 37538, Lusaka, Zambia; tel: +260-1-221 683; fax: +260-1-274 253.

Situated close to the rough main road that bisects Kafue National Park, Lufupa is the largest camp in this game reserve, well located for both game drives and bush walks. Although basic by comparison to most of the lodges in South Luangwa, Lufupa has recently been renovated and remains very sensibly priced, especially for long stays. $$

Mwaleshi Camp

P.O. Box 5, Mfuwe, Zambia; tel: +260-62-45018; fax: +260-62-45059; e-mail: remote.africa@satmail.bt.com

This bush camp is in remote North Luangwa National Park, on a perennial tributary of the Luangwa River. It is under the same management as Tafika Lodge and is normally visited as an excursion from Tafika. The long, rough road trip to the camp means that a minimum stay of four nights is recommended, and the focus, once there, is on walking rather than game drives. The camp is open mid-June through October. $$$$

Tafika Lodge

P.O. Box 5, Mfuwe, Zambia; tel: +260-62-45018; fax: +260-62-45059; e-mail: remote.africa@satmail.bt.com

Set on a scenic bend in the Luangwa River, Tafika combines bush architecture and an intimate atmosphere with comfortable facilities and world-class food. Tafika is remote from the main cluster of lodges around Mfuwe Bridge, and game drives and walks pass through parts of the national park used by few other operators. Microlight flights give a bird's-eye view over the river. The camp is open from May through November; river safaris can use Tafika from mid-February to mid-April. $$$$.

TOUR OPERATORS

Norman Carr Safaris

P.O. Box 100, Mfuwe, Zambia; tel: +260-62-45015; fax: +260-62-45025; e-mail: kapani@zamnet.zm

Based at Kapani Lodge, this longtime tour operator also runs three bush camps in the park.

Remote Africa Safaris

P.O. Box 5, Mfuwe, Zambia; tel: +260-62-45018; fax: +260-62-45059; e-mail: remote.africa@satmail.bt.com

This experienced company, based at Tafika Lodge, is particularly worth contacting for combined visits to South and North Luangwa, and for river safaris during the rainy season.

Robin Pope Safaris

P.O. Box 80, Mfuwe, Zambia; tel: +260-62-45090; fax: +260-62-45051; e-mail: popesaf@zamnet.zm

A local operator runs several lodges and camps in the Luangwa area and is especially worth contacting for foot safaris between late June and late September.

Sunvil Discovery

Sunvil House, Upper Square, Old Isleworth, Middlesex, TW7 7BJ, UK; tel: +44-20-8232 9777; fax: +44-20-8568 8330; e-mail: africa@sunvil.co.uk; web: www.sunvil.co.uk

Sunvil guides have extensive local experience and are a good first contact for customized safaris to Luangwa and elsewhere in the country.

Excursions

Kafue National Park

Zambian Tourist Office, P.O. Box 30017, Lusaka, Zambia; tel: +260-1-229 087; fax: +260-1-225 174; e-mail: zntb@zamnet.zm; web: africa-insites.com/zambia

Covering an area of 8,650 square miles (22,400 sq km) in western Zambia, Kafue is one of Africa's largest national parks, a vast tract of woodland and savanna bisected by the Kafue River and its seasonal floodplain. Kafue appears on surprisingly few tourist itineraries, given that the park is host to large populations of lions, leopards, buffalo, and elephants, together with numerous antelope, most notably roan, sable, red lechwe, puku, and sitatunga. A handful of lodges and the total wilderness atmosphere make Kafue an offbeat alternative to more popular destinations.

Lower Zambezi National Park

Zambian Tourist Office, P.O. Box 30017, Lusaka, Zambia; tel: +260-1-229 087; fax: +260-1-225 174; e-mail: zntb@zamnet.zm; web: africa-insites.com/zambia

Lower Zambezi National Park is effectively the Zambian counterpart to Zimbabwe's smaller but better publicized Mana Pools National Park. In recent years, it has emerged as Zambia's second most popular game reserve, particularly famous for its large herds of buffalo and elephants. The ultimate way to view game here is by canoe; many tour operators offer organized trips lasting up to 10 days. Fly-in and self-driven safaris are also popular.

North Luangwa National Park

Zambian Tourist Office, P.O. Box 30017, Lusaka, Zambia; tel: +260-1-229 087; fax: +260-1-225 174; e-mail: zntb@zamnet.zm; web: africa-insites.com/zambia

North Luangwa National Park, separated from South Luangwa by roughly 30 miles (48km) of farmland, protects similar habitats and an almost identical range of game. From a safari-goer's perspective, North Luangwa is far more isolated, functioning more like a private game reserve than a typical national park. Accommodations are limited to a handful of small, exclusive camps, and the park can be visited only with one of a few licensed operators. Private visits are forbidden.

Périnet
Madagascar

A cold mist thins, revealing the silhouettes of dove-gray trees against a white sky. The forest is quiet. High in the canopy an indri lemur, supported by the fork of two branches, straightens her back, yawns, and reaches out a long arm to break off a leafy twig: breakfast. The baby clinging to her back peers down with round, green eyes at a group of tourists. For half an hour or so, mother, infant, and other members of the family group feed languidly, conserving energy before the sun breaks through the mist, the light catching on their black-and-white coats. Indri, the largest of the lemurs and the only ones without tails, stand about 3 feet (1m) high and look something like teddy bears dressed in black socks and gloves, white arm-bands and leggings, and a tail coat that's a few sizes too small. ◆ All heads turn toward a faint moaning that sounds like the soughing of the wind through the trees; it's the call of a distant indri troop some 2 miles (3km) away.

Cut off from the mainland more than 100 million years ago, Madagascar is a grand experiment in evolution, filled with species found nowhere else on Earth.

The lemurs listen intently, moving their heads from side to side and staring out across the forest. Then the dominant female pushes her lips into a pink circle, throws her head back, and lets loose a wail. The volume of her song is extraordinary as it slides up and down the musical scale like an amplified harmonica. The singer's adolescent son joins in, a higher-pitched call with slightly less range, and then the infant's mother adds her voice to the choir. You can see the hairs rising on the arms of the tourists; this is spine-tingling stuff, the essence of Madagascar. ◆ The singing continues for a minute or two, then stops as suddenly as it started. It is time for the indri to

Indris are Madagascar's largest lemurs, with a haunting cry that echoes across Périnet's forested valleys. They usually travel in small family troops; their call defines the group's territory.

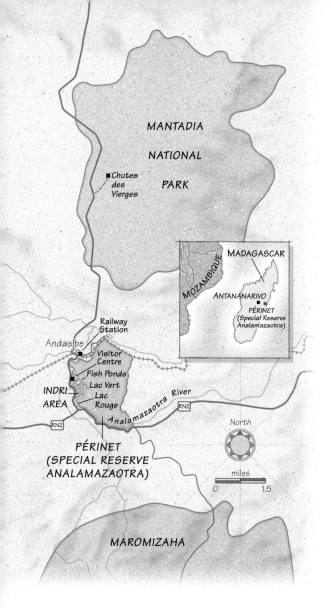

from mainland Africa about 165 million years ago, before the evolution of mammals, when dinosaurs dominated the earth. Some of Madagascar's plants and animals have evolved independently ever since the split, while others, like lemurs, reached the island much later as stowaways on logs or floating mats of vegetation. While these ancestral lemurs spread through the diverse habitats of their new home, their cousins on the mainland evolved in a very different direction and were eventually superseded by modern-day monkeys.

A similar scenario pertains to thousands of other species on Madagascar. As a rough estimate one can say that of the 200,000 living things on the island, 150,000 are found nowhere else in the world. Only about half of the birds are endemic, but all of the mammals, apart from introduced species, are unique to the island.

Indri are confined to the eastern forests of Madagascar but are habituated to people in only one reserve, **Périnet** (it is officially the **Special Reserve Analamazaotra**, but almost everyone calls it by its old colonial name), where two troops are found. Situated only four hours by a good road from the capital, Antananarivo, this is the most visited reserve on the island, and it has the best guides.

Périnet is often referred to as a rain forest, but at an elevation of 3,000 to 3,500 feet (900–1,100m) it's more properly classified as a montane forest. Compared with lowland rain forest, the canopy is lower, the temperature is cooler, leaves are smaller, and boughs are festooned with epiphytes and mosses. More light penetrates to the forest floor, encouraging the growth of shrubs, tree ferns, and bamboo. Lichen-covered vines are adorned with colorful fungi.

Altogether, there are nine species of lemurs in Périnet, although it's unlikely you will see them all.

move on. One animal climbs down from the high branches and, hugging the tree, her huge black feet flat against the trunk, springs backward, turns in midair, and lands with a thud on a tree 30 feet (9m) away. A crash of branches and another indri follows, then another, all bounding effortlessly from tree to tree, stopping only to eat a few leaves or stare down at the onlookers.

A Place Apart

Indri are one of 51 kinds of lemurs, a suborder of primates found only on Madagascar. Their isolation is due to the large-scale geologic forces that tore the island away

You may encounter gray bamboo lemurs feeding on bamboo near the warden's house, a troop of brown lemurs, and perhaps a sleeping avahi (woolly lemur) curled up in the fork of a tree. Bird-watching is excellent here too. Specialties include endemic species such as the velvet asity, a small black bird with emerald-green eyebrows, and the blue coua, which looks a bit like a blue jay with a bright blue patch of bare skin behind the eye, a characteristic of the entire family.

The Forest at Night

If time allows, stay in the park for an after-dark tour of the forest with a flashlight-bearing guide. A night walk usually turns up such nocturnal species as the greater dwarf lemur and the tiny mouse lemur. And if you're incredibly lucky you may spot an aye-aye.

A sunbird (left) feeds on nectar.

Madagascan tree frogs (top) have bulbous toes to cling to leaves and huge eyes for night vision.

The aye-aye's skeletal middle finger (right) is designed to extract insects from tree bark and large nuts. Local people are terrified of these lemurs, associating them with death.

This unusual lemur hunts grubs by tapping on trees and listening for cavities with its batlike ears. It then employs its most bizarre adaptation – a bony middle finger – to winkle the tasty morsels out of their hiding places.

Other creatures you may encounter at night are the jewel-like tree frogs, which are often found sitting on leaves, and the diminutive short-horned chameleon, no bigger than the last two joints of your little finger. Curiously, chameleons turn almost white at night, an evolutionary detour that

The Color of Love

When it comes to love, it's not difficult to see what's on a chameleon's mind. An amorous male advertises his interest in a potential mate by breaking into a display of bright and contrasting colors. If his timing is just right, the female will signal her receptivity by responding in kind. Otherwise, she'll brush him off by turning a discouraging shade of gray or black.

Nearly half of all chameleon species are found on Madagascar, and all are endemic to the island. These extraordinary lizards belong to a unique subfamily, Chamaeleoninae, that share a constellation of specialized adaptations, including pincerlike claws, eyes that swivel independently, and tongues that extend up to twice the length of their bodies to snap up insects. The males of some species have horns or nasal protuberances, and most species have prehensile tails.

Their best-known feature, however, is the ability to change color. Contrary to popular belief, they don't do it to camouflage themselves but as a response to environmental factors such as light and temperature or to communicate with other chameleons. Layers of specialized cells, each responsible for different hues, expand and contract differentially in order to produce the lizard's color-coded vocabulary. A tranquil chameleon, for example, is often green, an agitated chameleon, yellow. And the preferred hue of a jilted male chameleon? Well, that's a lizard of a different color.

Parson's chameleon (left) and Oustelet's chameleon (below) are among Madagascar's endemic creatures; 70 chameleon species have been recorded on the island.

Giraffe-necked weevils (opposite, top) are named for their extended necks.

Bridges and trails (opposite, bottom) lead visitors into the recesses of the forest.

seems to serve no adaptive function, though it does make them easy to see in the dark. Shine your flashlight on a sleeping chameleon and you can't miss it. This can't be said of a daytime search for these elusive animals, though boys living near the reserve collect the biggest species, Parson's chameleon, to earn a few coins posing with them for photos. Nearly two feet (.6m) long, brilliant green, and wearing the expression of disapproval common to all chameleons, they are some of the forest's most intriguing creatures.

Weird Bugs, Golden Lemurs

Adventurous visitors who want to extend their visit can travel south of Périnet to a 24,700-acre (10,000-hectare) forest known as **Maromizaha**, which offers a good day of hiking, spectacular views, and the best chance of seeing some of Madagascar's thousand or so bizarre and colorful weevils.

If you think of weevils in terms of brown things in the flour, wait until you see these. There are turquoise-blue weevils, purple weevils, brown weevils wearing fuzzy yellow tutus and, best of all, giraffe weevils, which make you wonder if Mother Nature was distracted when she created them. This insect has a jointed black neck that is at least four times the length of its bright red body. Unfortunately, its home at Maromizaha is imperiled. The forest is unprotected and is being cleared at an alarming rate.

Also in the area, about 15 miles (24km) north of Périnet, is the newly created **Mantadia National Park**, which is set at a higher altitude and consequently harbors different species. This is pristine primary forest. There are only a few constructed trails, and the hiking is sometimes rough, but this is a naturalist's gold mine, with many seldom-seen species of mammals, reptiles, and birds. There are indri here, though their coats are much darker than those in Périnet, as well as black-and-white ruffed lemurs. But the jackpot is the diademed sifaka, arguably the most beautiful lemur of all.

There are many species of sifaka, varying in color from entirely black to entirely white, but only the diademed sifaka is golden, with long, silky fur that is almost orange. Sifakas belong to the same family as indri, but are more slender and, like most other lemurs, have a tail they use for balance when leaping.

The park's steep trails offer gorgeous views across the forest and superb bird-watching, particularly for ground-rollers, vangas, and asitys. An easy two-hour trail leads up through the forest to a waterfall and lake. Bring your swimsuit for a cool dip in the pool beneath the falls.

Sadly, what remains of the island's last few patches of wilderness are threatened by

deforestation and poaching. Dozens of species have become extinct since humankind arrived 2,000 years ago, including a lemur the size of a gorilla and an ostrich-like bird that stood more than nine feet (3m) tall. Dozens more are endangered. Conservation measures have slowed but not stopped the loss of habitat. As always, the fate of this extraordinary place lies in the hands of its human stewards.

DETAILS

When to Go

Be prepared for rain at any time of year. The best time to visit is from April to May and from September to November, when midday temperatures are 70°F (21°C) to 80°F (27°C). The rain is heaviest from January to March, when cyclones can occur. Nights from June through August tend to be cool, around 50°F (10°C); bring a warm sweater or fleece or down vest. Some animals, including tenrecs and dwarf lemurs, hibernate during these months, when temperatures reach 60°F (16°C)to 70°F (21°C). Use insect repellent in all seasons and wear long pants to protect your legs from leeches.

Getting There

All international flights arrive in the capital, Antananarivo. There are no direct connections from the United States, and the only direct flights from Europe are on Air Madagascar and Air France, via Paris. The once-famous train from Antananarivo no longer runs all the way to Périnet, so travelers should take a bush taxi (*taxi-brousse*) or a bus for the three- to four-hour drive. You need your own vehicle to visit Maromizaha or Mantadia.

INFORMATION

Malagasy Embassies

United Kingdom: Hon Consulate, 16 Lanark Mansions, Pennard Road, London W12 8DT; tel: +44-20-8746 0134.

United States: 2374 Massachusetts Avenue, N.W., Washington, DC 20008; tel: 202-265-5525.

National Association for Management of Protected Areas

BP 1424, Antananarivo 101, Madagascar; tel: +261-20-224 1554; fax: +261-20-224 1539; e-mail: angap@bow.dts.mg

This is the government conservation body in Madagascar.

Tours Operateurs Professionnels

Espace DERA de l'Université, BP 8308, Antananarivo 101, Madagascar; tel/fax: +261-20-227 8859; e-mail: tpomad@dts.mg; web: www.madagascar-guide. com/top/index.html

CAMPING

Camping is not permitted within the reserve.

LODGING

PRICE GUIDE – double occupancy

$ = under $100 $$ = $100–$200
$$$ = $200–$300 $$$$ = $300+

Hotel Buffet de la Gare
Andasibe, Madagascar

Until 1993, this hotel, next to the train station in Andasibe, was the only place to stay. The elegant dining room has fresh flowers on the tables and a rosewood bar. The best accommodations are five bungalows in a meadow close to the forest. All have three or four beds and hot water. Less luxurious but perfectly adequate are seven chalet-type bungalows near the Buffet. The hotel does not have a phone, so booking a room in advance is difficult. $

Hotel Feon' ny Ala
Analamazaotra, Périnet, Andasibe, Madagascar.

The name means Window, or Voice, of the Forest. This lodge, with 18 bungalows and a camping area, is favored by serious naturalists; it's close enough to the reserve to hear the indri call. The Feon' ny Ala is 40 minutes from Andasibe, so plan to eat

your meals in the restaurant, or bring food with you from Tana if camping. The hotel does not have a phone, so booking a room in advance is difficult. $

Vakôna Forest Lodge

BP 750, Antananarivo, Madagascar; tel: +261-20-21394; fax: +261-20-23070; e-mail: izouard@bow.dts.mg; web: www.madagascar-contacts. com/vakona

Accessible only with your own vehicle, this luxury hotel has efficient management and good food. The main building holds an octagonal reception area, a bar, and a dining room with a huge fireplace in the middle. The 14 bungalows are quiet and comfortable. The lodge has its own small reserve and swimming pool; activities include horseback riding and viewing lemurs. $

TOUR OPERATORS

Boogie Pilgrim

Villa Michelet, Lot A11, Faravohitra, Antananarivo, Madagascar; tel: +261-20-25878; fax: +261-20-62556; e-mail: bopi@bow.dts.mg

A variety of tours are offered, including some by light aircraft.

Cortez Expeditions

25 Rue Ny Zafindraindiky, Antimena, Antananarivo, Madagascar; tel: +261-20-21974; fax: +261-20-24787; e-mail: cortez@dts.mg

One of the most experienced tour operators in Madagascar offers a variety of tours emphasizing natural history.

Cortez Travel Services

124 Lomas Santa Fe Drive, Solano Beach, CA 92075; tel: 619-755-5136 or 800-854-1029; fax: 619-481-7474; e-mail: cortez-usa@mcimail.com

This company specializes in Madagascar travel and has been running trips to the island for nearly two decades.

David Sayers Travel

54 High Street East, Uppingham, Rutland, LE15 9PZ, UK; tel: +44-1572-821 330; fax: +44-1572-821 072; e-mail: abrock3650@aol.com

Regular trips to Madagascar have a botanical emphasis.

Madagascar Airtours

33 Avenue de l'Indépendence, BP 3874, Antananarivo, Madagascar; tel: +261-20-24192; fax: +261-20-64190.

This agency has offices in most major towns. Specialized tours include natural history, bird-watching, cave exploration, trekking, mineralogy, river trips, sailing, and more.

Mad Caméléon

Lot II K6, BP 4336, Ankadivato, Antananarivo, Madagascar; tel: +261-20-63086; fax: +261-20-34420; e-mail: madcam@dts.mg

This small operator specializes in river trips, including exploration of the Manambolo River.

Malagasy Tours

Lot VX29, Avaradrova, Antananarivo, Madagascar; tel/fax: +261-20-35607.

The company runs specialized ethnobotany itineraries using local residents to explain the complexities of the Malagasy culture. Off-the-beaten-track explorations are also available.

Reef and Rain Forest Tours

1 The Plains, Totnes, Devon TQ9 5DR, UK; tel: +44-1803-866 965; fax: +44-1803-865 916; e-mail: reefrain@btinternet.com

A variety of tours are offered through this agency, which specializes in Madagascar.

Excursions

Ankarana Special Reserve

National Association for Management of Protected Areas, BP 1424, Antananarivo 101, Madagascar; tel: +261-20-224 1554; fax: +261-20-224 1539; e-mail: angap@bow.dts.mg

Sharp pinnacles of limestone karst, known in Madagascar as *tsingy*, have provided a perfect defense against the encroachment of humans in this western park. In canyons between the out-crops, deciduous trees harbor a wide variety of wildlife. Crowned and Sanford's brown lemurs are quite common, along with vociferous lepilemurs and the handsome ring-tailed mongoose. It's also a wonderful place for birding. Ankarana has no accommodations.

Berenty Private Reserve

Hotel Le Dauphin, P.O. Box 54, Taolagnaro, Madagascar; tel: +261-92-21238.

A small reserve bordering River Marmore, 50 miles (80km) from Fort Dauphin (Taolagnaro) in the southeast, Berenty is famous for its sassy ring-tailed lemurs, which sneak into the bungalows and leap on visitors' shoulders to eat bananas. Equally popular are the dancing sifaka lemurs, which bound across open areas on their back legs like displaced ballet dancers. This popular reserve combines excellent wildlife viewing with reasonably comfortable accommodations. In all, six species of lemurs are found here, along with many endemic birds, reptiles, and insects. It is also the best place to see Madagascar's "spiny forest" of giant cactuslike didierea trees.

Isalo National Park

National Association for Management of Protected Areas, BP 1424, Antananarivo 101, Madagascar; tel: +261-20-224 1554; fax: +261-20-224 1539; e-mail: angap@bow.dts.mg

The eroded sandstone Isalo massif lies in southern Madagascar between Fianarantsoa and Tulear (Toliara). Come here for the landscape, not the animals. Take in the golds and browns of the semidesert, and then cool off under a waterfall in lush green canyons. Isalo is hiking country, and the utter silence as you stride over the flat plateau surrounded by distorted rock formations is otherworldly. A luxury hotel on the edge of the park adds to the allure.

Lake Malawi
Malawi

CHAPTER **15**

Perhaps the best vantage in **Lake Malawi National Park** is afforded by the highlands of Cape Maclear's **Nankumba Peninsula** in late afternoon. It's a time and place that burns indelible images into the memory: the low sun staining the entire landscape with a luminous orange glow; the dusty plain below, surrounded by hills and dotted with bulbous baobab trees; and at the terminus of the plain, a curve of sandy beach and the cobalt blue waters of **Lake Malawi** beyond. ◆ There's invariably a light breeze out on the lake, dappling the water with cat's paws. On the beach, local villagers load their nets and launch their dugout canoes for a night of fishing. Hamerkop birds – dark brown with a blunt crest that somehow evokes dinosaurs – forage in the shallows, while dapper black-and-white pied king-fishers hover overhead nervously, diving periodically for fish. A fish eagle takes to the air and hunts along the shore of a nearby island, its brilliant white head and glossy, black wings reflecting

Wildlife and people share the shores of Africa's third-largest lake, home to a rainbow world of aquatic life and a dazzling variety of birds.

highlights of the fading sun. Its mate calls out, the plaintive cry carrying across the water – one of the most evocative sounds in Africa. ◆ Lake Malawi is the southernmost of the great chain of lakes that floods much of Africa's Great Rift Valley. The national park that incorporates portions of the lakeshore and numerous islands was established in 1980 with a primary goal in mind: to protect the myriad species of cichlid fish that inhabit the lake's pellucid waters. Lake Malawi is often compared to a huge tropical fish tank, and this is no exaggeration. A vast array of aquatic species thrive here, including the zebra fish – resplendent in various shades of blue accented by dark vertical

Lake Malawi, more like an inland sea than a lake, has stormy moods and tranquil days. Only fishermen ply this natural barrier between Malawi, Tanzania, and Mozambique.

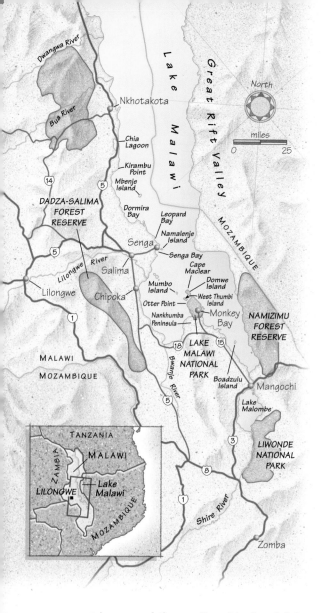

to paddle your own. Modern sea kayaks are available to rent at **Cape Maclear**. From there, you can venture out to the islands of **West Thumbi**, **Mumbo**, or **Domwe**, exploring their numerous coves, headlands, and beaches. Paddle close to the abundant outcroppings of smooth, gray boulders; shoals of fish tend to congregate around them and are easily visible through the crystalline water.

It's even more engaging to look at the fish from their own perspective. Calm, clear water makes Lake Malawi one of the world's premier freshwater dive sites. Both scuba and snorkel gear are available to rent, affording fantastic opportunites for examining the cichlids' brilliant coloration and foraging behaviors. At **Otter Point**, west of the main beach, the fish are so tame they'll eat bread from your hand.

Lake Malawi differs from most of Africa's national parks in that people are part of the protected environment. A few hundred Malawians live at Cape Maclear, earning their livelihoods in fishing and increasingly tourism. Although their village is outside the park's borders, and they're supposed to avoid the protected zones around the islands, they are very much a part of the day-to-day life of the park and interact easily with tourists. Learning something about their way of life and their traditional methods of fishing and farming adds immeasurably to the experience and should be a priority.

stripes – and the small multicolored fish known as mbuna. Not surprisingly, Lake Malawi is a source of cichlids for freshwater aquariums the world over.

The View from Below

You need a boat to best experience the lake and its stunning aquatic wildlife. Local villagers will row you around in their traditional fishing craft, but you may prefer

A white-faced duck (left) preens on a sandbank; listen for its shrill *swee-swee-sweeo*.

Though of critical ecological significance, the park protects only a small portion of the lake, which at 360 miles (580km) long and 50 miles (80km) wide is the third largest in Africa. The lake, in turn, is part of an even larger ecosystem: the Rift Valley trough. Escarpments frame the shores of the lake; sometimes the land descends in terraces to the shore, sometimes it plunges away in sheer cliffs. Beyond the escarpments are high plateaus of forest and grassland. To the south, Lake Malawi is drained by the **Shire River**, which connects a series of marshes and smaller lakes before joining the Zambezi River.

An elephant (opposite, top) grazes on the overgrown banks of the Shire River.

Little egrets (left) are stealthy hunters, waiting stock-still for prey at water's edge.

Golden beaches (below), warm water, and excellent scuba diving make landlocked Malawi an unusual beach destination.

Birder's Paradise

Malawi is almost as renowned for birds as for fish. Its rich and varied habitats and strategic location bordered by the vast rain forests of the Congo to the West, great savannas to the north and south, and the Indian Ocean to the east attract migratory

The hillocks behind the beach are richly cloaked in miombo woodland, affording food and shelter to a tremendous variety of birds, including turacos, hornbills, sunbirds, barbets, flycatchers, chats, and shrikes. A river wends its way between the hills, forming a marsh populated by ducks and crakes, as well as rarer species such as dwarf bittern and pygmy goose. This is also a foraging ground for crowned cranes, with their gracile, gray necks, crimson wattles, and magnificent golden crests.

Riparian forest crowds the banks of the river downstream from the marsh. Here, kingfishers perch on the overhanging branches, knifing into the water in flashes of orange and iridescent blue. Also haunting these coverts are Bohm's bee-eaters, brilliant green birds with bright red caps, long tail feathers, and curved bills. Africa's bee-eaters have formed symbiotic relationships with honey badgers and people, luring them to honeybee hives. When the hives are broken open for the honey, the bee-eaters feed on the grubs lodged in the discarded combs.

birds from much of the continent. More than 650 avian species have been recorded in Malawi, making it one of the world's stellar birding destinations.

One good place to combine birding with fish watching is **Senga Bay**, about 30 miles (48km) north of Cape Maclear. You can hire a boat to cruise the shoreline, or snorkel among the rocks. Many local mbuna differ from those near Cape Maclear. A big colony of white-breasted cormorants has commandeered **Namalenje Island**, a rocky jumble about a mile offshore. They're so numerous that they are gradually burying the island under a thick white cap of reeking guano.

The Emerald Forest

About 75 miles (120km) north of Senga Bay is **Nkhotakota Wildlife Refuge**, a 700-square-mile (1,810 sq km) redoubt of pristine miombo woodland and rugged escarpment.

A Rainbow of Fish

More than 600 fish species have been recorded in Lake Malawi, and biologists believe that up to 400 more have yet to be discovered – more than all the freshwater fish in Europe and North America combined. Even more remarkable, nearly all are endemic, occurring nowhere else on Earth.

Most belong to a huge family called *Cichlidae*. The most notable members are the many species of algae-eating rockfish known as *mbuna*. Each has evolved distinct anatomical features and feeding behaviors to exploit a slightly different aspect of the same ecological niche. The well-known zebra fish (*Psuedotropheus zebra*) feeds at right angles to the rock, combing through the algae with wide-spaced teeth to dislodge loose particles. *Ptropheops* has strong teeth designed to scrape off algae and feeds at an angle of 45 degrees, while *Labeotropheus fuellebori* has a very low mouth and serrated teeth, so it can scrape off algae while swimming with its body almost parallel to the rock.

Much like the Galapagos finches that Charles Darwin used to explicate his theory of natural selection, the fish of Lake Malawi are a testimony to the creative genius of evolution.

A fish eagle (top) strikes in the fish-filled waters off Cape Maclear.

Malawi cichlids (below) can change color, shape, and sex as they mature, making identification extremely difficult.

The reserve is an easy day trip from Lake Malawi and a must-see if you're in the area. Nkhotakota is almost impenetrable country, and few drivable tracks probe its lush forests. Buffalo, sable, and eland are here in abundance, small antelope like bushbuck and duiker tiptoe gently through the undergrowth, and elephants are increasing after years of poaching. The game is hard to spot in the dense bush, so your best chance of a sighting is by walking, not driving. Hiking the refuge also allows the visitor to utilize all the senses in appreciating one of the last great woodlands in East Africa. This is the Africa that once was, and it deserves to be savored.

Numerous rivers pour off the escarpment, cutting deep gorges and affording spectacular vistas of thundering whitewater framed by emerald forest. Giant kingfishers – stocky, foot-long birds with rapier beaks – hunt along these rapids, as do Pel's fishing owls, one of Africa's largest owls and the only one that preys on fish. With any luck, you may see one gliding silently over slow-running pools, clutching its prey in strong black talons. Their hoots and screeches resonate throughout the forest at dusk, providing a haunting farewell to visitors heading back to the lake.

Hippos (top) wallow in the shallows during the heat of the day and lumber onto land to feed at night.

Snorkelers (left) explore a rocky cove, where shoals of freshwater fish give the lake all the color of an ocean reef.

TRAVEL TIPS

DETAILS

When to Go

The best time to visit Malawi is during the dry season, May to September, when midday temperatures are generally 70°F (21°C) to 80°F (27°C). The rains last from October to April. The period just before the rains is best for game viewing as the bush is sparse, although temperatures are higher, reaching 95°F (35°C). Bird-watchers may consider visiting from October to December, during breeding time. Temperatures peak at 90°F (32°C).

Getting There

Most international flights land at Lilongwe, the capital of Malawi. The drive from Lilongwe to Senga Bay is about 80 miles (130km), to Cape Maclear about 120 miles (190km). Several safari outfitters in Malawi run customized, all-inclusive tours lasting from a few days to three weeks, and from luxurious to more straightforward options for those on a tighter budget. Most visit Lake Malawi, Liwonde, and Nyika National Parks. Driving yourself is also possible, with cars available through major rental companies or safari outfitters in Lilongwe. Distances are short and roads are relatively good, although vehicle standards are not always up to those in Europe or North America.

INFORMATION

Malawi Embassies

United Kingdom: 33 Grosvenor Street, London W1X 0ED, UK; tel: +44-20-7491 4172; fax: +44-20-7491 9916; e-mail: kwacha@malawihighcomm. prestel.co.uk

United States: 2408 Massachusetts Avenue, N.W., Washington, DC 20008; tel: 202-797-1007.

Malawi Tourism

4 Christian Field, London SW16 3JZ, UK; tel: +44-115-982 1903, fax: +44-115-981 9418; e-mail: enquiries@malawitourism.com

This is a reliable worldwide information service.

Ministry of Wildlife and Tourism

Department of National Parks, P.O. Box 30131, Murray Road, Lilongwe, Malawi; tel: +265-771295.

Information is limited at this government department.

CAMPING

Advance reservations are not necessary for camping anywhere in Malawi. Cape Maclear has several campgrounds along the beach, where facilities vary, although most of these cater to budget overland truck parties and can be lively. Senga Bay has one campground with amenities that is attached to a luxury hotel. Nkhotakota Wildlife Reserve has two basic campgrounds in wild and tranquil settings. There are also many cheap local guest houses, catering mainly to young or adventurous independent travelers, where reservations are not required.

LODGING

PRICE GUIDE – double occupancy

$ = under $100 $$ = $100–$200

$$$ = $200–$300 $$$$ = $300+

Chembe Lodge

P.O. Box 187, Monkey Bay, Malawi; tel/fax: : +265-633 489 or +265-584 334; e-mail: tumbuka@malawi.net

Large safari-style tents overlook Lake Malawi from the eastern end of the bay at Cape Maclear. Tents have verandas and thatched roofs; bathroom facilities are shared. There is a bar and restaurant. Scuba diving, dive instruction, snorkeling, and catamaran sailing are available. $

Club Makakola

P.O. Box 59, Mangochi, Malawi; tel: +265-584 244; fax: +265-584 417; e-mail: clubmak@malawi.net

This large hotel near Boadzulu Island, about 35 miles (56km) south of Cape Maclear, is at the southern end of Lake Malawi National Park. Facilities include a private beach, airport, nine-hole golf course, and swimming pool. Water sports, scuba diving, fishing, boat rides, and tours are available. $$

Livingstonia Beach Hotel

Central Reservations, P.O. Box 376, Blantyre, Malawi; tel: +265-744 022; fax: +265-744 483.

This hotel's lush gardens overlook Lake Malawi at Senga Bay. Boats can be rented and guided walks arranged. $$

Njobvu Safari Lodge

P.O. Box 388, Nkhotakota, Malawi; tel: +265-292 506.

Just outside the Nkhotakota Wildlife Reserve on the lakeshore, this lodge offers chalets with private baths, simple rooms, and a campground. Bird-watching guides are available. The owner organizes walking safaris to observe the elusive elephants. $

Nswala Lodge

P.O. Box 672, Blantyre, Malawi; tel: +265-620 629; e-mail: nswalasafaris@malawi.net

About 10 miles (16km) by rough road from Cape Maclear, this lodge has chalets (some with private baths) overlooking the lake and a campground. Activities include scuba diving and fishing. Bird-watching guides lead walks in the surrounding hills or along the lakeshore. $

Safari Beach Lodge

P.O. Box 1971, Lilongwe, Malawi; tel/fax: +265-277 406; e-mail: safwag@malawi.net

This simple guest house has double rooms with private baths

overlooking a beach. The hills nearby provide excellent bird-watching opportunities, and guides are available. $

TOUR OPERATORS

Central African Wilderness Safaris

P.O. Box 489, Lilongwe, Malawi; tel: +265-771 153; fax: +265-771 397; e-mail: info@wilderness.malawi.net

Customized safaris explore Malawi and Zambia. Hotel bookings, flights, and car rentals are also arranged. This company manages Mvuu Wilderness Lodge and Mvuu Camp in Liwonde National Park, and Chintheche Inn on Lake Malawi, from which Nkhotakota Wildlife Reserve can be reached.

Kayak Africa

P.O. Box 48, Monkey Bay, Malawi; tel: +265-584 456; e-mail: kayakafrica@earthleak.co.za

Based at Cape Maclear, this company rents kayaks by the day or longer and offers guided tours to islands within the national park, where it has simple camps.

Nyika Safari Company

P.O. Box 2338, Lilongwe, Malawi; tel: +265-757 379; fax: +265-757 316, e-mail: nyika-safaries@malawi.net

Safaris cover all of Malawi but specialize in the north. This company runs the lodge and all tourist activities at Nyika National Park, including hiking and riding horses. It also has a lodge at Vwaza Marsh Wildlife Reserve, south of Nyika, an excellent area for birding and viewing elephants.

Red Zebra Tours

P.O. Box 123, Salima, Malawi; tel/fax: +265-263 165; e-mail: redzebras@malawi.net

Based at a tropical fish farm outside Senga Bay, guides cater to serious fish watchers. Tours of a day or longer explore the lake, stopping to dive and snorkel at the best sites.

Excursions

Liwonde National Park

Malawi Tourism, 4 Christian Field, London SW16 3JZ, UK; tel: +44-115-982 1903; fax: +44-115-981 9418; e-mail: enquiries@malawitourism.com

Lake Malawi is drained to the south by the Shire River, which flows through Liwonde National Park. Notable mammals here include sable antelope and rhinos. Boat rides are a popular way to see the river's huge populations of hippos, crocodiles, and elephants, and bird-watching along the banks is always rewarding. Accommodations include Mvuu Wilderness Lodge and Mvuu Camp, which also has a campground. Both places are run by Central African Wilderness Safaris.

Mount Mulanje

Malawi Tourism, 4 Christian Field, London SW16 3JZ, UK; tel: +44-115-982 1903; fax: +44-115-981 9418; e-mail: enquiries@ malawitourism.com

Mount Mulanje is the highest part of Malawi, a rolling plateau surrounded by sheer escarpments, rising steeply above plains and tea estates in the south of the country. Mulanje is not a wildlife destination, although the flowers are spectacular, and some rare birds can be seen in the patches of forest. It is a wonderful wilderness area, with a network of hiking trails and simple log cabins for walkers. There is an unreliable reservation system for the cabins; most visitors just arrive, make arrangements, and start hiking the next day.

Nyika National Park

Malawi Tourism, 4 Christian Field, London SW16 3JZ, UK; tel: +44-115-982 1903; fax: +44-115-981 9418; e-mail: enquiries@malawitourism.com

This vast, high plateau in the north of Malawi is covered mainly by montane grassland. Mammals include zebras, eland, reedbuck, and roan antelope, and the park is surprisingly good for leopards. Bird life is fantastic, and Nyika is particularly noted for its wild orchids. Hiking is permitted, and safaris on horseback are an excellent way to appreciate this specialized wilderness. Accommodations include Chelinda Lodge and Chelinda Camp, which also has a campground. Both places, and the horse safaris, are run by Nyika Safari Company.

Selous
Game Reserve
Tanzania

CHAPTER **16**

Standing in the shade of a pom-pom borassus palm, a fisherman casts a fly in search of tiger fish. Flocks of gold, masked weaver birds fly around their hanging nests, their calls sizzling over the smoothly flowing waters of one of Africa's largest rivers, while a family of elephants wades into the shallows, splashing away the heat of the day. A young Egyptian goose, midstream, breaks the calm, flapping into panic as the chevron wake of a crocodile arrows near. The chase lasts longer than anyone would expect, covering a hundred yards of water, before the bird wins by a hair's breadth, and the thwarted croc subsides in the shallows. The gosling shoots up the sandy shore on webbed, road-runner feet, only to be chased again, this time by its mother, pecking and scolding in fear and relief. Even in the heart of one of Africa's largest protected wildlife areas, it is the small, domestic issues of life and death that count in an environment so vast that the nearest border is impossibly distant.

Dependable rains and a network of waterways sustain an impressive density of game in an untrammeled wilderness.

◆ The massive size of the **Selous Game Reserve**, nearly 17,500 square miles (45,300 sq km), is misleading. Although the animals can wander where they wish, conventional tourists with binoculars and cameras are restricted to the area north of the Rufiji River. The majority (88 percent) of the Selous, mainly miombo woodland lying to the south of the Rufiji River, is accessible only to licensed hunters using their own mobile camps. ◆ The northern, public area of the Selous, covering 2,086 square miles (5,403 sq km), still provides the experience of Africa at its most remote. At its heart is the **Rufiji River**, flowing from the west through the rocky 4-mile (6.4km) length of **Steigler's Gorge**. The river bellies out

A hyena's laugh is among the most chilling sounds of the African bush. This pup will stay near its den until it's old enough to fend for itself.

The map shows the Selous Game Reserve region with labels including: Rubeho Mountains, A7, Kidatu, TAZARA Railway North, B127, miles 0 40, Mbarika Mountains, Luguruka, Uluguru Mountains, Mgeta River, Matambwe Post, Kinganguru Post, Beho Springs, Beho River, Hot, Great Ruaha River, Steigler's Gorge, Rufiji River, ▽Siguri Falls, Luhombero River, SELOUS GAME RESERVE, Luhombero, Mpanga, Kidai Post, Mtemere Post, Ngwembe, Ngarimbi, Chema, Miembwe, Makungviro, Liwale, Mbarangandu, to Dar es Salaam, Beho Beho Camp, Selous Safari Camp, Impala Camp, Rufiji River Camp, Rufiji River, Utete, Indian Ocean, KENYA, TANZANIA, DAR ES SALAAM, SELOUS GAME RESERVE, ZAMBIA.

granted in 1982. While many wilderness areas have been preserved from human intrusion by a shortage of water, the Selous has no such problem. The land is greened by dependable rainfall, innumerable springs, and seepage pans. Twenty different species of tsetse fly, carrying sleeping sickness fatal to domestic cattle, have proved wildlife's friend here, keeping human habitation at bay. With diverse habitats and year-round water, the density of game in the northern Selous is second only to the Serengeti. Fewer than 4,000 visitors a year scatter across this varied wilderness, so this is one place where you are almost guaranteed to have the African bush to yourself.

Apart, that is, from the wildlife – ever present, though often shy and unused to man. Giraffes, Tanzania's national animal, gangle their way clear before peering back cautiously from their fragile height. There are 3,000 lions, but these are outnumbered by leopards, more plentiful here than anywhere else in Africa. Although as elusive as ever, Africa's most elegant cats are often spotted on the

as it heads east across the alluvial plains of the Selous toward the Indian Ocean, the broad flow shouldering aside trees and islands, breathing life into game-rich riparian forest, spreading bird-filled lakes and threading tributaries, oxbow lakes, and lagoons alive with fish, crocodiles, and hippos. Its constant flow fills and feeds a lattice of waterways that are both key to the beauty of the area and vital travel links in a land where roads are rare and rough.

To the north of the river, the ground shelves gently up through a broken landscape of isolated hills, providing rocky viewpoints over alluvial hardpan plain, riparian forest, spinoza, and miombo woodland. As it rises toward the **Uluguru Mountains**, the northern border of the protected area is marked by the parallel tracks of the TAZARA railway. Four times a week, a slow, noisy train trundles past.

Alone in the Bush

This remote reserve richly deserves its status as a World Heritage Site,

The serval (left) relies on its acute hearing to track down prey. It can bring down game as large as a duiker but is often satisfied with lizards and rodents.

Female and young lions (opposite, top) hunt as a team.

A Meller's chameleon (opposite, bottom) waits patiently for prey to come into range of its long flicking tongue.

rocky cliffs of **Steiglers' Gorge**, following rocky fault lines to the rapids to drink.

The open floodplains and hardpan beds are tracked by herds of a hundred or more buffalo. More than 110,000 of these mighty herbivores, horns curved like a Doris Day hairdo, live in the reserve – the largest population in Africa. Elephants, their numbers decimated by poaching in the 1980s, here tend to keep to small breeding groups, breaking down trees to create the mosaic of vegetation regrowth essential for a full and varied ecosystem. The other target of commercial poachers, the browsing black rhinos, are more elusive. Tracks are often seen, but the surviving animals are understandably shy.

Grazing animals are plentiful, with many species specific to the Selous. The Selous wildebeest is grayish-yellow in color. Strangely, those seen south of the Rufiji usually have a white chevron on their nose, while only one percent of the wildebeests north of the river share this mark. Eland in the Selous carry larger horns than elsewhere in Africa, while sable antelope tend to be smaller, with shorter horns. Other ungulates include impalas, Lichtenstein's hartebeests, and the greater kudu, with spiral horns and lateral white flank stripes. Warthogs track through the bush, tails held high, while bushpigs are most often seen in the early morning.

Painted Dogs

The endless expanses of the Selous provide a generous sanctuary for the world's most endangered carnivore, the painted hunting dog. Nearly half the world's wild dogs live in the Selous in sociable, interactive packs, most often found resting through the heat of the afternoon. Wait a while and they rouse, licking and scrapping as they tease each other into hunting mode. Then, with a strange, un-doglike chirping song, they move off fast, to hunt remorselessly in packs ranging in size from 10 to 60 animals. With their stamina and intelligence they are the most feared of Africa's predators. Finding an area of bush devoid of all game is a good indication that hunting dogs are near.

The varied habitats and plentiful waterways of the Rufiji area make it a paradise for birds, with more than 440 species recorded. Among the oxbow lakes, lagoons, and channels, storks, herons, terns, and waders flock and flutter through the air, and the spectacular African skimmer flashes across the water's surface, trawling with its lower jaw for fish. Malachite kingfishers blaze with color on lower branches, while the tall borassus palms are vantage points for fish eagles and Dickinson's kestrels, and nesting homes for slender palm swifts. As night

get around. Light, aluminum boats are perfect for journeys along the narrow waterways that link lakes and lagoons to the main river, threading through pods of hippos and sending crocs slithering down into the water. Despite the density of predators, walking safaris are a leading attraction. Armed park rangers can be booked to accompany gentle strolls lasting just a few hours or overland camping safaris lasting days.

Are Guns Good?

Conservation methods that blend photographic tourism and commercial hunting are central to the survival of Selous. Tourists with cameras, floating down the middle of the Rufiji River, quickly recognize the difference in animal

falls a new range of birds appears: Pel's fishing owl and the white-backed night heron.

Away from the water, the acacia woodlands echo with the bubbling cries of laughing doves and the deep calls of ground hornbills, with racket-tailed rollers and the flashing colors of white-fronted bee-eaters lending color and enchantment to the scene. High overhead, bateleur and martial eagles ride the thermals in search of prey.

The only settlements are two campsites to the north and six lodges widely spaced along the 30-mile (48-km) length of the Rufiji River. Game drives by four-wheel-drive vehicle are perhaps the best way to get close to wildlife but aren't the only way to

behavior caused by the presence of hunters. On the northern, protected bank, the game shies away cautiously at the sight of humans; to the south they run from sight.

In this remote wilderness, it is generally agreed that hunting is essential for the survival of the Selous's wildlife. The game reserve's twin advantages, size and isolation, are also its most pressing problems. Any hopes that photographic tourism could fund effective policing of the Selous's border were dashed when hunting was banned in 1973. Professional hunters left the area and poachers flooded in. Throughout the 1980s the park saw some of the world's worst scenes of commercial poaching, with the

Nature's Garbage Disposal

Vultures don't circle dying prey. They've got too much sense. In the search for food, they'll soar with spread-feathered ease, but when they spot a dying animal they settle on a nearby tree to watch and wait.

Nature's cleaners perform a vital function in the ecology of the bush. When the predators move on, the vultures move in, pecking carrion into clean-picked bones. In the air they are as graceful as any other raptor, soaring effortlessly for hours. When they spot a rotting carcass they arrow down with such speed their feathers set off a humming roar of purpose.

Viewed close up, however, they have little of the elegance of other raptors. Heads and necks tend to be thinly feathered or bald – much easier to keep clean – beaks are sharp and hooked, and legs weak and tottery. They always seem to know what is happening: unseen communication spreads word of a kill far and wide. Where one vulture appears, others are sure to follow, and their hissing and squealing over carrion provide some of the bush's most memorable dramas.

Hyenas and vultures (above) perform a vital role in clearing the bush of fallen game. Vultures remove flesh and hyenas crunch bones until little remains.

Dung beetles (right) mold animal droppings into balls. They lay their eggs in the balls, which nourish pupating larvae.

Black rhinos (opposite) fell to poachers in great numbers when the Tanzanian tourist industry collapsed in the 1970s and '80s.

A ground hornbill (below) carries away a pilfered egg.

black rhino population dropping from 3,000, the largest in Africa, to a few scattered individuals. Elephant numbers fell from 120,000 in the 1970s to less than 30,000 in 1991.

Since hunting has been reinstated, poaching has dropped dramatically, due to the increased activity of commercial hunters, with the elephant population recovering to 54,000 and rhinos, once again, being occasionally seen. Expensive trophy fees now make up 80 percent of the Selous's revenue, with careful quota management minimizing the impact on endangered species.

Management, however, is not a word that is easily applied to one of Africa's last, untamed wilderness areas. Each year the wet season closes the park to even the hardiest four-wheel-drive, washing out roads and flooding airstrips. The Rufiji swells in the gray privacy of torrential rain, tearing down trees and battering out a new pattern of lakes and waterways in the sandy soil, and rewriting the map of a land where man is a mere visitor. As the rains steam from the dirt roads of the Selous, each dry season brings new wonders of nature, washed fresh for the most important residents: the wildlife.

TRAVEL TIPS

DETAILS

When to Go

The best time to visit Selous is during the slightly cooler season from late June through October, when high temperatures are 80°F (27°C) to 85°F (29°C), the game stays near the river, and the bush dries out to a thin, transparent scree. The rainy season runs from November to May, with highs up to 95°F (35°C). The early rains are not too severe, and a drier interlude in January and February can offer a good chance to experience the bush in blossom. It's also a great time for bird-watching. From the end of March through May, Selous sees heavy rains; the reserve is inaccessible, and the tourist camps are closed.

Getting There

Travelers fly into Tanzania via the capital, Dar es Salaam. From there, it is 150 miles (240km) to the entry at Mtemere. A four-wheel-drive vehicle is needed for driving around the reserve, and rentals are available at the airport. It takes about eight hours to reach the entrance; the last 47 miles (74km) are on a dirt road.

Usual access is by plane to airstrips at Beho Beho, Mbuyu, Rufiji River Camp, Mtemere, Selous Safari Camp, and Steigler's Gorge. Several local airlines fly into the reserve, including Air Tanzania (P.O. Box 543, Dar es Salaam, Tanzania; tel: +255-51-110 245; fax: +255-51-46545; e-mail: mdir@airtanzania.com); Coastal Travels (P.O. Box 3052, Dar es Salaam, Tanzania; tel: +255-51-117 959; fax: +255-51-118 647; e-mail: coastal@twiga.com); and Precision Air (P.O. Box 70770, Dar es Salaam, Tanzania; tel: +255-51-130 800; fax: +255-51-113 036; e-mail: info@precisionairtz.com).

INFORMATION

Tanzania Embassies

United Kingdom: 43 Hertford Street, London W1Y 8DB; tel: +44-20-7499 8951; fax: +44-20-7491 9321; e-mail: Balozi@tanzania-online.gov.uk

United States: 2139 R Street, N.W., Washington, DC 20008; tel: 202-939-6125; fax: 202-797-7408; e-mail: tanz-us@clark.net

Tanzania National Parks

P.O. Box 25295, Dar es Salaam, Tanzania: tel: +255-51-866 064; fax: +255-51-861 007; e-mail: tanapa@habari.co.tz

Tanzania Tourist Office

United States: 205 East 42nd Street, Suite 1300, New York, NY 10017; tel: 212-972-9160; fax: 212-682-5232.

CAMPING

Selous Game Reserve

Tanzania National Parks, P.O. Box 25295, Dar es Salaam, Tanzania: tel: +255-51-866 064; fax: +255-51-861 007; e-mail: tanapa@habari.co.tz

The only way to visit the Selous on a budget is by camping in either established camps such as those at Mtemere and Beho Beho or at special campsites where prices are somewhat higher. Campsites are unfenced, and wild animals roam freely; independent travelers must hire a park ranger to ensure their safety.

LODGING

PRICE GUIDE – double occupancy

$ = under $100 $$ = $100–$200
$$$ = $200–$300 $$$$ = $300+

Mahale Tented Camp

P.O. Box 150, Usa River, Tanzania; tel/fax: +255-811-512 312; e-mail: greystoke@luxurious.com

This lodge in Mahale National Park can be reached only by charter flight. All meals and game-viewing activities are included in the price. $$$$

Mwagusi Safari Camp

World Archipelago, 55 Fulham High Street, London SW6 3JJ; tel: +44-20-7471 8780; fax: +44-20-7384 9549; e-mail: worldarc@compuserve.com

Ten tents in a magnificent setting overlook the Sand River in Ruaha National Park. All meals and game-viewing activities are included in the price. $$$$

Ruaha River Lodge

Foxtreks Limited, P.O. Box 10270, Dar es Salaam, Tanzania; tel: +255-811-327 706.

This less expensive alternative to Mwagusi has bandas (chalets) set on a rocky kopje, with fine views of the surrounding landscape. All meals and game-viewing activities are included in the price; access is by air only. $$

Rufiji River Camp

Hippo Tours and Safaris, P.O. Box 13824, Dar es Salaam, Tanzania; tel: +255-51-71610; fax: +255-51-75165; e-mail: hippo@twiga.com

Twenty tents under thatch roofs, set high over the river, offer great views and serve as a base from which to explore the reserve. Meals are included in the price, but game drives and boat trips cost extra. $$$$

Sand Rivers Selous

P.O. Box 24133, Nairobi, Kenya; tel: +254-2-882 521; fax: +254-2-882 728; e-mail: Bonham.Luke@swiftkenya.com

Eight individually designed bedrooms overlook the Rufiji River. Activities are tailored to guests' special requirements. Steigler's Gorge is within a day's drive; bush camping, fishing, and walking safaris offer alternatives to game drives by vehicle or boat. $$$$

Selous Safari Camp

Tours and Trade International BVI, 47 Albemarle Street, London

W1X 3FE, UK; tel: +44-1367-253 810; fax +44-1367-253 812; e-mail: enidtti@compuserve.com

Formerly known as Mbuyuni, this camp is set on a river with walk-in tents under thatch roofs built on wooden decks. It offers immediate access to some of the most beautiful lakes and waterways at the heart of the reserve, crowded with game and birds. Walking and fishing safaris can be arranged. Prince Charles stayed in tent number eight. $$$$.

TOUR OPERATORS

Coastal Tours
P.O. Box 3052, Dar Es Salaam, Tanzania; tel: + 255-51-117 959; fax: +255-51- 118 647; e-mail: safari@coastal.cc

Coastal offers flights and a full range of tour services.

Hippo Tours and Safaris
P.O. Box 13824, Dar Es Salaam, Tanzania; tel: +255-51-71610; fax: +255-51-75165; e-mail: hippo@twiga.com

Hippo Tours operates at the budget end of the market but generally funnels visitors to Rufiji River Camp, which it owns.

Tropical Trekking
P.O. Box 2047, Arusha, Tanzania; tel: +255-57-507 011; fax: +255-57-508 226; e-mail tropicaltrekking@cybernet.co.tz

United Kingdom: Suite F1, Hartsbourne House, Carpenters Park, Watford, Herts WD1 5EF, UK; tel: +44-20-8428 8221; fax: +44-20-8421 1396; e-mail: tropicaltrekking@aol.com

Guides specialize in Tanzania, including treks up Mount Kilimanjaro and encounters with chimpanzees in Mahale National Park.

Excursions

Mahale National Park
Tanzania National Parks, P.O. Box 25295, Dar es Salaam, Tanzania: tel: +255-51-866 064; fax: +255-51-861 007; e-mail: tanapa@habari.co.tz; web: www.ruaha.org or www.ruaha.com

This park, where Jane Goodall conducted her pioneering chimpanzee research, is one of the few places in the world where you can get close to chimps. Travel to the spectacular forested hills east of Lake Tanganyika is expensive, and park fees are very high. The only way to see the chimps on a budget involves using the erratic services of Air Tanzania.

Mount Kilimanjaro
Tanzania National Parks, P.O. Box 25295, Dar es Salaam, Tanzania: tel: +255-51-866 064; fax: +255-51-861 007; e-mail: tanapa@habari.co.tz; web: www.ruaha.org or www.ruaha.com

Sixty thousand visitors climb Mount Kilimanjaro every year, making Africa's highest mountain (19,453 feet/5,929m) Tanzania's most visited park. Six trekking routes reach the top; the ascent takes five to six days, with mountaineering experience opening up further options. It helps to be fit, although the most common problem that climbers encounter is altitude sickness, which is not related to general health. The most popular trail is the Maranga Route, although the best views are from the more demanding Machame Route.

Ruaha National Park
Tanzania National Parks, P.O. Box 25295, Dar es Salaam, Tanzania: tel: +255-51-866 064; fax: +255-51-861 007; e-mail: tanapa@habari.co.tz; web: www.ruaha.org or www.ruaha.com

Almost as large as Selous but fully protected against hunters, Ruaha National Park is one of Africa's finest yet least visited wilderness areas. The park's spine is formed by the watershed of the Nzombe and Ruaha Rivers, full and flooding in the wet season, isolated lakes linked by sandy riverbeds when dry. The park is especially good for viewing predators, with plenty of lions and cheetahs. Varied habitats attract a huge variety of birds. Since it's expensive to reach, you will virtually have the park to yourself.

Serengeti and Ngorongoro Crater
Tanzania

CHAPTER **17**

Even in the dry season, the **Seronera River** holds the promise of shade and water. Born as a series of springs on the **Serengeti Plains**, this modest stream trickles from pool to pool, fringed by a ribbon of Senegal palms and graceful fever trees whose lemon-yellow trunks glow in the late afternoon sun. Doves chant. Orioles call with fluting voices. It is as peaceful as an English park. ◆ And yet, the air sizzles with tension. Sprawled in the branches of a sausage tree, a leopard waits for darkness before setting out on its nocturnal hunt. At river's edge, lions peer hungrily over the tall grass at herds of wildebeests and zebras grazing on the plains. Millions of herbivores migrate through the **Seronera Valley** every year on their way to and from Kenya's **Masai Mara National Reserve**, and always the big cats are waiting. ◆ It is the ancient drama of this great migration that makes the Serengeti one of the world's premier game parks. Few places can match the staggering number of plains animals or the sense of boundless

A sea of grass at a pair of celebrated game parks sustains millions of hoofed animals and the predators that feed on them.

freedom one feels while traveling across the amber grasslands. Little wonder that the Masai called it *Siringit* – the place where the land runs on forever. ◆ One of the earliest – and still one of the best – descriptions of the Serengeti was penned by American hunter Stewart Edward White in 1913: "It is hard to do that country justice," he wrote. "From the river it rolls away in low sloping hills, as green as emeralds beneath trees spaced as in a park. And the game. Never have I seen anything like that game." ◆ About seven years later, another American hunter, Leslie Simpson, motored across the Serengeti in a Model A Ford, blazing a trail

A stand of acacias shade a herd of Cape buffalo roaming the floor of Ngorongoro Crater; the walls of the caldera tower above them.

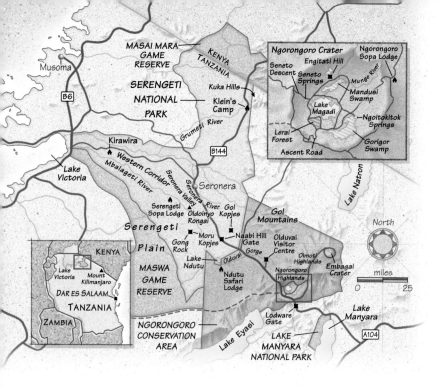

lodge is ensconced in a large grove of acacias overlooking **Lake Ndutu**, whose saline waters attract throngs of flamingos. A lion pride lives in the woods, and servals, small African cats, hunt in the reeds of a nearby marsh.

A half-hour drive northeast of Naabi Hill is **Gol Kopjes**, a wonderland of granite inselbergs and rolling plains. The outcroppings are like islands in a sea of grass. They serve as watchtowers for cheetahs and surefooted klipspringers, roosts for barn owls, and refuges for birthing lionesses. Agama lizards bask on the sun-warmed rocks, and sunbirds sip nectar from scarlet leonotis flowers that bloom among the boulders.

These short-grass plains of the southern Serengeti are at their loveliest from October to March or April, when the vegetation is lush and the wildebeests have returned from the Masai Mara. That begins to change in May, when parched winds signal the onset of the dry season. Game retreats to the **Western Corridor** or into the woodlands north of the Seronera Valley. It isn't just the wildebeests and zebras that leave the southern plains at this time. With them travel eland, topi, kongoni, giraffes, and skittish herds of Thompson's gazelles as well as the big cats that feed on them.

June and July are usually the best months to explore the Western Corridor, a region of parklike plains between the **Grumeti** and **Mbalageti Rivers**. Here game tends to linger, exploiting the abundant grass. At **Kirawira**, a watering site on the Grumeti River, some of the largest crocodiles in Africa lie in wait for the wildebeests that come to drink.

Wildlife is harder to spot in the acacia glades and thorn thickets of the northern woodlands, but this is the place to look for

for generations of hunters and game viewers. Even then, it was clear that the golden age of African wilderness was passing, but it wasn't until 1951 that the Serengeti became a national park. Today it is a World Heritage Site and Biosphere Reserve encompassing 8,078 square miles (20,922 sq km) – an area larger than Switzerland.

Grass and Granite

For most visitors, the first glimpse of the Serengeti comes on the drive down from the **Ngorongoro Highlands** to the southeast. The plains spread out below; the **Gol Mountains** rise on the northern horizon. On entering the park at its southern gateway, **Naabi Hill**, one finds nothing but grass in every direction. A 30-minute drive to the south leads to **Ndutu Lodge**, the only place to stay in the park's southern sector. The

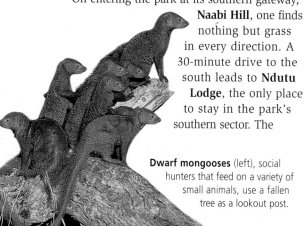

Dwarf mongooses (left), social hunters that feed on a variety of small animals, use a fallen tree as a lookout post.

A **vervet monkey** (left) feeds on a tissue flower; though plants make up most of a vervet's diet, it will eat lizards, eggs, and insects if given the opportunity.

Bachelor lions (below) often hunt together until they are strong enough to win a pride of their own.

elephants and buffalo. Some of the park's biggest buffalo herds can be seen around **Klein's Camp**, a pristine area at the foot of the **Kuka Hills**.

One of the best places in the Serengeti for year-round game-viewing is the Seronera Valley in the very center of the park. Here the high-country breezes ripple through miles of waist-high red oat grass broken only by a few scattered hills such as **Nyaraswiga** and **Oldoinyo Rongai**. Abundant vegetation attracts a great variety of species, including giraffes, buffalo, warthogs, and reedbucks, which, in turn, sustain resident leopards and large lion prides.

One of the park's most scenic game drives leads south of the Seronera Valley to the **Moru Kopjes**, an archipelago of granite islands about 9 miles (15km) south of the **Serengeti Sopa Lodge**. Fig trees and candelabra euphorbias sprout from the tumbled rocks, while the abundant caves and crevices shelter all manner of creatures, including leopards, goshawks, and yellow-winged bats. One of the kopjes is adorned

with Masai cave paintings, some more than 200 years old. On another stands the extraordinary **Gong Rock**. Strike it with a stone and listen to its bell-like chimes resonate across the plains. The Serengeti is full of such wonders. But in the end it is the sheer multitude of living things that makes this one of the most remarkable parks in Africa.

A Hidden World

But even the Serengeti pales in comparison to **Ngorongoro Crater**, a fabulous lost world teeming with wildlife southeast of the park in the **Ngorongoro Conservation Area**. The crater is the world's largest intact caldera – a geologic relic created about three million years ago by the collapse of a volcanic cone that may have stood taller than Kilimanjaro. Ash sent aloft by the cataclysm settled onto the Serengeti Plains, resulting in the rich soil that feeds lush grasses to this day.

The crater is a gigantic natural stadium, an almost perfect circular depression 11 miles (18km) in diameter surrounded by steep palisades. Visitors usually approach from the south, passing through the highland cloud forest on the outer slopes until the ground falls away and the crater yawns before them.

At first, one sees only sunlight and shadow spilling across the crater floor 1,700 feet (520m) below, but binoculars bring details into view. Scattered across the plains are 10,000 wildebeests, 5,000 zebras, 3,000 buffalo, and myriad other creatures. A pink blush along the soda-encrusted shores of **Lake Magadi** is a vast colony of flamingos feeding on brine shrimp. A dark speck far out in the golden grass is one of Tanzania's few remaining black rhinos.

A memorial crowned with a buffalo skull stands at a viewpoint near the entrance to the crater, commemorating the men who have given their lives for wildlife conservation, including two rangers shot dead by poachers in 1978. Along the western rim is another stone marker, this one erected in memory of Bernard and Michael Grzimek, father-and-son German zoologists whose pioneering work in the 1950s focused international attention on the conservation of Tanzania's wildlife.

Into the Depths

All but one of Ngorongoro's safari lodges are situated on the southwest sector of the crater rim. The exception is the **Ngorongoro Sopa**

The Wildebeest Migration

For the Serengeti wildebeest, life is an endless journey, chasing the rains to stay alive. The only constant point in this annual cycle of birth and death is calving time, which peaks in February around Naabi Hill in the far south of the park. The short grasses that grow on these open plains are rich in the minerals that build healthy bones in newborn calves.

When the rains end in May and the grass is exhausted, the herds begin their long march north – an epic trek to the dry-season grazing grounds in Kenya's Masai Mara reserve. On their way through the Western Corridor and the northern woodlands, they face a variety of dangers, from poachers' snares to crocodiles and lions. Once in the Mara, they normally stay from July to October, when the onset of the rains draws them south again. By the time they reach the calving grounds, they may have covered 1,875 miles (3,000km), making this one of the longest overland migrations in the animal kingdom.

A Cape buffalo (opposite, top), fresh from a mud bath, takes a momentary break from grazing.

A wildebeest calf (left) must be able to follow its mother shortly after birth to keep up with the herd.

chats, wheatears, rosy-breasted long-claws, and Jackson's widow birds.

Sometimes a huge shaggy head rises from the grass – a male lion rousing itself for a view of the plains. The Ngorongoro lions suffered a severe setback in 1998, when the crater flooded with torrential El Niño rains. Washed out of their territories, many of the lions left and never returned, halving the population to just 32 adults. Fortunately, a bumper crop of cubs has been produced since the flood, and the population seems to be rebounding.

As significant as lions are to the Ngorongoro ecosystem, they are not the crater's most efficient predators. That crown belongs to the spotted hyena. Several clans of these formidable hunters roam the crater floor. Hyenas hunt in packs, some chivvying their prey by nipping at the snout and flanks, others severing the hamstrings with their powerful jaws. By this method, they are able to bring down animals as large as adult zebras.

Lodge, on the opposite side. It takes an hour longer to reach but has its own access track leading down to the crater floor.

Everyone else enters the crater by driving down the steep track from the western rim to **Seneto Springs**, where Masai boys water their cattle. Unlike the Serengeti, which is reserved solely for wildlife, about 40,000 Masai inhabit the sprawling 2,500-square-mile (6,480-sq-km) conservation area around the crater itself. In fact, *Ngorongoro* is probably a Masai name, though its origins are clouded. One explanation holds that its clanging syllables evoke the sound of Masai cattle bells.

Grasslands dominate the crater floor. During the dry season, which typically runs from June through October, they are the same tawny color as the lions that prey on the herds of wildebeests, zebras, buffalo, kongoni, eland, gazelles, and warthogs. But the rains transform these dusty plains. Overnight, lush carpets of emerald turf appear, strewn with drifts of white cycnium flowers. Gray-crowned cranes bugle mournfully to one other, and white storks arrive from Europe to join flocks of larks, pipits,

A black rhino (opposite, bottom) finds refuge in easily patrolled Ngorongoro Crater.

Marabou storks (right) are primarily scavengers; their pendulous throat sacs are most likely used in courtship.

Noticeably absent from the crater are giraffes, topi, and impalas. It is presumed that the crater walls are too steep for the giraffes to negotiate and that there is insufficient forage to support large herds of topi and impalas. Also absent are elephant cows and calves, though you will see mature bull elephants – six-ton veterans carrying some of the heaviest tusks in Africa. Look for them grazing under the lacy canopies of yellow-barked acacias in the **Lerai Forest** in the southern portion of the crater or wallowing in the reedbeds of the **Mandusi Swamp** on the caldera's far western edge.

It's worth stopping at the hippo pool on the edge of the swamp. Bird life is prolific here. Black crakes are often seen scuttling on orange feet over the backs of semisubmerged hippos. Sacred ibis forage along the water's edge, and saddle-billed storks spear frogs in the reeds.

Lake Magadi, an alkaline lake a short distance from the swamp, has even greater concentrations of birds. Flamingos get star

Olduvai and the Leakeys

Situated about halfway between Serengeti National Park and Ngorongoro Crater, **Olduvai Gorge**, a fissure in the earth 300 feet (90m) deep, is a vital link in the fossil history of humankind. Anthropologist Louis Leakey discovered pebble tools during his first expedition to the gorge in 1931, but it took 29 years before the toolmaker was found.

One of the first major breakthroughs came in 1959, when Leakey's wife, Mary, uncovered a skull fragment that belonged to a 1.75-million-year-old hominid later classified as *Australopithecus boisei*, a robust, bipedal creature with apelike features. The very next year, the Leakeys' son Jonathan stumbled across teeth and bone fragments that led to the discovery of a more lightly built and humanlike specimen that was roughly the same age as the first. Its name, *Homo habilis*, "handy man," reflected the Leakeys' contention that it was a primitive member of the human family and the maker of the simple tools that Louis had found decades earlier.

Even more exciting discoveries followed. In 1976, members of a team led by Mary Leakey found two sets of hominid footprints at Laetoli, just south of Olduvai. The tracks date to about 3½ million years ago and confirm that early human ancestors walked on two feet well before developing large brains. Richard Leakey followed up on his mother's discovery in 1984 with "Turkana Boy," a nearly complete specimen of *Homo erectus*, unearthed north of Olduvai in Kenya.

A modest visitor center at the gorge interprets the Olduvai fossils and chronicles the Leakeys' remarkable and often controversial career.

Louis Leakey (far left) established a key link in human evolution when he discovered stone tools at Olduvai Gorge. His wife, Mary, later unearthed skull fragments belonging to a robust, apelike creature dubbed Zinjanthropus (left) by the Leakeys but subsequently classified as *Australopithecus boisei*.

Olduvai Gorge (below), site of the Leakeys' most significant work, is a fossil treasure house.

An elephant (opposite, top) browses on water plants near a pod of hippos at a Ngorongoro pool.

Egyptian vultures (opposite, below) bide their time before feasting on scraps left by predators.

billing, but there are also rafts of red-billed teal, flurries of plovers, and myriad long-legged waders, including avocets, greenshanks, and black-winged stilts, all assiduously probing the mud for crustaceans and burrowing insects.

Time for a Bite

At midday, everyone heads for the nearest picnic spot. There are only two official sites – one overlooking the reed-fringed pools of **Ngoitokitok Springs** to the north of the **Gorigor Swamp**, and another, shadier spot in the Lerai Forest. Both sites can get quite crowded. It's best to eat inside your vehicle rather than risk being mugged by the black kites and vervet monkeys who have dis-covered that the picnic baskets of gullible tourists make for easy pickings.

If you want to get away from competing safaris, head north of the **Munge River**, which flows down from the **Olmoti Highlands**. Eland favor the hillsides north of the Munge, and relatively few visitors make the effort to explore this terrain.

You'll find stunning views of the crater from the flat summit of **Engitati Hill**, called the Golan Heights by some Tanzanian guides. From here, it's often possible to make out black rhinos resting in the grasslands below. More than 100 rhinos lived in the crater throughout the 1960s, but by 1986 all but a few had been slaughtered by poachers. Since then, these magnificent beasts have edged back from the brink, and the population now stands at about 19, making Ngorongoro the best place in Tanzania to see them.

At the end of the day, all tourist vehicles must leave the crater, laboring up the one-way egress track that begins at the edge of the Lerai Forest. By sunset, Ngorongoro is once again the sole province of its native inhabitants.

TRAVEL TIPS

DETAILS

When to Go

The dry season (June to October) is followed by short rains in November and December, another dry spell in January and February, and the long rains of March through May. Although the park is close to the equator, temperatures on the Serengeti Plain are tempered by altitude. For much of the year, you can expect temperatures from 70°F (21°C) to 80°F (27°C). The rim of Ngorongoro Crater is 7,333 feet (2,235m) above sea level, so nights are cold.

Getting There

Kilimanjaro International Airport, an hour's drive west of Arusha, is the entry to northern Tanzania's safari circuit. There are direct flights from Europe, but most travelers connect via Nairobi or Dar es Salaam. Ngorongoro is a four-hour drive from Arusha; it's another three hours to Serengeti. Light aircraft also serve the parks. For details, contact Regional Air Services, CMC Building, Sokoine Road, P.O. Box 14755, Arusha; tel: +255-57-2541; fax: +255-57-4164; or Precisionair, P.O. Box 1636, Arusha; tel: +255-57-6903; fax: +255-57-3204; e-mail: precision-ark@cybernet.co.tz

INFORMATION

Tanzania Embassies

United Kingdom: 43 Hertford Street, London W1Y 8DB; tel: +44-20-7499 8951; fax: +44-20-7491 9321; e-mail: Balozi@tanzania-online.gov.uk

United States: 2139 R Street, N.W., Washington, DC 20008; tel: 202-939-6125; fax: 202-797-7408; e-mail: tanz-us@clark.net

Tanzania National Parks

P.O. Box 3134, Arusha, Tanzania; tel: +255-57-3471 or +255-57-4082; fax +255-57-8216; e-mail: tanapa@habari.co.tz

Chief Warden, P.O. Box 25295, Dar es Salaam, Tanzania: tel: +255-51-866 064; fax: +255-51-861 007.

Tanzania Tourist Offices

United States: 205 East 42nd Street, Suite 1300, New York, NY 10017; tel: 212-972-9160; fax: 212-682-5232.

CAMPING

Independent camping is not permitted in Serengeti National Park or Ngorongoro Crater Conservation Area.

LODGING

PRICE GUIDE – double occupancy

$ = under $100 $$ = $100–$200
$$$ = $200–$300 $$$$ = $300+

Gibb's Farm

P.O. Box 6084, Arusha, Tanzania; tel: +255-57-6702 or +255-57-8930; fax: +255-57-8310; e-mail: ndutugibbs@nabari.co.tz

A coffee farm near Karatu on the edge of the Ngorongoro cloud forest offers wonderful home cooking, an idyllic garden, and 15 twin-roomed cottages. Gibb's Farm is popular with birders. $$$

Kirawira

Serena Hotels, P.O. Box 2551, Arusha, Tanzania; tel: +255-57-8175 or +255-57-6304; fax: +255-11-4155; e-mail: serena@habari.co.tz

This tented lodge deep in the Western Corridor overlooking the Grumeti River has 25 spacious tents with private baths and ceiling fans. There is also a swimming pool. $$$$

Klein's Camp

CCAfrica, P Bag X27, Benmore 2010, South Africa; tel: +27-11-809 4300; fax: +27-11-809 4400; e-mail: bookings@ccafrica.com; web:www.ccafrica.com

This hideaway among the Kuka Hills on the Serengeti's north-eastern edge has eight twin-bed cottages with private baths, and a swimming pool. $$$$

Manyara Serena Lodge

Serena Hotels, P.O. Box 2551, Arusha, Tanzania; tel: +255-57-8175 or +255-57-6304; fax: +255-11-4155; e-mail: serena@habari.co.tz

Sixty-seven rooms with private baths are at the edge of the Rift Valley escarpment, overlooking the park. A pool is on the premises. $$$

Migration Camp

P.O. Box 409, Dar es Salaam, Tanzania; tel: +255-51-36134 or +255-51-44491; fax: +255-51-44332.

Sixteen tents with private baths are set on a rocky kopje overlooking the Grumeti River in the park's northern sector. There are timber walkways, viewing platforms, and a swimming pool. $$$$

Ngorongoro Crater Lodge

CCAfrica, P Bag X27, Benmore 2010, South Africa; tel: +27-11-809 4300; fax: +27-11-809 4400; e-mail: bookings@ccafrica.com; web:www.ccafrica.com

Sumptuous accommodations are divided into two camps with 12 suites, and a Tree Camp with six suites on the crater rim. Features include butler service, four-poster beds, and lavish bathrooms with freestanding tubs. $$$$

Ndutu Safari Lodge

P.O. Box 6084, Arusha, Tanzania; tel: +255-57-6702 or +255-57-8930; fax: +255-57-8310; e-mail: ndutugibbs@nabari.co.tz.

This is the only lodge for exploring the southern short-grass plains, with 32 simply furnished rooms. The food is excellent. $$$

Ngorongoro Sopa Lodge

Sopa Management, P.O. Box 1823, Arusha, Tanzania; tel: +255-57-6886 or +255-57-6703; fax: +255-57-8245; e-mail: info@sopalodges.com

The only lodge on the eastern rim has its own access route to the crater floor. It offers 100 centrally heated suites and a swimming pool. $$

Serengeti Sopa Lodge

Sopa Management, P.O. Box 1823, Arusha, Tanzania; tel: +255-57-6886 or +255-57-6703; fax: +255-57-8245; e-mail: info@sopalodges.com

Situated in the park's best game-viewing area between the Moru Kopjes and the Seronera Valley, the lodge has 100 rooms with private balconies and baths. A swimming pool is on the grounds. $$

TOUR OPERATORS

Gibb's Farm Safaris

P.O. Box 6084, Arusha, Tanzania; tel: +255-57-6702 or +255-57-8930; fax: +255-57-8310; e-mail: ndutugibbs@nabari.co.tz

Experienced guides lead private luxury camping safaris at Serengeti, Ngorongoro, and Tarangire.

Hoopoe Adventure Tours

P.O. Box 2047, India Street, Arusha, Tanzania; tel: +255-57-7011 or +255-57-7541; fax: +255-57-8226.

Private camping and lodge safaris venture around northern Tanzania. Facilities include Hoopoe's own comfortable tented Kirurumu Lodge overlooking Lake Manyara.

Serengeti Balloon Safaris

The Adventure Center, P.O. Box 12116, Arusha, Tanzania; tel: +255-57-8578; fax: +255-57-8997.

Hour-long flights over the Serengeti take off daily at dawn and are followed by an open-air champagne breakfast.

Excursions

Arusha National Park

Tanzania National Parks, P.O. Box 3134, Arusha, Tanzania; tel: +255-57-3471 or +255-57-4082; fax: +255-57-8216; e-mail: tanapa@habari.co.tz

Covering just 20 square miles (50 sq km), Arusha is one of Tanzania's smallest and most beautiful parks, less than a 30-minute drive from the town of the same name. Much of it is montane rain forest, the home of black-and-white colobus monkeys and forest birds such as Narina's trogon. Its most spectacular features are the Momella Lakes and Ngurdoto Crater – a miniature Ngorongoro, one mile across. From its rim you can enjoy views of Kilimanjaro and, on a clear day, the giant ash cone of Mount Meru.

Lake Manyara National Park

Tanzania National Parks, P.O. Box 3134, Arusha, Tanzania; tel: +255-57-3471 or +255-57-4082; fax: +255-57-8216; e-mail: tanapa@habari.co.tz

Flamingos, elephants, and tree-climbing lions are the stars of this Rift Valley park, a two-hour drive from the town of Arusha. Driving 22 miles (35km) from the gateway town of Mto-wa-Mbu to Maji Moto Hot Springs takes you from groundwater forest to acacia woodlands and grassy floodplains alive with game and 350 species of birds. Most vehicles stick to the northern sector, so the area south of the Endabash River is usually more peaceful.

Tarangire National Park

Tanzania National Parks, P.O. Box 3134, Arusha, Tanzania; tel: +255-57-3471 or +255-57-4082; fax: +255-57-8216; e-mail: tanapa@habari.co.tz

Elephants and baobab trees – giants of the animal and vegetable kingdoms – dominate Tarangire. Covering 525 square miles (1,360 sq km) of plains, thornbush, swamps, and palm groves, this is Tanzania's fourth-largest park, only 70 miles (112km) southwest of Arusha but surprisingly uncrowded. June through October is the peak time for tourists, when the Tarangire River is the only water for miles around and thousands of animals move in from the Masai Steppe. Lions and leopards are the top predators. Tsetse flies can be a nuisance.

Masai Mara National Reserve
Kenya

CHAPTER **18**

On the high plains of Masai Mara, not far from **Governor's Camp**, is a seasonal watercourse known as **Bila Shaka Lugga**, a Swahili term that means roughly "without fail." It was named by safari guides, who knew that lions could almost always be found there. But the same can be said for much of the Mara. No matter where you stay, lion sightings are virtually guaranteed on every game drive. From the **Siria Escarpment** in the west of the reserve to the **Ngama Hills** in the east, no less than 22 prides hold sway, each with its own territory of grass and thickets. ◆ Some seasoned travelers regard the Mara as the Times Square of game reserves, perpetually abuzz with tourists. But in few other places can travelers view wildlife in such breathless close-up, or encounter it in such abundance, especially when migrating zebras and wildebeests pour in from Tanzania's Serengeti Plains. Wild animals don't recognize political frontiers; humans force boundaries upon them.

The plains tremble as wildebeests and zebras advance toward the Mara River. The great migration has begun.

But here wildlife is allowed to roam freely across the border, uniting the two parks into a single ecological unit that supports the heaviest concentration of large mammals on the planet. ◆ That's why, every summer, one hears the same question at every camp and lodge in the Mara: When will the migration begin? By July, the answer is already marching across the plains, as hundreds of thousands of hoofed animals cross the Serengeti toward their dry-season refuge in the Mara's wild meadows, where oat grass ripened by rain and sunshine stands tall enough to hide a prowling lion. ◆ At first it is just a trickle, an advance guard of zebras, a few columns of wildebeests, crossing the Tanzanian border and spilling out across the plains. But soon

Wildebeests stampede across the Mara River. Lurking crocodiles, powerful river currents, and the simple press of bodies make this one of the most dangerous moments in their annual migration from the Serengeti.

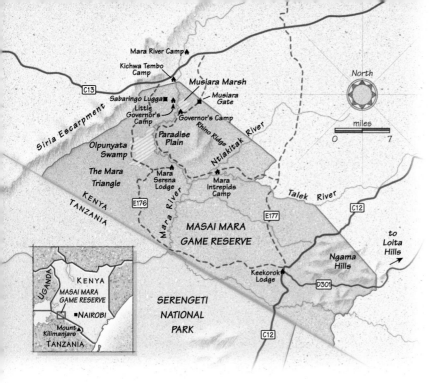

Warthogs trot across the plains with tails erect like radio antennae. Herds of toffee-gold impalas, the most elegant of the antelope, browse along the fringes of the bush, while statuesque topi watch solemnly from termite mounds. Black rhinos, elephants, and big cats are also full-time residents, adding drama to every game drive.

A wide array of habitats is represented in the Mara, each with a unique complement of flora and fauna. Hippos occupy the deeper pools of the Mara River, while Nile crocodiles bask on flat rocks and sandbars. Monitor lizards favor dead tree trunks as vantage points. Acacia woodlands attract giraffes, which browse on the feathery leaves regardless of the vicious thorns, while impalas, olive baboons, and a variety of other animals feed on the fallen seed pods.

But it is out in the Mara's boundless grasslands that the best game viewing is to be found. This is the haunt of the rangy, sway-backed cheetah, the fastest animal on Earth, and its favorite prey, the dainty, tail-twitching Thomson's gazelle. From all around rise the sounds of the plains – the booming voices of ground hornbills, the demented

the trickle becomes a flood as the main body of the migrating herds comes thundering in. For the next three or four months they remain in the Mara, a deafening, grunting army, chomping and trampling the grass, stampeding across the **Mara River** in search of fresh grazing, and providing predators with a season of plenty until the onset of the "short rains" in October and November draws them south again.

If you want to witness the great migration in full swing with its spectacular river crossings and glut of lion kills, then August and September are prime time in the Mara. Yet even when the Serengeti herds have departed, the Mara still puts on an unrivaled pageant of predators and prey. For a start, many thousands of wildebeests that used to migrate to the **Loita Hills** outside the reserve now stay here year-round, as do many other animals.

A cheetah (right) sharpens its claws on a truck's tailgate; it's not unusual for the cats to approach safari vehicles.

shrieking of crowned plovers, the squeal of zebra stallions calling to their mares, and, at first light, the spine-tingling rumble of lions.

Masai Homeland

It was the Masai who first named these plains the Mara, or Spotted Land, a reference to the acacia glades that once freckled the grasslands before fire and elephants created today's open vistas. The Masai tended cattle here for 200 years, until rinderpest wiped out their livestock in the mid-1800s. When Europeans arrived in the early 20th century, they found only wilderness teeming with game.

In short order, the Mara became a favored destination of trophy hunters – an uncontrolled free-fire zone that finally led to the creation of the region's first wildlife sanctuary, the **Mara Triangle**, consisting of all the land west of the Mara River in the present-day reserve. In 1961 another 500 square miles (1,300 sq km) were added, bringing the total

to 590 square miles (1,530 sq km), but not before hunters had shot all but a handful of male lions on the plains around **Keekorok**. By then, the Masai had returned to reclaim their ancestral grazing lands. Though the region is technically a game sanctuary, the presence of these red-robed herdsmen adds immeasurably to the magic of the Mara; they are as much a part of the ecosystem as the herds of wild game.

Zebras (above) seek safety in numbers and are often found in the company of wildebeests.

Snorts and grunts are the language of the topi (right), an antelope closely related to hartebeests, who join the annual migration in the thousands.

The Big Picture

One of the best viewpoints in the Mara is the rim of the Siria Escarpment, whose 1,000-foot-high (300-m) walls march away to the Serengeti, creating a natural boundary along the reserve's northwestern edge. From here you see the Mara as it must appear to the bateleur eagles and vultures who glide on the thermals that curl up the sides of the escarpment. Sprawled below are the plains and marshes of the Mara Triangle. Stately giraffes move between the scattered parasol shapes of desert date trees, skeins of wildebeests dot the plains like threaded beads, and the Mara River winds sinuously toward the faraway hills around Keekorok to the south.

The Triangle is the wettest sector of the Mara–Serengeti ecosystem. More than 50 inches (130cm) of rain are recorded here annually, most of it falling from March through May, when the sodden black soil makes driving impossible over much of the reserve. But as the rains end, the Mara emerges as the greenest place on Earth, and wildlife responds exuberantly, courting and breeding with mad abandon.

Weaver birds swirl in buttercup clouds around their hanging-basket nests. Kori bustard cocks strut purposefully across the plains, displaying their puffed-up throat sacs to potential mates, and red-collared widow-birds in extravagant breeding plumage flaunt their long black tailfeathers as they flush from the grass.

Your Part of Paradise

The average visitor seldom spends more than three days in the Mara – hardly enough time to explore the entire reserve. Most game viewing is concentrated within an hour's drive of the lodges, so what you see depends very much on where you stay. One thing is certain: a resident pride of lions will patrol whatever locale you choose. Other sightings are serendipitous: a leopard lounging in a fig tree, a troop of banded mongooses rippling through the grass, or a family of bat-eared foxes playing outside their burrow.

While all visitors want to view game, few want to view other game viewers. One of the best places to avoid other vehicles is **Mara Intrepids**, a camp hidden in a grove of African olive trees on the banks of the **Talek River**. Intrepids is set in a wedge of rolling savanna between the Talek and **Ntiakitak Rivers**, making it difficult for tourists from other camps to reach the area. The resident lions, known as the Ol Kiombo pride, are almost always active, and cheetahs prowl the plains to the south.

At the northern tip of the preserve in the original Mara Triangle is **Kichwa Tembo Camp**, which offers excellent game viewing on the plains along the Mara River and in the meadows of nearby **Sabaringo lugga**. **Mara Serena Lodge**, about 10 miles (16km) south of Kichwa Tembo on a ridge overlooking the river's west bank, also provides excellent and varied viewing. The hippo pools below the lodge are some of the best in the preserve, and a foray into nearby **Olpunyata Swamp** invariably produces elephants, buffalo, and waterbucks.

Camps and lodges like **Mara River Camp** actually lie in the Masai rangelands outside the reserve's northern borders, but don't let this deter you. Since there is no boundary fence, you would never know if you were inside or outside the reserve, and the game is just as prolific. Indeed, the acacia wood-

lands and rocky ridges to the north and east of **Musiara Gate** are renowned for the best leopard sightings in Kenya.

Just inside the reserve, on the east bank of the Mara River, is **Governor's Camp**, its spacious tents shaded by tall trees. High in the canopy, green pigeons and black-and-white casqued hornbills forage for fruit, and a flash of crimson wings reveals a Livingstone's turaco. Governor's Camp is the only place in Kenya to see this spectacular forest bird which, along with its red pinions, has a green head and body, an extravagant crest, and a blue tail.

If you want to follow the big cats, a few days at Governor's puts you at the heart of the action. **Musiara Marsh**, almost in sight of camp, is rife with lions, which can be heard roaring and bellowing most nights. Sometimes they even visit the local

A gathering of little bee-eaters (opposite, top) warm themselves in the morning sun.

Agama lizards (opposite, bottom) are often seen sunning themselves on rocks during the day; they dart away at the first sign of trouble.

An elaborate Masai head-dress adorned with feathers and cowrie shells (right, top) is a symbol of warrior status.

Raised around wildlife (below), Masai trackers can detect the faintest animal spoor in the bush.

Warriors in Red

With their red robes and elaborate ochre hairstyles, the Masai are the most recognizable of Kenya's many tribal groups. They are thought to have migrated into the Mara–Serengeti region from North Africa some 500 years ago and now number about 250,000, divided into about a dozen regions, each with its own dialect and customs. In the Mara, the Il Purko Masai is the dominant group.

The Masai believe that God chose them to be custodians of the world's cattle, an indication of just how central the animals are to Masai life. Milk and blood are the staples of their diet, dung is used to plaster their huts, and cattle are the principal measure of wealth. They are also well known for their prowess as warriors. Though Masai boys are no longer permitted to prove their bravery by spearing lions, they still endure the pain of circumcision in an elaborate rite of passage that signals their transformation into *il-morani*, or warriors. Only later do they shave off their shoulder-length plaits and marry, often to more than one wife.

Despite their resistance to government settlement programs, the Masai haven't been able to avoid the incursions of the outside world. Large tracts of Masailand have been subdivided, fenced, and planted with crops – a situation that threatens both the Masai and the wildlife with which they share their home. For the moment, however, the majority of these proud people cling tenaciously to their nomadic way of life.

airstrip, lolling in the shade of the parked Cessnas. Others keep watch from **Rhino Ridge**, due east of camp, or lie up in the croton thickets of **Paradise Plain** to recover from a night of hunting.

Wildlife Crossing

A lonely tract of rolling grassland between Governor's Camp and the Mara Serena Lodge leads to a ford on the Mara River that is the site of one of the greatest wildlife spectacles on the planet. Forced into a geographical bottleneck, tens of thousands of zebras and wildebeests pour across the river here in an avalanche of wildly plunging bodies. Though awe-inspiring in every detail, this is not an event for the faint-hearted. Crocodiles kill many animals, latching onto their snouts and pulling them down into the muddy water. Many others are drowned in the crush, or injured so severely that they soon fall victim to the ever-vigilant lions and hyenas.

The plains are bare by the time the migrating herds return south at the end of the dry season, the lush grasses reduced to yellow stubble by millions of mouths and hooves. But in October and November the short rains fall again, and overnight the grasslands return to life. This is the season the Masai call *ilkiserat*, the time of the grass rains, when topi, the fastest antelope on the plains, give birth to their gingery fawns, and the hills around Keekorok in the southwest corner of the park are as green as Ireland.

When driving in the Keekorok area, keep an eye open for black rhinos. During the heat of the day, these lumbering dreadnoughts often retreat into thickets of croton and wait-a-bit thorn, where they lie as motionless as great gray boulders, waiting for the air to cool before rousing themselves to feed. Black rhinos are browsers, using their prehensile upper lips to pluck leaves from shrubs and trees. They are one of the few animals who feed on the cactuslike candelabra euphorbia tree.

In the early 1970s, more than 100 black rhinos roamed the Mara. A decade later only 11 survived. The rest had been slaughtered by poachers for their horns, which were literally worth their weight in gold. But since 1983, rigorous patrols by armed rangers have enabled the Mara's black rhinos to creep back from the brink of extinction. Their numbers now stand at 33, making this the largest free-ranging population in East Africa.

Keekorok is the oldest and biggest lodge in the Mara. Its game-viewing tracks can get busy at times, but the scenery is glorious, a beautiful amalgam of rolling hills and savanna. This is one of East Africa's few departure points for hot-air balloon safaris. Soaring skyward into the African dawn is a singular way to view game and allows passengers to glimpse the enormity of the Mara ecosystem from above.

A safari balloon (top) drifts over the grasslands.

A rock python (left) squeezes the life out of a Thomson's gazelle, tightening its coils with every exhalation of its prey.

An "off-duty" lion (right) snoozes through the heat of the day. If prey is plentiful, lions may rest as much as 20 hours a day.

TRAVEL TIPS

DETAILS

When to Go

The best time to visit is during the wildebeest migration, which coincides with the reserve's dry season (July to October). The herds usually arrive in July, although weather and wildebeest do not always obey the rules – as when El Niño rains disrupt the seasons. July can be relatively cool and overcast (65°F/18°C to 70°F/21°C). Expect late-afternoon downpours as thunderstorms build up during the short rains of October and November. December through February is hot and sunny, with temperatures around 80°F (27°C) until the onset of the long rains, which normally fall from April to June. Some lodges close at this time, and flooding renders many areas impassable.

Getting There

International flights from the United States and Europe travel to the Kenyan capital, Nairobi. Masai Mara is 45 minutes by light aircraft from Nairobi's Wilson Airport. Airkenya (tel: +254-2-605 745; fax: +254-2-602 951; e-mail: resvns@airkenya.com) operates two flights a day. Most lodges have their own airstrips, and it is not uncommon to see lions as soon as you step out of your aircraft. The alternative to flying is a grueling five-hour drive – longer in wet weather – although it does give you a chance to see more of the country.

In addition to game drives, there are balloon safaris most days from Little Governor's Camp, Fig Tree Camp, and Keekorok, Mara Serena, and Mara Sarova Lodges. Book through your tour operator or lodge.

INFORMATION

Kenya Embassies

United Kingdom: 45 Portland Place, London W1N 4AS; tel: +44-20-7636 2371; fax: +44-20-7323 6717.

United States: 2249 R Street, N.W., Washington, DC 20008; tel: 202-387-6101; fax: 202-462-3829.

Kenya Tourist Offices

United Kingdom: 25 Brooke's Mews, off Davies Street, London W1Y 1LG; tel: +44-20-7355 3144; fax: +44-20-7495 8656; e-mail: kcomm45@aol.com; web: africanvacation.com/kenya

United States: 424 Madison Avenue, New York, NY 10017; tel: 212-486-1300; fax: 212-688-0911; or 9150 Wilshire Boulevard, Suite 160, Beverly Hills, CA 90212; tel: 310-274 6635; fax: 310-859 7010; e-mail: consulate@aol.com; web: africanvacation.com/kenya

CAMPING

Independent camping is not permitted in Masai Mara National Reserve.

LODGING

Governor's and Little Governor's Camps

P.O. Box 48217, Nairobi, Kenya; tel: +254-2-331 871; fax: +254-2-726 427; e-mail: govscamp@africaonline.co.ke

Governor's Camp, Africa's first permanent, luxury safari camp, has 38 roomy tents, some on the riverbank, others facing the plains, all with private bathrooms and hot water. Little Governor's, a boat ride away across the Mara River, is more intimate, with 17 tents. $$$$

Keekorok

Sheraton Kenya Hotels, P.O. Box 47557, Nairobi, Kenya; tel: +254-2-540 780; fax: +254-2-545 954; e-mail: sheraton-kenya@net2000.co.ke.

The Mara's oldest, busiest lodge has 70 rooms with private baths, a swimming pool, and a wildlife observation hide. $$

Kichwa Tembo

CCAfrica, P Bag X27, Benmore 2010, South Africa; tel: +27-11-809 4300; fax: +27-11-809 4400; e-mail: bookings@ccafrica.com; web:www.ccafrica.com

The camp has 45 spacious tents with private baths set in riverine forest at the foot of the Siria escarpment. An open, thatched dining room and swimming pool overlook the Mara plains. $$

Mara Intrepids

Heritage Hotels, P.O. Box 78888, Nairobi, Kenya; tel: +254-2-716 628; fax: +254-2-212 878; e-mail: heritagehotels@form-net.com

This secluded, tented lodge has a bar, dining room, swimming pool, and 30 tents with four-poster beds and private baths. A high-rise hide at the edge of the plains provides good game viewing. The price includes activities and meals. $$$$

Mara Serena

Serena Hotels, P.O. Box 48690, Nairobi, Kenya; tel: +254-2-710 511; fax: +254-2-718 100; e-mail: 62578620@eln.attmail.com

This 74-room hilltop lodge offers some of the best views in the Mara. A swimming pool is on the premises. $$

Sarova Lion Hill Lodge

Sarova Hotels, P.O. Box 72493, Nairobi, Kenya; tel: +254-2-716 688; fax: +254-2-715 566; e-mail: gmm@sarova.com.ke

All rooms have private verandas at this comfortable lodge on the eastern shore of Lake Nakuru. A swimming pool is on the grounds. $$

TOUR OPERATORS

Cheli and Peacock

P.O. Box 39806, Nairobi,
Kenya; tel: +254-2-748 307;
fax: +254-2-750 225; e-mail:
helipeacock@africaonline.co.ke;
web: www.chelipeacock.com

Expert guides offer customized,
mobile, tented safaris.

Cottar's Safari Service

P.O. Box 44191, Nairobi, Kenya;
tel: +254-2-884 508; fax:
+254-2-882 234; e-mail:
cottars@form-net.com

For four generations, the
Cottar family has been offering
luxury "Out of Africa"-style
safaris with lodging at its private
Mara homestead.

Kenia Tours and Safaris

Jubilee Insurance Building, 4th
Floor, Kaunda/Wabera Street,
Nairobi, Kenya; tel: +254-2-223
699; fax: +254-2-217 671; e-mail:
kenia@africaonline.co.ke

The company offers a choice of
seven-day road safaris, including
Masai Mara, Aberdares, and other
game reserves. Transport is by
minibus or four-wheel-drive
vehicle. Accommodations range
from camping to safari lodges.

Safari Camp Services

P.O. Box 44801, Nairobi, Kenya;
tel: +254-2-228 936; e-mail:
safaricamp@form-net.com;
web: www.kenyaweb.
com/safari-camp/

Budget safaris to the Masai
Mara and the Rift Valley
lakes are run by veteran
operator Dick Hedges.

Wildlife Journeys and Expeditions

8 Comeragh Road,
London W14 9HP, UK;
tel: +44-20-7381 8638;
fax: +44-20-7381 0863; e-mail:
wwj@wjournex.demon.co.uk

Fly-in and horseback safaris cover
the region from the Loita Hills
to the Mara River. Customized
itineraries are also available.

Excursions

Aberdares National Park

*Kenya Wildlife Services, P.O. Box 40241,
Nairobi, Kenya; tel: +254-2-501 081; fax:
+254-2-504 171; e-mail: kws@kws.org;
web: www.kws.org*

The Aberdare Mountains, 112 miles (180km)
north of Nairobi, cover an area of spectacular
scenery on the edge of the Rift Valley, with
rivers and trout streams cascading down
thickly forested valleys. Vast moorlands, with
giant alpine heathers and lobelias, link the
two highest peaks, Ol Doinyo Lasatima
(13,353 feet/4,070m) and Kinangop (13,030
feet/3,972m). The Ark and Treetops are forest lodges built on
stilts beside a water hole. At night the clearing becomes a floodlit theater, with sightings of elephants, rhinos, and leopards.

Mount Elgon

*Kenya Wildlife Services,
P.O. Box 40241, Nairobi,
Kenya; tel: +254-2-501
081; fax: +254-2-504
171; e-mail: kws@kws.
org; web: www.kws.org*

Mount Elgon is a sleep-
ing volcano straddling
the Kenya–Uganda

border, a 294-mile (470-km) drive from Nairobi. At 14,178 feet
(4,321m), it is East Africa's fourth-highest mountain and is host
to one of Kenya's most stunning forest parks. Birding is outstanding, with gorgeous blue Ross's turacos and monkey-
eating crowned eagles on the must-see list. But the main
attraction is Kitum Cave, where elephants come every night to
dig for salt. Elgon is also great for trekkers. No special equipment is needed, but be prepared for rain and cold weather.

Rift Valley Lakes

*Kenya Wildlife Services, P.O. Box
40241, Nairobi, Kenya; tel: +254-2-
501 081; fax: +254-2-504 171; e-mail:
kws@kws.org; web: www.kws.org*

North of Nairobi, a necklace of lakes
renowned for bird life is strung along
the Great Rift Valley. Most famous is
Lake Nakuru, whose shores are often

fringed with cotton-candy clouds of lesser flamingos. There
is also a good chance of seeing black and white rhinos, lions,
leopards, and Rothschild's giraffes. Naivasha, a 90-minute
drive from Nairobi, is a freshwater lake with a checklist of 400
birds. Stay here to explore nearby Hell's Gate National Park.
Other lakes to visit are Bogoria, Elmentaita, and Baringo.

Tsavo and Amboseli National Parks

Kenya

Skittering and dancing with the wind, a swarm of dust devils crosses Amboseli's dusty plains. Sandy soil spins high into the air, whirling across a flat, treeless landscape. Shouldering through the miniature tornadoes, a herd of elephants tramps with sturdy determination across the sunbaked earth from its Masai homeland to the necklace of swamps and lakes at the heart of Amboseli. ◆ **Tsavo and Amboseli National Parks** in southeast Kenya could hardly be more different. Amboseli is small and spectacular, clustered around a swampy core that spreads into a seasonal lake. Blessed by views of snowcapped **Mount Kilimanjaro**, it is a prime source of water for miles around. Good sightings of game, especially elephants, are guaranteed, but in the dry season, the sheer density of the herds crowding its 153 square miles (396 sq km) turns most of the park into a dust bowl. The density of tourists, in season, can also be high. ◆ If peace is what you're after, follow a Goliath

Bull elephants vie for dominance, cheetahs devour their prey, and Masai tribesmen tend their cattle under the gaze of Kilimanjaro, Africa's highest mountain.

heron as it flaps off to the east, 50 miles (80km) across the **Chyulu Hills** to Tsavo. This is Kenya's largest park, spreading north from the Tanzanian border. Together, its two separate units, Tsavo East and West, protect an area the size of Massachusetts. Skimming high overhead, our heron looks down on volcanic cones and open plains, searching out lush springs bubbling with water and seasonal lakes glazed pink by flamingos. To the north, the landscape dries into a shelving wilderness of scrubland and lava flows, studded with baobab trees and tracked by elephant herds and other game drawn to the waters of the **Galana** and **Athi Rivers**.

A young lion can keep up with the pride at about seven months of age but remains dependent on its mother for food and protection for 16 months.

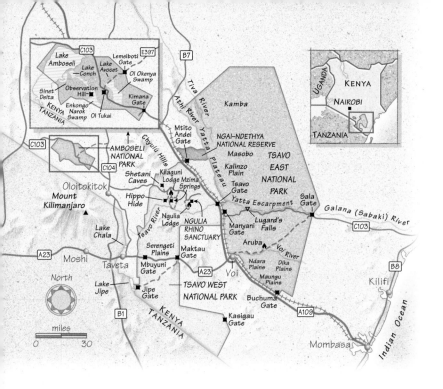

"language" of the world's largest land mammal. From the height of Observation Hill, binoculars bring the lattice of dirt tracks into focus, and it is easy to identify your lodge, locate the largest herds, and plan a game drive.

To the west of this viewpoint is **Lake Amboseli**, often little more than the damp core of a soda plain. The tan speck of a safari vehicle rushes to meet a plane at the airport, 3 miles (5km) to the north. To the east the **Ol Tukai** area, where most of the lodges are surrounded by game fences, is dark with Amboseli's few remaining trees, flanked by the emerald greens of **Enkongo Narok** and **Ol Okenya** swamps. Beyond are the grazing lands of Masai tribesmen and, blued and hazed by distance, the rounded cones of the Chyulu Hills.

Views of Kili

Back at Amboseli, a good place to start a tour is at the top of **Observation Hill**, a perfectly conical volcanic plug rising 100 feet (30m) above the plain, with sweeping views of the park. To the south the towering bulk of Mount Kilimanjaro, Africa's tallest mountain, snowcapped and garlanded with woodland, marks Tanzanian territory. Views of the mountain are usually clearest in the morning and evening.

The woody thunk of tusk striking tusk echoes across the plain below, indicating a fight between bull elephants: a primeval conflict, slowed by the size of the combatants. There are more than 1,000 elephants based in the park, and it is here that Cynthia Moss, with her Elephant Research Project, is conducting Africa's longest-running study of elephant communication, decoding the

Crowded Land

The great attraction of Amboseli is the sheer volume of game. From ground level the shimmering perspectives of animal upon animal across an open plain can be truly overwhelming. As early as 1883, the explorer Joseph Thompson wondered "how can such large

Egrets (right) feast on insects stirred up by a passing herd of elephants.

numbers of game live in this extraordinary desert." The answer is that most come mainly to drink. The pressure of the wild population, and safari vehicles driving off authorized tracks, has damaged the ground cover while the evaporation of springs into the oven-hot air seems to be worsening a salinity problem that has caused Amboseli's few trees to die and fall onto the dusty salt flats.

For grazing, the animals spread out toward the Chyulus, sharing their feed with herds of cattle belonging to Masai pastoralists, or they go south to the acacia **Tortilis**, fringing the lower slopes of Kilimanjaro. The open terrain within Amboseli doesn't provide cover for predators, and in this busy reserve you usually have to share the headline animals. A cheetah close to a road will be ringed by safari vehicles, usually minivans with pop-up roofs, bristling with cameras. Even a sleeping hyena can draw quite a crowd. Change your focus to

Equatorial snow (right) crowns the peak of Kilimanjaro, an extinct volcano about a million years old.

Sunset (above) reddens the sky over Amboseli, silhouetting an acacia tree.

the smaller animals and you will find yourself alone. Observing the graceful romance between slender crowned cranes, their spiky crests a Day-Glo orange, or the dainty steps of a blacksmith plover fluttering into the air with a metallic *klink klink* of alarm, can provide just as much pleasure.

Craters, Cones, and Lava Flows

It is much easier to escape into the vastness of Tsavo. A difficult track threads directly from Amboseli, through the Chyulus, to Tsavo West, but even with four-wheel-drive in the dry season it's not always passable. Access is usually by road from Nairobi or Mombasa; on scheduled flights from Nairobi, three times a week; or by charter flights to small and

exclusive lodges in isolated settings. The more developed area, **Tsavo West**, is nearer to Amboseli, stretching in a huge C with its back to Kilimanjaro. Bordered to the south by the Tanzanian border and reaching up to the Galana River, Tsavo West protects 3,500 square miles (9,065 sq km) of tall grassy plains, heavily vegetated volcanic cones, and woodland scenery. The volcanic soil supports a huge variety of plants and, because it filters rainwater into permanent springs, an equally wide range of wildlife. The Big Five are represented, though most of the remaining black rhinos have been moved for their own safety into the central **Ngulia Sanctuary**. It is the variety of animals that is key to Tsavo West's appeal. A slender gerenuk, teetering on its hind legs as it reaches up to nibble upper leaves, the sleek, padding form of a black-backed jackal trailing lions, or the shy, twitching ears of a bat-eared fox – all are part of a living mosaic.

Most travelers restrict their visits to the more developed area between the **Tsavo River** and the main Mombasa highway. Highlights include **Mzima**

Springs, which consists of two lakes linked by a small rapid that are fed by rainwater draining through the porous rock of the Chyulu Hills. The springs provide a welcome opportunity to escape the confines of your safari vehicle along a marked trail through tall yellow-barked fever trees, but the area is a bit overdeveloped. A pipeline diverts much of the water to Mombasa, and a hippo hide, set in the water at one end of the upper pool, has sent all the hippos to the other. Visitors goggle through glass greened with algae at lake fish who goggle straight back. The water hole at **Kilaguni Lodge** attracts a steady stream of game and is a dramatic backdrop for guests enjoying a drink or meal. Nearby **Ngulia Lodge** features the same cast of wildlife but is also known for its autumn bird migration, when hundreds of thousands of European migrants flutter through the area. Keen bird-watchers gather on the terrace, adding exotic migrants to the checklist of 440 bird species already recorded in Tsavo.

The area's geological past is unmistakable, with craters and cones providing countless vistas of broken woodland and stretching plains. In the background, the brooding bulk of Mount Kilimanjaro is often visible, but nearer volcanoes are much younger, with many, including those that form the Chyulu Hills, only 500 years old. Although there are no active volcanoes, the last eruption, just 200 years ago, sent the **Shetani** lava flows blistering across the bush. It's perhaps not surprising that Shetani, in the local language, means "devil," as the glowing trails of molten rock sizzling and spitting through the bush must have been a terrifying sight. The huge petrified streams of pumice are only now being broken down by a few hardy plants. The lava flows are threaded by caves up to 12½ miles (20km) long. They are favorite leopard lairs, so you'll need a guide to explore them; ask at the park headquarters near **Mtito Andei Gate** on the Nairobi road.

A hippo calf (opposite, top) stays close to its mother, whose powerful jaws are a formidable defense against crocodiles.

A malachite kingfisher (left) clings to a reed at water's edge.

A gerenuk's long neck (right) enables it to nibble shoots beyond the reach of other gazelles.

Impalas (below) rely on speed and agility to elude pursuers.

Tsavo East offers an altogether wilder experience: so wild, in fact, that the greater part of the park, northeast of the Galana River, has been closed to visitors for many years and is only now opening up, slowly, to small groups on private camping safaris. Photographers, however, will find animals much more shy in a region where poachers held sway through much of the 1970s and '80s. The section of Tsavo East that is open to the public, the southern plains around the **Voi River** and north as far as the Galana, is nearer to Mombasa than Nairobi but still attracts few safari tours.

Graceful Gazelles

Delicate and graceful, gazelles are the McDonald's of the bush: fast food to most of Africa's predators. With a fragile, ethereal beauty and delicate, targetlike markings, these small antelope roam Africa's plains in gentle herds, nervously snacking on tender shoots and fluttering long eyelashes at passing safari vehicles. Fast and agile, they can outrun most animals if they spot the danger in time; when frightened, they leap dramatically into the air, reaching heights of 10 feet (3m) and easily clearing a game-viewing vehicle. Off-guard, however, a few fast swipes by a well-placed lion will turn them quickly into lunch, while their young are favorite prey of Africa's raptors and smaller cats.

For safety, they browse in bachelor herds or harems guarded by a single dominant ram. They also often graze with baboons, whose speed at spotting danger keeps predators at bay. It's not a great defensive tactic – even baboons quite like eating young impalas.

Impalas, growing up to 3 feet (1m) tall, with golden coats and black-and-white markings on their rumps, are the most common and beautiful of Africa's gazelles. Stumpy, stripy, flashing tails provide visual markers to help these social animals follow each other through the bush. The smaller springbok (in southern deserts), Thomson's gazelle, and the desert-living Grant's gazelle (in East Africa) share the impala's distinctive black lateral stripes. The tiny dik-dik, whose face is the closest to the cartoon deer Bambi, grazes close to the sandy floor while the more solitary long-necked gerenuk (of East Africa) can stand upright on its rear legs and nibble away at vegetation usually reserved for giraffes.

TRAVEL TIPS

DETAILS

When to Go

The temperature remains stable for much of the year, reaching highs of 80°F (27°C) to 90°F (32°C). There are usually two rainy seasons: three-month-long rains from April to June (part of the Asian monsoon) and six-week-long short rains in November and December. Rain causes the wildlife to disperse and closes *murrum* (dirt) roads in and around both Amboseli and Tsavo. To see the big herds, visit when the land has dried out, from January to March or from July to October. Although animals are harder to spot when the bush is freshly greened by rain, savings can be substantial at the better lodges, especially for people traveling on their own.

Getting There

The two main airports that serve this region are in Nairobi and Mombasa. Tsavo straddles the main Nairobi–Mombasa Road and is about 150 miles (240km) from either city. Amboseli is best reached on the road from Nairobi via Namanga, a four- to five-hour drive in the dry season. Scheduled flights link Nairobi with Tsavo and Amboseli (Airkenya Aviation, Wilson Airport, P.O. Box 30357, Nairobi, Kenya; tel: +254-2-605 745; fax: +254-2-602 951; e-mail: info@airkenya.com). The direct route between Tsavo and Amboseli across the Chyulu Hills is almost impassable, even in the dry season. To travel from one to the other, it is best to return to the main Nairobi Road or charter a plane and travel by air.

INFORMATION

Amboseli National Park

P.O. Box 18, Namanga, Kenya; tel: +254-302-22251; fax: +254-302-22250.

Kenya Embassies

United Kingdom: 45 Portland Place, London W1N 4AS, UK; tel: +44-20-7636 2371; fax: +44-20-7323 6717.

United States: 2249 R Street, N.W., Washington, DC 20008; tel: 202-387-6101; fax: 202-462-3829.

Kenya Tourist Offices

United Kingdom: 25 Brooke's Mews, off Davies Street, London W1Y 1LG, UK; tel: +44-20-7355 3144; fax: +44-20-7495 8656; e-mail: kcomm45@aol.com; web: africanvacation.com/kenya

United States: 424 Madison Avenue, New York, NY 10017; tel: 212-486-1300; fax: 212-688-0911; or 9150 Wilshire Boulevard, Suite 160, Beverly Hills, CA 90212; tel: 310-274-6635; fax: 310-859-7010; e-mail: consulate@aol.com; web: africanvacation.com/kenya

Kenya Wildlife Services

P.O. Box 40241, Nairobi, Kenya; tel: +254-2-501 081; fax: +254-2-504 171; e-mail: kws@kws.org; web: www.kws.org

Tsavo East National Park

P.O. Box 14, Voi, Kenya; tel: +254-147-2228; fax: +254-147-30034.

Tsavo West National Park

P.O. Box 71, Mtito Andei, Kenya; tel: +254-302-22483.

CAMPING

Kenya Wildlife Services

P.O. Box 40241, Nairobi, Kenya; tel: +254-2-501 081; fax: +254-2-504 171; e-mail: kws@kws.org; web: www.kws.org

The park authority has campsites in Amboseli, Tsavo East, and Tsavo West, but they are not especially well sited and, if traveling independently, you will need to bring your own tents, cooking utensils, and camping gear.

LODGING

PRICE GUIDE – double occupancy

$ = under $100 $$ = $100–$200

$$$ = $200–$300 $$$$ = $300+

Finch Hattons

P.O. Box 24423, Nairobi, Kenya; tel: +254-2-604 321; fax: +254-2-604 323; e-mail: finchhattons@iconnect.co.ke

This lodge in Tsavo West, built around a natural spring and pool, is always teeming with hippos and birds. Wooden platforms on stilts support 35 walk-in tents. Two- and three-night packages include game drives. $$$$

Galdessa

P.O. Box 24397, Nairobi, Kenya; tel: +254-2-577 018; fax: +254-2-564 945; e-mail: mellifera@swiftkenya.com

Eight bandas (chalets) overlook the Galana River and the Yatta Plateau in a remote part of Tsavo East. $$$$

Ol Donyo Wuas

P.O. Box 24133, Nairobi, Kenya; tel: +254-2-882 521; fax: +254-2-882 728; e-mail: bonham.luke@swiftkenya.com

Staying here combines a wilderness experience with the added depth of life on a Masai community ranch that overlooks Amboseli from the Chyulus. $$$$

Ol Tukai

P.O. Box 40075, Nairobi, Kenya; tel: +254-2-540 780; fax: +254-2-545 948.

One of the few lodges within Amboseli National Park, accommodations here are grouped within fences that protect some of the few remaining trees. $$$

Tortilis Camp

P.O. Box 39806, Nairobi, Kenya; tel: +254-2-748 307; fax: +254-2-750 225; e-mail: chelipeacock@attmail.com

Seventeen walk-in tents on platforms surround a main lodge set high over the plains, just outside Amboseli's border. The tents have views of Mount Kilimanjaro. $$$$

TOUR OPERATORS

Balloon Safaris

P.O. Box 43747, Nairobi, Kenya; tel: +254-2-502 850 or +254-2-504 192; fax: +254-2-501 424; e-mail: ballons@africaonline.co.ke

Hot-air balloons take riders through the Taita Hills between Tsavo East and Tsavo West.

Cheli and Peacock

P.O. Box 39806, Nairobi, Kenya; tel: +254-2-748 307; fax: +254-2-750 225; e-mail: chelipeacock@attmail.com

Guides lead mobile tented safaris; the company also has luxury lodges.

Patrick Reynolds

P.O. Box 56923, Nairobi, Kenya; tel: +254-2-571 661; fax: +254-2-571 665; e-mail: bushhome@ africaonline.co.ke

Walking safaris around the Tiva River offer the chance to get close to game.

Richard Bonham Safaris

P.O. Box 24133, Nairobi, Kenya; tel: +254-2-882 521; fax: +254-2-882 728; e-mail: bonham.luke@swiftkenya.com

Safaris travel by horseback outside park boundaries from a base lodge or mobile camp.

UTC

P.O. Box 42196, Nairobi, Kenya; tel: +254-2-227 847; fax; +254-2-216 871; e-mail: utcn@africaonline.co.ke

Minibus safaris depart daily from Nairobi and Mombasa.

Excursions

Marine Reserves

Kenya Wildlife Services, P.O. Box 40241, Nairobi, Kenya; tel: +254-2-501 081; fax: +254-2-504 171; e-mail: kws@kws.org; web: www.kws.org

Offshore marine parks at Malindi, Watamu, and Wasini offer much-needed protection to Kenya's fragile Indian Ocean coral reefs. Of these, the best and farthest from human settlement is Wasini in the far south near the fishing village of Shimoni. Snorkeling and diving here are usually arranged through Kisite Dhow Tours (tel: +254-127-2331). In the north, there is a marine park with diving clubs and hotels off the popular resort town of Malindi, although silt from the Galana River often coats the reef in sand. Watamu, 21 miles (35km) south, has three beachfront hotels overlooking the protected reef. Diving here is arranged by Aqua Ventures (tel: +254-122-32008). The waters are clear from December through April. From May to November, trade winds cover the shore in seaweed, especially in the north.

Mount Kenya

Kenya Wildlife Services, P.O. Box 40241, Nairobi, Kenya; tel: +254-2-501 081; fax: +254-2-504 171; e-mail: kws@kws.org; web: www.kws.org

Mount Kenya is the second-highest mountain in Africa, a long-extinct volcano eroded into a jagged outline of challenging peaks permanently frosted with snow and glaciers. It's a rewarding climb with many exotic plant and animal species. Most fit people can climb to Point Lenana, at an elevation of 16,358 feet (4,986m), though it's far from easy. The slightly higher Batian and Nelion Mountains will challenge experienced climbers.

Samburu National Reserve

Kenya Wildlife Services, P.O. Box 40241, Nairobi, Kenya; tel: +254-2-501 081; fax: +254-2-504 171; e-mail: kws@kws.org; web: www.kws.org

On the fringes of the Northern Frontier District in the arid north of Kenya, Samburu is just remote enough to avoid the crowds. The permanent water of the Ewaso Nyiro River attracts plenty of game, including desert-dwellers such as Grant's gazelle and gerenuk, known as the "giraffe antelope" for its long neck. The colorful Samburu people, closely related to the Masai, add a fascinating human dimension to the region. The best place to stay is Larsens Tented Camp, P.O. Box 40075, Nairobi, Kenya; tel: +254-2-540 780; fax: +254-2-543 810.

Bwindi
Impenetrable Forest
National Park
Uganda

CHAPTER 20

Bwindi Impenetrable Forest seems to have sprung from the mind of Edgar Rice Burroughs during his most perfervid Tarzan fantasies – a place of soaring trees festooned with epiphytes, lianas, and creepers, entirely suffused by a dim, emerald light. In some places the verdure is so thick that visitors must hike on solid mats of vegetation that tremble and flex with every step, threatening to break through and dump the unwary hiker into unseen depths below.   ◆   This is a shadowy place, and wildlife is usually heard before it is seen. Birds soar above the canopy, trilling, screeching, whistling. Leaves rustle and branches snap as the resident primates, including colobus monkeys and chimpanzees, forage in the treetops. Vagrant hoots and mutterings waft through the foliage.   ◆   In areas where the forest thins, the powerful equatorial sun beats down on thickets of giant bamboo and meadows strewn with extravagantly colorful wildflowers like giant heliconia. It is here, at the edge of the forest, that you will find the object of

A tough trek through dense rain forest yields a great reward – a haunting encounter with the world's last mountain gorillas.

your journey – family groups of mountain gorillas, basking in the sun, contemplating the clouds of gaudy butterflies, grazing placidly on the vegetation, and engaging in spirited horseplay.   ◆   Bwindi Impenetrable Forest – or Bwindi Impenetrable Park, as it is sometimes called – encompasses 128 square miles (332 sq km) in the **Kigezi Highlands** of southwestern Uganda. Designated as a national park in 1991, it lies at the heart of the African high plateau and varies in altitude from 3,700 feet (1,100m) to its 8,000-foot (2,400-m) apex at **Rwamunyoni Peak**. It is a profoundly dramatic landscape, consisting of steep hills and narrow gorges where streams tumble down a

Mountain gorillas inhabit dense highland rain forests. Living in family groups under a dominant male, they graze during the day and curl up at night in nests of branches and leaves.

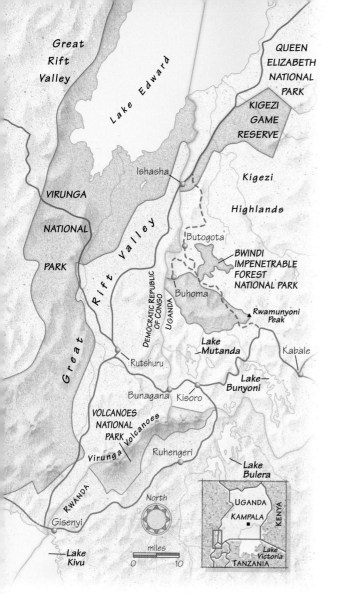

Uganda, a situation that was only exacerbated when the national park was established and the people within its borders were forced to relocate. The park is therefore under unrelenting pressure – not just from farmers seeking to expand their fields but from hunters, beekeepers, and collectors of medicinal plants and basketry materials. Of all these threats, hunters of bush meat are the most problematic, at least in the short term. They rely heavily on snares, an indiscriminate method of hunting that kills protected species such as mountain gorillas and chimps as well as antelope, which are the intended prey.

In order to enlist the support of the local population in conserving Bwindi and its spectacular wildlife, a program has been instituted that permits beekeeping and the sustainable harvest of wild plants within the forest. Local communities also benefit from tourism; villagers receive a percentage of the fees that visitors pay to enter the park.

Gorilla tourism is the legacy of primatologist Dian Fossey, who pioneered research on the animals in the 1980s. In order to facilitate her work, Fossey endeavored to habituate the animals to her presence, a method that has worked not only with gorillas but also with numerous other mammalian species, including chimpanzees and meerkats. Once the animals are convinced by long experience that humans are benign, they allow even strangers to approach in close proximity.

To avoid interfering with the gorillas' foraging and social interaction, visitors are allowed to spend no more than an hour with any one group, and no group may be visited more than once by tourists in any 24-hour period. Parties are limited to six visitors and must be led by a park guide.

More Bark than Bite

Gorillas live in family groups of females, their offspring, and subadult males, all led by a mature male, or "silverback," named after the silvery-gray fur on their backs and shoulders. A mature male mountain gorilla is an exceedingly impressive animal, standing slightly less than 6 feet (2m) tall and weighing up to 425 pounds (193kg). Gorillas have squat

succession of silvery waterfalls. The high rainfall, tropical climate, mixture of lowland and montane forests, and rich soils make this one of Africa's most productive ecosystems. Gorillas are the star attractions, but Bwindi also teems with other wildlife, including 120 types of mammals, 346 varieties of birds, and more than 200 kinds of butterflies.

People of the Forest

The fertile soils of the Bwindi region grow maize and cassava as readily as trees and wildflowers, and this is proving a dilemma for the wildlife. The area surrounding the park is one of the most heavily populated in legs but long, muscular arms, thick trunks, and massive chests. Adult males have a ridge of bone at the top of their skulls that anchors their jaw muscles, giving them a bite of formidable power. Silverbacks have a legitimate need for such a capability. Each is the defender of his group and must be ever alert to rival males intent on stealing his mates.

Their extraordinary strength means that competing silverbacks would do great harm to each other if they ever engaged in total combat. Gorillas have consequently developed a broad repertoire of ritualized behavior, such as chest drumming, foot stamping, and mock charges, to obviate the need for actual fighting. They tear up vegetation and stuff it in their mouths or throw it at rivals; they howl, beat the ground, and generally raise a ruckus to express their profound displeasure with rivals. This extravagant behavior once led to

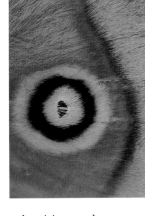

Butterflies (right) bring iridescent color to the rain forest's "symphony of green."

A baby gorilla (below) plays with its mother. Gorillas are indulgent parents; even silverback males tolerate rambunctious juveniles.

the popular misconception that gorillas are fierce and murderous beasts. Today we know that the opposite is true. Gorillas are actually shy and retiring, and their displays of aggression are largely a ruse to avoid physical confrontation.

Family groups stake out a home range that encompasses 10 to 15 square miles (26–39 sq km). They are nomadic within

their territories, feeding and resting as they move. Their diet is almost entirely vegetarian, consisting of a wide range of flora, which includes wild fruits, celery, bamboo, and nettles.

In the evening, they construct nests by bending over branches and lining the concavities with grasses or leaves; the lighter animals sleep higher in the canopy than the heavier ones. Gorillas tend to foul their nests during the night, and never sleep in the same place twice.

A large family of gorillas can number up to 30 individuals and leaves a distinct and recognizable trail as it moves through the jungle. Bwindi's guides can easily follow this track, and they can also estimate the progress and direction of a group from earlier sightings. If a guide is unable to find a group, he will locate the previous night's nests, then track from there; the success rate for finding habituated groups is quite high.

A Growing Threat

Though some contrarians differ, most scientists think the gorillas living in Bwindi are the same subspecies of mountain gorilla found in the Virunga Volcanoes region that straddles the borders of Rwanda, the Democratic Republic of the Congo (formerly Zaire), and Uganda. Whether the populations consist of one or two subspecies, one thing is certain: there are only about 630 mountain gorillas left. Bwindi shelters 300 of the animals, and Virunga sustains about 330. Unhappily, the two refuges are biological islands, separated by 15 miles (24km) of farmland. This is minimal habitat at best, raising serious doubts about the long-term survivability of the species. Compounding the threat is the expanding human population, and the

Gorilla Guardian

Dian Fossey is known throughout the world for her pioneering research on gorillas and their behavior. Born in California in 1932, she first saw wild gorillas on a trip to Africa in 1963. Later, Louis Leakey encouraged Fossey to initiate a long-term field study of the animals in their natural environment as he had chimpanzee expert Jane Goodall.

After a brief sojourn in the Congo, she moved to Rwanda and established a research camp, Karisoke, in 1967. There, she spent years tracking gorillas up and down the steep slopes of the Virunga Volcanoes despite chronic health problems, including bouts with emphysema and a fear of heights.

It wasn't until two beloved gorillas, Digit and Uncle Bert, were killed in 1978 that she changed tack from pure science to "active conservation," launching an often controversial campaign against poachers that alienated some of her supporters in the West. Articles in *National Geographic*, television appearances, and the publication in 1983 of her book *Gorillas in the Mist* (later a popular movie), focused world attention on the gorillas' plight but gave her little protection against the hatred of poachers. She was found murdered at Karisoke in 1985 and was buried at the camp's cemetery next to her beloved gorillas. Her epitaph summed up the motivation behind her remarkable career: "No one loved gorillas more."

A frog (top) relies on camouflage to hide from predators in the forest's leaf litter.

Dian Fossey (left), seen here engaged in social grooming, studied gorillas by gradually habituating them to her presence.

Guereza (right), also known as black-and-white colobus monkeys, can eat up to a third of their weight in leaves a day.

slow rate of reproduction among gorillas.

A female mountain gorilla will not have her first baby before the age of 10. The gestation period is long – 8½ months – and she will bear young only once every three or four years at best. Nor is it particularly easy for mountain gorillas to conceive; the females are fertile for only three or four days out of every month. Though infant gorillas develop more quickly than humans, they are still virtually helpless when born, and remain heavily dependent on their mothers until they are three or four years old.

The biggest problems facing the gorillas, however, are political rather than biological. Bwindi and Virunga lie in one of the world's most politically unstable regions. The Democratic Republic of the Congo is currently embroiled in a bitter civil war, Rwanda is recovering from genocidal warfare between the ruling Tutsis and rebel Hutus, and Tutsi and Hutu conflict threatens to flare up in Uganda. A rebel attack on the park in 1999 cost the lives of eight tourists and a park warden. As a result, tourism to the gorilla refuges has diminished, and that has throttled a much-needed source of revenue. The park suffers almost immediately: snares are set to obtain bush meat, and gorilla poaching becomes ever more attractive. In 1995, for instance, four adult gorillas from the Kyaguliro Group were speared to death at Bwindi, and an infant appears to have been abducted. Particularly distressing is the fact that this group was habituated to humans and, as a result, was easy to approach. If the killings continue, scientists and government officials will have to reconsider the wisdom of letting gorillas and people interact.

TRAVEL TIPS

DETAILS

When to Go

Uganda's equatorial climate, tempered by altitude, is pleasant at all times of the year, rarely exceeding 80°F (27°C) or falling below 55°F (13°C). From March to May and from October to November, however, the rain can be relentless and may make some dirt roads impassable or confine their use to drivers of four-wheel-drive vehicles.

Getting There

Several airlines have direct flights to Uganda's main international gateway, Kampala, though many travelers prefer to fly into Nairobi. Most tour operators collect passengers from the airport. From Kampala, Bwindi is a day's drive, partly on paved roads and partly on dirt roads. Driving yourself is possible, but the last part of the journey through mountainous, cultivated lands can only be driven slowly, so be sure to leave Kampala early. The route can be especially difficult during the rains. The only convenient way to visit the Bwindi gorillas at present is as part of an organized tour.

There are currently two habituated groups of gorillas in the park and, with only six people allowed to visit each group on any one day, the waiting list tends to be long. Book your place well before leaving home and pay the necessary deposit of $30 per person (the full cost is $250 per person). The activity can be strenuous, with up to nine hours of walking on steep hillsides that are invariably slippery with wet mud and rotting vegetation. You will need a good pair of walking boots and clothes you can get dirty. It may rain but is unlikely to be cold.

Travel advisory: Security can be an issue here, due to political unrest. The government is mindful of the value of tourism and is making every effort to ensure the security of visitors to Bwindi, sometimes sending army personnel out with gorilla trackers. However, rebels have attacked tourist camps in the past, and visitors are urged to consult their embassies for the latest travel advisories before making their plans.

INFORMATION

Uganda Embassies

United Kingdom: Uganda House, 58–59 Trafalgar Square, London WC2N 5DX, UK; tel: +44-20-7839 5783; fax: +44-20-7839 8925.

United States: 5911 16th Street, N.W., Washington, DC 20011; tel: 202-726-7100 or 202-726-7101; fax: 202-726-1727.

Uganda Tourist Board

P.O. Box 7211, Kampala, Uganda; tel: +256-41-242 196; fax: +256-41-242 188; e-mail: utb@starcom.co.ug

United States: 336 East 45th Street, New York, NY 10017-3489; tel: 212-949-0110; fax: 212-682-5232.

Uganda Wildlife Authority

P.O. Box 3530, Kampala, Uganda; tel: +256-41-346 290; fax: +256-41-236 291.

CAMPING

Independent camping is not permitted in the park.

LODGING

PRICE GUIDE – double occupancy

$ = under $100 $$ = $100–$200
$$$ = $200–$300 $$$$ = $300+

African Pearl Safaris Homestead

P.O. Box 4262, Kampala, Uganda: tel: +256-41-346 287 or +256-41-233 566; fax: +256-41-346 287; e-mail: apsafari@swiftuganda.com

Five simple cottages share showers and toilets. Full board is included. $$

Community Bandas

Uganda Wildlife Authority, P.O. Box 3530, Kampala, Uganda; tel: +256-41-346 290; fax: +256-41-236 291.

The national park's own accommodations, these bandas (simple chalets) are built from local materials, have shared facilities, and accommodate eight people each. The price covers the bed only. $

Mantana Tented Camp

Entebbe, Uganda; tel/fax: +256-42-20152; e-mail: masio@calva.com

United States: 10818 McComas Court, Kensington, MD 20895; tel: 202-244-4395; fax: 1-202-244-4676; e-mail: mantanausa@juno.com

Bwindi Camp, a little more than a mile (1.6km) from park headquarters, offers seven double rooms, each with a private bath and an open veranda. The price includes all meals. $$$

Volcanoes Mobile Tented Camp

27 Lumumba Avenue, P.O. Box 22818, Kampala, Uganda; tel: +256-41-346 464; fax: +256-41-341 718; e-mail: volcanoes@infocom.co.ug

United Kingdom: Volcanoes, P.O. Box 16345, London SW1X 0ZD, UK; tel: +44-20-7235 7897; fax: +44-20-7235 1780; e-mail: volcanoes@mailbox.co.uk; web: www.volcanoessafaris.com

Volcanoes Mobile Camp, just outside Bwindi National Park, has comfortable tents with their own private facilities. The price includes all meals. $$$

White Horse Inn

P.O. Box 51, Kabale, Uganda; tel: +256-486-23336 or +256-486-23339; fax: +256-486-23717.

Surrounded by well-kept gardens, this colonial-style hotel is set on a hill over-looking town and has 40 bed-and-breakfast rooms. $

TOUR OPERATORS

Mantana African Safaris

Entebbe, Uganda; tel/fax: +256-42-20152; e-mail: masio@calva.com

United States: 10818 McComas Court, Kensington, MD 20895; tel: 202-244-4395; fax: 202-244-4676; e-mail: mantanausa@ juno.com

Experienced drivers and guides lead safaris throughout Uganda's parks and reserves.

Volcanoes

27 Lumumba Avenue, P.O. Box 22818, Kampala, Uganda; tel: +256-41-346 464; fax: +256-41-341 718; e-mail: volcanoes@ infocom.co.ug

United Kingdom: P.O. Box 16345, London SW1X 0ZD, UK; tel: +44-20-7235 7897; fax: +44-20-7235 1780; e-mail: volcanoes@mailbox.co.uk; web: www.volcanoessafaris.com

Multiday safaris, using luxury four-wheel-drive vehicles and carefully trained guides, stay at Mount Gahinga Rest Camp, Sipi Falls Rest Camp, Travellers Rest Hotel, Bwindi Camp, and other selected lodges and camps throughout Uganda. Itineraries can be customized to suit participants' travel plans and special interests.

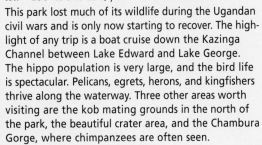

Excursions

Kibale Forest National Park

Uganda Wildlife Authority, P.O. Box 3530, Kampala, Uganda; tel: +256-41-346 290; fax: +256-41-236 291.

This large and accessible area of equatorial rain forest, about 200 miles (320km) west of Kampala, is said to contain the world's highest concentration of primates. Its 11 primate species include black-and-white colobus monkeys, red colobus monkeys, galagos, and more than 500 chimpanzees. You stand a good chance of seeing a group of these habituated chimps during a guided forest walk. Also watch for elephants and admire the park's magnificent rain forest trees.

Mgahinga Forest National Park

Uganda Wildlife Authority, P.O. Box 3530, Kampala, Uganda; tel: +256-41-346 290; fax: +256-41-236 291.

This park, about the same size as Bwindi, borders both the Congo and Rwanda and protects Uganda's section of the important Virunga Volcanoes area, inhabited by more than half of the world's population of mountain gorillas. High-altitude savanna woodland, montane forest, and bamboo clothe the slopes, while dwarf heath vegetation is found near the summits. Visits to the gorillas are subject to the same strictures as in Bwindi but with the added proviso that visits cannot take place if no habituated groups are in Uganda's section of the Virungas. Security is a major consideration in this area.

Queen Elizabeth National Park

Uganda Wildlife Authority, P.O. Box 3530, Kampala, Uganda; tel: +256-41-346 290; fax: +256-41-236 291.

This park lost much of its wildlife during the Ugandan civil wars and is only now starting to recover. The highlight of any trip is a boat cruise down the Kazinga Channel between Lake Edward and Lake George. The hippo population is very large, and the bird life is spectacular. Pelicans, egrets, herons, and kingfishers thrive along the waterway. Three other areas worth visiting are the kob mating grounds in the north of the park, the beautiful crater area, and the Chambura Gorge, where chimpanzees are often seen.

Murchison Falls
National Park
Uganda

C H A P T E R
21

t is the quintessential African river scene. The **Victoria Nile** flows wide and sluggish through a tangle of tall grass and acacia trees. Hundreds of hippopotamuses laze in the shallows. Every so often, one of these aquatic giants breaks from its sedentary bathing to emit a series of animated snorts and grunts, or to indulge in a cavernous yawn, revealing a truly terrifying set of incisors. A monstrous crocodile lies open-jawed on a sandbar; without warning, this grimly efficient predator, a survivor from the age of the dinosaurs, slides silently into the river, its menacing presence reduced to a pair of tiny, unblinking eyes and the faintest of ripples. ◆ Birds are everywhere. African skimmers glide over the water, their neat monochrome plumage offset by garish red beaks. Standing motionless on a tiny papyrus island is a 5-foot-tall (1.5-m) goliath heron, a study in concentration until an abrupt downward lunge of its bill signals the demise of an unfortunate frog. Plovers, wagtails, and dikkops scurry along the shore, while a pied kingfisher hovers high above the river, and a flock of red-throated bee-eaters twists kaleidoscopically around the sandbank in which they breed. Deep in the riverside tangle, a jarring, churring duet reveals the presence of a pair of black-headed gonaleks, gloriously handsome with their rich crimson breasts. From somewhere in the distance comes the high, wild cry of a hunting fish eagle. ◆ This particular stretch of the Nile has changed little in mood since 1864, the year in which the **Murchison Falls** were "discovered" and named by Sir Stanley Baker, the legendary big-game hunter and incidental explorer, who – in what must be the most idiosyncratic honeymoon of the Victorian era – spent years charting

The legendary Nile flows through a lightly visited reserve recovering from years of political turmoil.

Murchison Falls throws up a cloud of spray as the Victoria Nile pours through a fissure in the Rift Valley escarpment.

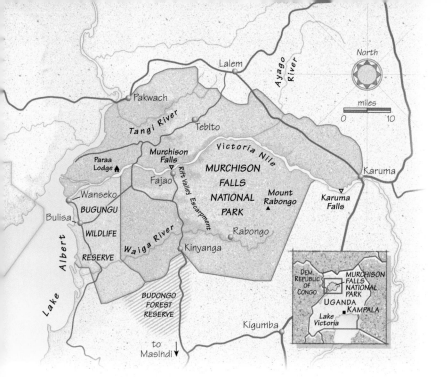

North

Lalem

Pakwach

Tangi River

Tebito

Victoria Nile

Paraa
Lodge ▲

Murchison
Falls ▽

MURCHISON

Fajao

FALLS

Wanseko

NATIONAL

BUGUNGU

PARK

Mount
Rabongo ▲

Karuma

Karuma
Falls ▽

Bulisa

WILDLIFE

Rabongo

Waiga River

Kinyanga

RESERVE

Rift Valley Escarpment

Ayago River

miles

0   10

DEM.
REPUBLIC
OF
CONGO

MURCHISON
FALLS
NATIONAL
PARK

UGANDA

KAMPALA

BUDONGO
FOREST
RESERVE

Lake
Victoria

Kigumba

to
Masindi ▼

Lake Albert

track but probably attracting fewer visitors in a year than would pass through the Masai Mara in the course of a quiet week. In the 1960s, by contrast, Murchison Falls was as popular as any game reserve on the continent: a cinematic slice of African wilderness, teeming with game, and boasting a clutch of outstanding tourist lodges. That all changed in 1971, when Idi Amin seized power and initiated a 15-year cycle of coup and counter-coup from which Uganda is still recovering. Under Amin and his successors, the country's once-booming tourist industry ground to a standstill, and every last tourist lodge in Murchison Falls was gutted by guerrillas.

Lodges can be resurrected. So, given the right circumstances, can an ailing tourist industry. But there is no way to recover the rhinos that were poached to extinction during Uganda's 15 years of madness, and it will take decades for many of the park's other large mammal populations to be restored to their late-1960s highs. Incredible as it may seem today, Murchison Falls in its heyday boasted Africa's densest concentration of

the southern course of the Nile in the company of his young wife. Sadly, however, the section of this mighty river protected within **Murchison Falls National Park** is the only one where wildlife still holds sway over humanity and livestock. As such, it possesses a liberating, almost fantastic quality, allowing one to shed the prosaic realities of modern Africa and be swept exhilaratingly into the Africa of wildlife documentaries.

Once and Future Park

These days, Murchison Falls occupies a fringe position on the African tourist map – not wholly off the beaten

Black-and-white colobus monkeys (above) typically live in troops of six to 10 animals in territories of 60 acres (24 hectares) or less.

A wildlife-watching boat (right) plies calm Nile waters.

Nile crocodiles (right), often seen lazing on the riverbank, may seem lethargic, but they can strike with lightning speed.

elephants, an estimated 16,000 animals within an area of 1,483 square miles (3,841 sq km). By the late 1980s, no more than 500 elephants remained. Over the same period, buffalo numbers plummeted from 26,000 to fewer than 1,000. Who knows where it might have ended had it not been for the coup that brought President Museveni to power in 1986 and restored order to Uganda?

The Nile's Finest Mile

A rare constant in the tumultuous recent history of Murchison Falls, Frances Oyo Okot has, for almost 40 years, piloted launch trips from the park head-quarters at **Paraa** upriver to the base of the 141-foot (43-m) waterfall for which the park is named. In the 1960s, 11 passenger boats plied this stretch of river. Now there is only one, the *Kiboko* (Swahili for "hippo"), but game viewing from its spacious deck remains a highlight of any Uganda tour. Oversized crocs, snorting hippos, and prodigious bird life can be taken for granted, as can sightings of buffalo, waterbuck, and Uganda kob. Passengers are often entertained by a herd of elephants coming down to drink, while a lucky few might glimpse a troop of black-and-white colobus monkeys leaping gracefully between the branches of a ficus grove near the base of the waterfall.

Even more enduring is Murchison Falls itself, described by Baker as the most spectacular thing to happen to the world's longest river along its 4,160-mile (6,700-km) journey from Lake Victoria to the Mediterranean. The term *waterfall* does Murchison scant justice. The water here doesn't fall so much as explode: an immense frothing plume that gathers irresistible for-ward momentum as the Nile is expelled, crashing and roaring, through a narrow crack in the Rift Valley escarpment. It's a thrillingly primal sight viewed from the launch. Clamber up densely vegetated cliffs to the rocky viewpoint above the falls, and the force of the water is simply devastating.

The Nile downstream of Paraa is the best

The Source of the Nile

The source of the Nile perplexed Egyptians, Greeks, and Romans (Ptolemy claimed that the Nile rose in the Mountains of the Moon), and became the Holy Grail of 19th-century geography. In the 1770s, James Bruce traced the Blue Nile to its source at Ethiopia's Lake Tana. But the source of the White Nile, the longer by more than 1,000 miles (1,600km), remained a mystery well into the next century, inspiring some of the most grueling journeys undertaken by Victorian explorers.

Explorers John Hanning Speke (left) and Richard Burton (below, left) were rivals in their search for the Nile's source. Speke later shot himself after being ridiculed for claiming that the Nile flows from Lake Victoria.

Fueled by rumors of great lakes and snowcapped peaks deep in the heart of central Africa, John Hanning Speke and Richard Burton became the first Europeans to reach Lake Tanganyika, in 1858. Later that year, Speke "discovered" Lake Victoria, claiming it as the probable source of the Nile. Burton backed Tanganyika. In 1863, Speke visited the north shore of Lake Victoria and established that a substantial river exited from the lake. Burton was scornful, claiming that Speke had actually seen two different lakes. In 1864, on the eve of a public debate with Burton, the much-maligned Speke died of a self-inflicted gunshot wound.

Speke was vindicated more than 10 years later by Henry Morton Stanley, who finally connected the dots between Africa's aquatic landmarks and proved that Lake Victoria was "the largest inland sea on the continent of Africa." Stanley would write that "I must give [Speke] credit for having understood the geography of the countries we traveled through better than any of us who so persistently opposed his hypothesis."

place in Africa to seek out what is arguably the ultimate sighting on the continent's bird list. This is the shoebill, a heavily built slate-gray bird which, like an escapee from behind the looking glass, sports an extravagant bill fixed in a permanent Cheshire Cat smirk. Many bird-watchers come to Murchison Falls with the sole aim of seeing a shoebill, whose exalted status is a result not only of its bizarre appearance but also of its lack of close genetic allies, its highly localized distribution, and the inaccessibility of the papyrus swamps it frequents. A small motorboat is used to take tourists downriver from Paraa, where, on a good day, one might encounter shoebills on four or five occasions. And on a bad day? Well, persistence normally pays, but the guides tell a cautionary story of an American birder who waved a $100 bill at them and said the money was theirs the moment he

saw a shoebill. One wonders who was more disappointed, the guides or the birder, when after three days the banknote still hadn't changed hands.

Rebirth

Away from the river, Murchison Falls is a game reserve split in two by the river. South of the Nile, a cover of dense, scrubby woodland gives way to rain forest at **Rabongo** in the southeast. Game here is scarce, to the extent that practically any sign of mammalian activity is cause for minor celebration. Tsetse flies, by contrast, are abundant. Africa's miniaturized answer to the vampire bat takes much of the credit for the national park's existence, since it was an outbreak of tsetse-

borne disease that forced the colonial administration to evacuate people from the area in 1907, paving the way for it to become a game reserve. Think on this and say a quick "thank you" before whacking the nearest tsetse with a heavy object.

Game drives to the north of the river are a lot more fun. Tsetse flies are mercifully few in this area of rolling grassland and tall borassus palms, and the relatively dense game evokes some idea of what this park was like in its heyday. The handsome Uganda kob is the stock grazer, while Jackson's hartebeest, a doleful looking antelope with stumpy, spiral horns, is sometimes seen standing sentinel on a termite mound. Twitchy as only a small antelope can be, oribi are frequently encountered in pairs or trios, freezing at the approach of a vehicle, before sneezing their distinctive alarm call and belting off into the distance. The area north of the river is one of the few places in East Africa where the terrestrial patas monkey is common, while about 500 Rothschild's giraffes constitute what is possibly the last viable breeding population of a race whose markings fall between those of

The shoebill stork (left), also known as the whale-headed stork, is one of the world's rarest and most distinctive birds.

Jackson's hartebeests (below) set up scouts in prominent positions while the rest of the herd grazes in peace.

the Masai and reticulated giraffes of Kenya.

Anyone who visited Murchison Falls in the 1960s would be saddened to see how little game is left. But these things are never as clear-cut as they seem. Expert opinion is that the park has never been in better ecological shape than it is now, paradoxically a product of the wholesale poaching, which allowed the vegetation to recover from degradation linked to elephant overpopulation. And animal numbers have visibly increased since the early 1990s. Estimates suggest that the elephant population has doubled to roughly 1,000 over recent years. Lions, at one point threatened with local extinction, now number between 50 and 100. The dramatic economic and social recovery of Uganda under its current leadership has been well documented; it is a success story mirrored in microcosm by the revival of Murchison Falls in the 1990s.

DETAILS

When to Go

Murchison Falls can be visited in any season, with temperatures remarkably similar year-round – about 80°F (27°C) at midday and 60°F (16°C) at night. Some roads may be impassable during the rains, from late March to May and from mid-September to November, but the waterfall is always impressive, and game is plentiful north of the river. For birders, the European winter is the optimum time to visit, as resident bird populations are boosted by migrants.

Getting There

The nearest international airport is in Kampala, but most travelers fly into Nairobi, which has more international connections. Most tour operators specializing in Uganda include Murchison Falls. For those wishing to visit independently, the park headquarters at Paraa is a full day's drive from Kampala via Masindi. The road to Masindi is fairly well maintained, but a four-wheel-drive vehicle is necessary to travel farther. Travelers using public transportation should take the bus from Kampala via Masindi to Bulisa, where bicycles can be rented to cover the last 20 miles (30km) to Paraa.

Launch trips to the base of the falls run twice daily if there's a demand, and can be organized at short notice at park headquarters. Motorboat trips to look for shoebills can also be arranged at short notice; mornings are most likely to be productive. Visitors who don't have their own transportation can join one of the game drives that run out of Sarova Paraa Lodge.

Travel advisory: Uganda has enjoyed a high level of internal stability since President Museveni took power in 1986, but it does border some of the most volatile countries in Africa. Check with your embassy for travel advisories; reliable tour operators should provide warnings if the situation deteriorates.

INFORMATION

Uganda Embassies

United Kingdom: Uganda House, 58–59 Trafalgar Square, London WC2N 5DX, UK; tel: +44-20-7839 5783; fax: +44-20-7839 8925.

United States: 5911 16th Street, N.W., Washington, DC 20011; tel: 202-726-7100 or 202-726-7101; fax: 202-726-1727.

Uganda Tourist Board

P.O. Box 7211, Kampala, Uganda; tel: +256-41-242 196; fax: +256-41-242 188; e-mail: utb@starcom.co.ug

United States: 336 East 45th Street, New York, NY 10017-3489; tel: 212-949-0110; fax: 212-682-5232.

Uganda Wildlife Authority

P.O. Box 3530, Kampala, Uganda; tel: +256-41-346 290; fax: +256-41-236 291.

CAMPING

There is a campsite with facilities at Paraa, and primitive sites elsewhere in the park.

LODGING

PRICE GUIDE – double occupancy

$ = under $100 $$ = $100–$200
$$$ = $200–$300 $$$$ = $300+

Nile Safari Camp

P.O. Box 2288, Kampala, Uganda; tel: +256-41-258 273; fax: +256-41-233 992, e-mail: iou@swiftuganda.com

Situated on the south bank of the Nile, this tented camp has an authentic bush setting. Hippos and elephants are often seen from the wooden deck and swimming pool, and the birding is excellent – shoebills reside sporadically on an island in front of the lodge. Prices include full board. $$–$$$

Paraa Rest Camp

P.O. Box 3530, Kampala, Uganda; tel: +256-41-346 290; fax: +256-41-236 291.

This national park camp lies near park headquarters, above the jetty for the launch trip to the base of the falls. Traditional huts come with bedding and mosquito nets. There are communal washing facilities for campers, and chalets with private baths. Basic meals and drinks are sold at a kiosk. $

Rabongo Camp

P.O. Box 3530, Kampala, Uganda; tel: +256-41-346 290; fax: +256-41-236 291.

This underused rustic retreat, on a river in the Rabongo Forest, is accessible only to those who drive themselves. Monkeys are prolific, and activities include chimp tracking and forest birding. Visitors stay in log cabins or bring their own tents; food must be brought from outside the park. $

Sambiya Lodge

P.O. Box 5187, Kampala, Uganda; tel: +256-41-233 596; fax: +256-41-344 855, e-mail: afritour@swiftuganda.com

Guests stay in air-conditioned rooms or tented accommodations at this lodge, which is near the top of the falls and the chimp-tracking center at Kanyiyo Pabidi in the Budongo Forest. $–$$

Sarova Paraa Lodge

P.O. Box 22636, Kampala, Uganda; tel: +256-41-251 211; fax: +256-41-251 209.

This modern lodge, on the Nile facing park headquarters, is conveniently located for game drives north of the river. $$$

TOUR OPERATORS

Abercrombie and Kent

United Kingdom: Sloane Square House, Holbein Place, London

SW1W 8NS, UK; tel: +44-20-7559 8600; fax: +44-20-7730 9376; e-mail: info@abercrombiekent. co.uk; web: www. abercrombiekent.com

United States: 1520 Kensington Road, Oak Brook, IL 60523-2141; tel: 800-323-7308; e-mail: info@abercrombiekent.com

This global giant with 32 offices worldwide operates in 100 countries, including Uganda, and has a large safari program.

Afritours and Travel

P.O. Box 5187, Kampala, Uganda; tel: +256-41-344 714 or +256-41-233 596; fax: +256-41-344 855; e-mail: afritour@ swiftuganda.com

This Kampala-based company offers package tours around Uganda and is also worth contacting for four-wheel-drive rentals.

Premier Tours

217 South 20th Street, Philadelphia, PA 19103; tel: 800-545-1910; fax: 215-893-0357; e-mail: info@premiertours.com

This is one of the few American companies offering Uganda tours.

Volcanoes Tours

P.O. Box 22818, Kampala, Uganda; tel: +256-41-346 464, fax: +256-41-341 718; e-mail: volcano@swiftuganda.com

This recently established company is based in Kampala and is rapidly acquiring a good reputation among safari tourists.

Wild Frontiers

P.O. Box 844, Halfway House, South Africa 1685; tel: +27-11-315 4838; fax: +27-11-315 4850; e-mail: wildfront@icon.co.za

This South African company has its own ground operation in Kampala and runs a variety of natural-history and birding tours to Uganda and elsewhere in East Africa.

Excursions

Budongo Central Forest Reserve

Uganda Wildlife Authority, P.O. Box 3530, Kampala, Uganda; tel: +256-41-346 290; fax: +256-41-236 291.

Budongo Forest lies along the southern border of Murchison Falls National Park, making it an excellent stop on your way from Kampala. Budongo protects Uganda's largest chimpanzee population and several other primate species, along with a dazzling array of forest birds. Guided chimp and bird walks are available at Kanyiyo Pabidi Tourist Site on the main road between Masindi and Paraa. About 25 miles (40km) west of Masindi, Busangiro Tourist Site offers inexpensive huts and is within striking distance of the so-called Royal Mile, possibly the best forest birding site in Uganda. A feature of this area is the chilling nocturnal call of the tree hyrax.

Kidepo Valley National Park

Uganda Wildlife Authority, P.O. Box 3530, Kampala, Uganda; tel: +256-41-346 290; fax: +256-41-236 291.

Situated in the arid northeast of Uganda, this remote and alluring park is arguably the country's best-kept game-viewing secret. Of 86 mammal species recorded here, almost 30 occur nowhere else in Uganda, such as cheetahs, greater kudu, and oryx. The two-day drive from Kampala passes through areas where there is a slight but real security risk. There is no public transport, so the only practical way to reach Kidepo is by chartered flight, staying at the well-appointed Apako Lodge. This trip is best arranged through a reputable tour operator.

Lake Mburo National Park

Uganda Wildlife Authority, P.O. Box 3530, Kampala, Uganda; tel: +256-41-346 290; fax: +256-41-236 291.

This relatively new national park protects a network of lakes and swamps set in an area of acacia woodland that once served as the royal hunting ground of the Ankole aristocracy. Plains animals such as zebras, impalas, eland, buffalo, and waterbuck are common, and it's the best place in Uganda to see savanna birds more normally associated with Kenya and Tanzania. When approaching the park, watch for the domestic Ankole cattle, noted for their immense horns. An attractively rustic camp with huts and camping facilities lies at the center of the park, about a five-hour drive west of Kampala.

Bale
National Park
Ethiopia

The chill, thin air of the **Sanetti Plateau** can leave the visitor gasping for breath. So, too, can the otherwordly beauty of this strange montane landscape, which conforms to media-generated images of Ethiopia only in its apparent bleakness. It is not that the Sanetti Plateau is arid – on the contrary it receives an average annual rainfall of 45 inches (114cm) – but rather that, perched at a lofty elevation of 13,000 feet (4,000m), it supports such an unfamiliar mix of plant life. There are no trees as such, no expansive green meadows. Instead, the plateau is shrouded in the muted vegetation characteristic of Afro-alpine moorland: a pastel montage of lichen-covered rocks, tussocks of gray and white everlasting Helichrysum shrubs, clumped forests of shoulder-high heathers, and the prehistoric-looking giant lobelia. ◆ The Sanetti Plateau is the elevated centerpiece of 850-square-mile (2,200-sq-km) **Bale National Park** in southeastern

Ethiopia's geographical isolation has left this highland park an untouched wonderland of giant plants and endemic wildlife.

Ethiopia. It can be reached on foot or by donkey from the park headquarters at **Dinsho**, though Sanetti is also accessible by car. An extravagantly scenic road ascends from the sleepy regional capital of **Goba** to the northern edge of the plateau, crossing slopes aflame with red and orange aloes, where francolins and guinea fowl scurry in front of the vehicle, and sunflower-yellow flocks of black-headed siskin sing canary-like from the undergrowth. ◆ Perhaps 30 minutes out of Goba, the vehicle will reach the plateau and the highest all-weather road in Africa. One doesn't go long here without encountering life. Spot-throated plovers and blue-winged geese, both endemic to Ethiopia, fuss away at the fringes of the shallow tarns. The

The Bale Mountains shelter a unique range of plant and animal species on high-altitude plateaus and moorland at the northern extent of the Great Rift Valley.

The Simien wolf, like many creatures found in Bale National Park, is unique to Ethiopia. To understand the high level of endemism that characterizes the country's ecology, one need only look at its geography. At the heart of Ethiopia lies a block of mountainous highlands, averaging more than 6,000 feet (1,800m) in altitude and covering an area twice that of Great Britain. Giddily scenic, the **Ethiopian Highlands** are isolated on three sides by desert, and have thus developed something of an island ecology. For instance, at least 30 of the more than 800 bird species recorded in Ethiopia are unique to the country, and a spate of recently described species suggests that several "new" endemics await discovery. And while the country is essentially part of the Afro-tropical ecozone, it has also absorbed many Palearctic elements. Nowhere is this phenomenon more noticeable than in the evergreen forests at Dinsho on the northern foothills of the Bale range. Interspersed with patches of open grassland and seasonal marsh, the forest around Dinsho has a positively Mediterranean quality, underscored by the herby aroma of fallen hagenia leaves. Several endemic birds are found here: the secretive Abyssinian catbird attracts attention to itself with its busily melodious song, while parties of colorful black-winged lovebirds flap and squawk through the canopy, and white-winged black tits creep inconspicuously along the juniper branches. Dinsho is also the last major stronghold of the mountain nyala, one of Africa's rarest large antelope. Far from being an Ethiopian version of the southern African nyala, the mountain nyala has close genetic links with the greater kudu, which it strongly resembles, though

vehicle may surprise a pair of tiny gray duiker as they forage between clumps of heather, or startle a bristly-coated klipspringer. On occasion, a solitary golden jackal or leopard ranges up to these heights. So, it is claimed by locals, does the Abyssinian lion, an elusive creature with a luxuriant dark mane. The abundance of raptors in the skies above the plateau is not unrelated to the proliferation of giant mole-rats on the ground below. A somewhat hamsterlike bundle of flesh and fur, the giant mole-rat weighs in at 4½ pounds (2kg) and is reputedly found nowhere else but on the Sanetti.

For the giant mole-rats, danger comes not only from the sky but also from the plateau's most characteristic terrestrial carnivore: the Simien wolf. Visit Sanetti in the early morning and you are almost certain to encounter this coyote-like creature, its rich chestnut contrasting with the pale vegetation. The Simien wolf is also known as the Simien fox, Ethiopian wolf, red dog, and Abyssinian jackal, but by any name it boasts the dubious distinction of being the world's most endangered canine. The Simien wolves of Bale represent roughly half of the global population, estimated at 500 animals, and may be the only viable gene pool in existence.

it has a shaggier coat, less distinct side-stripes, and smaller horns.

The Sanetti Plateau and the Dinsho area comprise two of the three major habitats protected within Bale National Park. The third is **Harenna Forest**, which lies at the southern base of the Sanetti Plateau. Harenna has yet to be the subject of full scientific exploration: a pioneering herpetological expedition recently found several hitherto undescribed reptile and amphibian species, while a cursory visit by mammalogists resulted in the discovery of two endemic shrews. Harenna Forest also supports an abundance of guereza and grivet monkeys as well as bushpigs, giant forest hogs, bushbuck, leopards, lions, and possibly a small population of African hunting dogs.

It would be facile to compare Bale to the better-known savannah reserves of East Africa. Bale is not a conventional safari destination, though to any serious nature lover it must rank as one of the continent's finest and most alluring montane reserves. And what you do see at Bale, you

tend to see well, due to the inexplicable fearlessness of the wildlife, a phenomenon epitomized by the behavior of Rouget's rail. African rails are renowned for their skulking habits and are notoriously difficult to find even where they are common. Not so Rouget's rail, which habitually stuns visiting birders by strutting around the Sanetti Plateau like a model on a catwalk.

Much the same can be said of the park's two star attractions: the mountain nyala and Simien wolf. The former has hit on a defense strategy so risible that one could be forgiven for wondering why it wasn't hunted to extinction years ago. Confronted by a human intruder, the mountain nyala will sneak off behind the nearest bush, duck low for a few seconds, then – like a child playing peek-a-boo – crane its long neck over the vegetation to check out the situation, unfailingly revealing its presence in the process. And those who are fortunate enough to encounter a Simien wolf at close quarters will find this handsome canine to be even more confiding. There is something thrilling, and not a little sad, attached to the sensation of looking into the brown eyes of one of the world's rarest animals, and finding therein the trusting innocence of a domestic puppy.

The mountain nyala (top), a rare antelope discovered only in 1908, is found in large herds in Bale National Park.

The Simien wolf (right) is hunted by farmers who erroneously believe it threatens their livestock.

TRAVEL TIPS

DETAILS

When to Go

Bale National Park is pleasant year-round, although October and November are the optimal months. The temperature remains more or less constant year-round, 60°F (16°C) to 70°F (21°C) at midday, 50°F (10°C) at night. Small rains from late January to early March and long rains from July to early September sometimes restrict travel options in remote parts of Ethiopia, but these are also the times when the countryside is at its most beautiful, and there are fewer tourists. For birders, Ethiopia is most rewarding from October through March, when seasonal migrants from Europe boost the resident bird populations.

Getting There

Several international carriers fly to Addis Ababa in Ethiopia, and Ethiopian Airlines has flights connecting Addis Ababa to Goba, the regional center of Bale. Most tour operators specializing in Ethiopia can arrange driving safaris to Bale from Addis Ababa. For independent travelers, buses to Goba stop a 10-minute walk from the park headquarters at Dinsho, where inexpensive hiking or donkey trekking excursions can be arranged for visiting the Sanetti Plateau and elsewhere in the national park.

Travel advisory: Ethiopia is regarded as a "difficult" country to travel in. This is partly due to the long distances, rough roads, and basic facilities, partly to a general level of hassle unusual elsewhere in Africa. Travelers who fly between major centers and stay at nominally upscale hotels are generally less affected by this than those who use public transportation and stay at local lodgings.

Protracted hostilities between Ethiopia and Eritrea have reduced the number of tourists visiting Ethiopia, but the fighting has not directly affected areas regularly visited by tourists. For current information, check your embassy's travel advisories.

INFORMATION

Ethiopian Airlines

Churchill Road, P.O. Box 1755, Addis Ababa, Ethiopia; tel: +251-1-517 000; fax: +251-1-611 474; web: www.ethiopian-airlines.com; e-mail: info@ethiopian-airlines.com

United Kingdom: Fourth Floor, Foxglove House, 166 Piccadilly, London W1V 9DE, UK; tel: +44-20-7491 2125; fax: +44-20-7491 1892.

United States: 405 Lexington Avenue, New York, NY 10174; tel: 800-445-2733 or 212-867-0095; fax: 212-692 9589.

Embassies

United Kingdom: 17 Princes Gate, London SW7 1PZ, UK; tel: +44-20-7589 7212; fax: +44-20-7584 7054.

United States: 2134 Kalorama Road, N.W., Washington, DC 20008; tel: 202-234-2281; fax: 202-328-7950.

CAMPING

Camping is permitted at the park rest house at Dinsho.

LODGING

Accommodations in southern Ethiopia are generally restricted to local guest houses. The choice, in most towns of any size, is abundant, and several houses can be found in Dinsho, Robe, and Goba, the most strategic settlements in the vicinity of Bale National Park.

Dinsho Resthouse

Department of Natural Resources, P.O. Box 386, Addis Ababa, Ethiopia; tel: +251-1-515 970.

This rustic, Swiss-built chalet is in the heart of the forest at the park headquarters, about half a mile (1km) from the main road and the bus route between Addis Ababa and Goba. It offers endless hiking possibilities as well as good birding and game viewing from the garden. Basic local meals can be taken at restaurants in Dinsho village, and there are cooking facilities for those who bring their own supplies. $

Ghion Hotel Chain

P.O. Box 1643, Addis Ababa, Ethiopia; tel: +251-1-513 222; fax: +251-1-515 381.

The Addis Ababa Ghion is one of the better large hotels in the Ethiopian capital, and the showpiece of a relatively upscale hotel chain represented in all the main tourist centers of northern Ethiopia. $$

Goba Ras Hotel

P.O. Box 1632, Addis Ababa, Ethiopia; tel: +251-1-517 060; fax: +251-1-517 533.

This government hotel on the outskirts of Goba is reasonably comfortable and has most of the basics: hot running water, cold drinks, and acceptable food. $

TOUR OPERATORS

Experience Ethiopia Travel

P.O. Box 9354, Addis Ababa, Ethiopia; tel: +251-1-519 291; fax: +251-1-519 982.

This Addis Ababa-based company is well equipped to tackle anything from a standard tour of the northern historical circuit to trekking and four-wheel-drive trips to more remote parts of the country like Bale National Park.

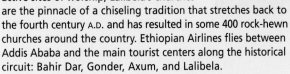

Journeys by Design

2 Marchmont Gardens, Richmond, Surrey TW10 6ET, UK: tel: +44-208-332-2928; fax: +44-208-948-6588; web: www.journeys bydesign.co.uk

This British company specializes in customized trekking tours of the Bale Mountains in search of the Simien wolf, mountain nyala, and other rare animals.

Unusual Destinations

P.O. Box 97508, Petervale 2157, South Africa; tel: +27-11-706 1991; fax: +27-11-463 1469; e-mail: unusdest@global.co.za; web: www.unusualdestinations.com

This South Africa-based company specializes in customized tours to several of Africa's more out-of-the-way countries, such as Ethiopia, Madagascar, and Eritrea.

Yumo Tours

4 Seymour House, 19 Hanson Street, London W1P 7LN, UK; tel/fax: +44-20-7631 5337; e-mail: yumo@dial.pipex.com; web: www.yumo.net

This British tour operator has its own ground operation and years of hands-on experience dealing with the practicalities of traveling in Ethiopia.

Excursions

Awash National Park

Ethiopian Embassy, 2134 Kalorama Road, N.W., Washington, DC 20008; tel: 202-234-2281; fax: 202-328-7950.

This relatively accessible game reserve protects a patch of dry acacia savanna in the Rift Valley east of Addis Ababa. Common mammals include Beisa oryx, Soemmering's gazelle, Swayne's hartebeest, Salt's dik-dik, greater and lesser kudu, and Hamadryas and Anubis baboons. Lions are present in small numbers. The beautiful carmine bee-eater and Abyssinian roller are conspicuous among roughly 400 recorded species of birds. The park is a straightforward three- to five-hour drive from Addis Ababa; accommodations are found at Kereyou Lodge, perched on the edge of the Awash River Gorge.

Lalibela

Ethiopian Airlines, Churchill Road, P.O. Box 1755, Addis Ababa, Ethiopia; tel: +251-1-517 000; fax: +251-1-611 474; web: www.ethiopian-airlines.com; e-mail: info@ethiopian-airlines.com

Northern Ethiopia's magnificent historical circuit incorporates the 2,500-year-old city of Axum, the medieval island monasteries of Lake Tana, and the 16th-century castles in Gonder. The highlight, however, is undoubtedly Lalibela, where a subterranean complex of 12 churches was hand-carved into the rocks in the 13th century. Still active sites of worship, Lalibela's churches are the pinnacle of a chiseling tradition that stretches back to the fourth century A.D. and has resulted in some 400 rock-hewn churches around the country. Ethiopian Airlines flies between Addis Ababa and the main tourist centers along the historical circuit: Bahir Dar, Gonder, Axum, and Lalibela.

Simien Mountain National Park

Ethiopian Embassy, 2134 Kalorama Road, N.W., Washington, DC 20008; tel: 202-234-2281; fax: 202-328-7950.

Ethiopia's premier hiking and mule-trekking destination, this World Heritage Site is notable for its rugged scenery of gaping ravines and craggy peaks, including Africa's fourth-highest mountain, the 15,400-foot (4,700-m) Ras Dashen. A relatively impoverished fauna includes the very rare Simien wolf and walia ibex. Most hikers encounter the gelada baboon, an Ethiopian endemic with a flowing mane and red chest patch. Treks ranging from two to 10 days can be arranged through local tour operators or at park headquarters in Debark, which lies a half-day bus ride from the city of Gonder.

Red Sea
Egypt

t is a typically calm morning in Egypt's deep south. The sun shines strongly, and the sea is calm – good omens for the day's diving. The desert shoreline is punctuated only by the white tents of a dive safari camp silhouetted against the deep blue of the sea. Behind the camp, the mountains of the **Eastern Desert** stretch out to the horizon. ◆ A group of divers is busy on shore, gearing up on a large tarpaulin spread out on the beach to prevent sand from getting into the equipment. Zipped, buckled, and double-checked, they wade through the shallows and are transferred by Zodiac to a dive boat moored in the bay. Forty minutes later, the dive boat is tying up to a buoy at **Elphinstone Reef**. ◆ Elphinstone is one of a series of dramatic offshore seamounts that characterize the southern **Red Sea**. Carpeted in hard and soft corals, the reef acts as a magnet for marine life of every description, from tiny blennies taking cover in coral crevices to the deadly lionfish, its elegant red-and-white

Pristine coral reefs bursting with life and color await divers off Egypt's desert shores.

pectoral fins waving gently as it floats a few feet above the reef, safe in the knowledge that its poisonous dorsal fins will protect it from predators. Royal angelfish – resplendent in a coat of yellow, blue, and black stripes – and gaudy butterflyfish add splashes of color to the undersea palette. Coral groupers, their coral-pink skins dappled with vivid vermilion spots, hover beneath overhangs waiting for a tasty morsel to pass by. The strong currents bring in scores of pelagics such as giant trevallies and silver-sided jacks, hunting in huge shoals that sweep across the reef in a flash of silver and blue scales. The sheer multitude of fish virtually guarantees that the ocean's mightiest predators are never far away: up to seven species of shark can be seen here.

Clownfish will go to great lengths to protect their eggs, which are laid around the base of their sea-anemone homes; the tiny fish will even challenge divers who swim too near.

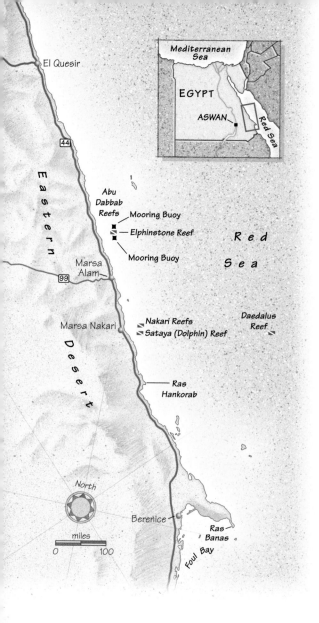

predators approach each other, only to swerve away at the last moment. The wrasse disappears over the edge of the reef, while the eel glides across the coral, eventually secreting itself into a convenient hole.

The divers descend farther along the sloping plateau until, at about 80 feet (25m), it abruptly stops. They fin across a stretch of open water and, at 100 feet (30m), arrive at an isolated outcrop, standing like a lonely sentinel at Elphinstone's northernmost tip. A school of barracuda knifes through the current, while a shark circles the outcrop below. It's impossible to tell in the gloomy depths what species it is, and, with their time up, the divers reluctantly swim back across the reef and into the shallows.

Edge of the Deep

After a surface interval spent lounging around on deck, it is time for a second dive. The boat motors over to a mooring buoy at the southern plateau, and the divers again don their gear, splash over the side, and swim to the reef.

The **southern plateau** tapers off more steeply than its northern counterpart. Its sheer walls are festooned with soft corals that plunge abruptly into the depths. Just 10 minutes into the dive and the sound of the dive leader banging a knife against her tank alerts the group to something unusual.

The divers scan their surroundings and lock on to a silvery shape approaching from the south. It is an oceanic whitetip shark, easily identified by its large, rounded dorsal fin and broad, white-tipped pectorals. The divers watch warily as it swims against the current toward them before veering off and disappearing from whence it came. The group moves back to the shelter of the reef where a friendly Napoleon wrasse approaches; it hangs around for a while, apparently unperturbed by the flashing cameras before gracefully finning away to explore elsewhere.

The metallic clang of knife on tank signals the return of the whitetip shark, and again they turn their attention to the open water. This time they get a better look. Honed by 400 million years of evolution, the shark's

Into the Blue

The divers make final adjustments to their gear and then drop one by one into the blue. They descend on Elphinstone's **northern plateau** and almost immediately encounter a cloud of fairy basslets, each a bright point in a golden shoal of thousands, retreating as one into the safety of the shadows.

Small schools of bluescale emperors and yellow-band fusiliers hover above the reef. Below them, a giant moray swims sinuously across the plateau. Coincidentally, a Napoleon wrasse approaches from the other direction. The divers watch in fascination as the two

streamlined body slices effortlessly through the sea, its open mouth revealing rows of razor-sharp teeth. Fortunately, its natural prey doesn't include humans, but it still circles curiously before departing for a more productive hunting ground. The divers return to their boat, babbling excitedly as they strip off their equipment and prepare for the journey home.

From Shore or Sea

Elphinstone is one of a series of offshore reefs in the southern Red Sea that teem with marine life. To the north are the **Abu Dabbab Reefs**, and to the south is **Daedalus Reef**, some 60 miles (90km) offshore. Beyond that, sprawling along the coastline opposite **Marsa Nakari**, are the **Nakari Reefs** and **Sataya (Dolphin) Reef**.

Until recently the only way to reach these reefs was on a live-aboard dive boat operating

A school of gold anthias (left) flees from a diver in a coral-encrusted trench.

Fire lionfish (below) are one of the Red Sea's most beautiful but dangerous denizens; their long, curved spines are loaded with potentially fatal venom.

out of one of several small ports on the Egyptian coast. But thanks to the success of dive resorts elsewhere on the Red Sea, there are now several options for lodging in this remote southern region and exploring the reefs on day trips.

The southern Red Sea also offers fine opportunities for shore diving and snorkeling. Apart from hotel developments and the occasional port, the coastline is almost entirely unspoiled, with pristine reefs reachable from any number of entry points. Most of the resorts have excellent "house reefs," often just a few steps from the dive center, which

are especially convenient for night dives.

There are typically two shore dives per day – either on the house reef or farther afield, depending on weather conditions. Safari trucks usually load up about 8:30 A.M. A dive guide gives a detailed briefing upon reaching the designated site, and then it's a simple matter of strolling into the sea and slipping beneath the surface.

Many of the fringing reefs are pitted with caverns and swim-throughs, usually leading out through the reef onto a wall sloping down to depths of 15 to 50 feet (5–15m). Coral outcrops pepper the seabed, interspersed with fragile acropora corals spreading out in huge tablelike shapes. Beefy coral groupers lurk beneath rocky overhangs, and colorful basslets shroud the reef in vast shoals. Blue-spotted stingrays scud across the sand in search of mollusks, while enormous parrotfish patrol the reef edge, gnawing noisily on coral polyps.

It's a world unlike any other, a living city filled with life forms that are utterly alien and yet oddly familiar. Scientists tell us that life began in the sea and that coral reefs are among the oldest habitats on Earth. If that's true, then exploring the coral reefs of the Red Sea isn't merely a grand adventure but a return to an ancient home.

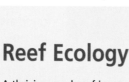

Reef Ecology

A thriving coral reef is one of the most glorious sights on the planet, bursting with color and life and supporting a dazzling array of plants and animals. In the Red Sea alone, there are more than a thousand species of reef fish and hundreds of kinds of invertebrates.

Though often mistaken for plants, corals are actually tiny animals called polyps that resemble sea anemones. Reef-building corals secrete rigid, outer skeletons that fuse with each other and surrounding rubble. Over millennia, as new generations of coral grow on the remains of the old, intricate forms and patterns develop. These limestone structures, the largest built by living things, provide food and shelter for a host of creatures that evolve together into a tightly knit and highly efficient ecological unit.

Among the most fascinating relationships between species are those that benefit both organisms. Coral polyps, for example, depend upon symbiotic, single-celled algae that reside in their tissue and help manufacture nourishment. Clownfish defend themselves from predators by living among the stinging tentacles of sea anemones and, in return, attract prey for the anemone to feed on. And more than 50 species of cleaner fish and shrimp thrive solely by removing detritus and parasites off the scales and even the teeth of much larger fish who would ordinarily swallow them whole.

Though coral reefs are one of nature's most productive ecosystems, they are also among the most fragile. Because they grow in nutrient-poor water, they are extremely vulnerable to environmental disturbances, including those caused by careless divers. It's essential that divers minimize their impact on the environment by maintaining neutral buoyancy, preventing gauges and tank from banging against the reef, and mooring boats to buoys rather than dropping anchor. As the saying goes, visitors should endeavor to take only pictures, leave only bubbles.

Coral polyps (left) resemble plants but are actually small, stationary animals.

A clownfish (below) nestles in the stinging tentacles of an anemone. A mucus coating protects the fish from harm.

A Napoleon wrasse (right) can weigh as much as 420 pounds (190kg) but is usually wary of divers in spite of its huge size.

TRAVEL TIPS

DETAILS

When to Go

There is good scuba diving year-round in the southern Red Sea, but the best time to go is in spring or fall. Summer (May to September) is generally hot and dry, with air temperatures as high as 113°F (45°C) and sea temperatures about 81°F (27°C). Winter (October to April) is cooler, with air temperatures around 68°F (20°C) and sea temperatures falling as low as 64°F (18°C). Visibility is generally around 65 feet (20m), with only slight seasonal variations. Plankton blooms in the summer months can occasionally cloud the water.

Getting There

Until a proposed airport at Marsa Alam is in place, the main gateway to the southern Red Sea is Hurghada, which is reached by a connecting flight from Cairo or by charters from Europe. The roads from Hurghada to Marsa Alam are good, and the ride on public transportation takes up to four and a half hours, including transfers. Driving yourself is possible, but the drive from Cairo is long, hot, and arduous; most tour operators arrange transfers from Hurghada, and all of them shuttle divers from hotel to boat.

Travel Advisory

In summer, divers should bring either a one-millimeter Lycra skinsuit or a three-millimeter neoprene wetsuit. In winter, a 5-millimeter or 7-millimeter wetsuit is recommended, depending on your susceptibility to the cold. The winter wind chill on the offshore reefs can be significant, so you will need a fleece top to keep you warm between dives. Thick-soled neoprene booties are a must for shore diving to protect your feet while crossing the top of the reef. This is a remote area, so bring spare equipment. Diving gear can be rented on site, but it is better to have your own mask, snorkel, and fins.

INFORMATION

Egyptian Tourist Authority

Misr Travel Tower, Abbassia Square, Cairo, Egypt; tel: +20-2-285 4509; fax: +20-2-285 4363; web: http://touregypt.net

United Kingdom: Egyptian House, 170 Piccadilly, London W1V 9DD, UK; tel: +44-20-7493 5283; fax: +44-20-7408 0295; e-mail: egypt@freenetname.co.uk

United States: 8383 Wilshire Boulevard, Suite 215, Beverly Hills, CA 90211; tel: 213-653-8815; fax: 213-653-8961; e-mail: egypt@etala.com; 630 Fifth Avenue, Suite 1706, New York, NY 10111; tel: 212-332-2570; fax: 212-956-6439; e-mail: egypttourst@aol.com

Egyptian Embassies

United Kingdom: 26 South Street, London W1Y 6DD, UK; tel: +44-20-7499 3304; fax: +44-20-7491 1542; web: www.egypt-embassy.org.uk

United States: 3521 International Court, N.W., Washington, DC 20008; tel: +1-202-895-5400; fax: +1-202-244-4319.

LODGING

PRICE GUIDE – double occupancy

$ = under $100 $$ = $100–$200
$$$ = $200–$300 $$$$ = $300+

Kharamana Resort

Blondie Beach, Marsa Alam, Egypt; tel: +20-195-100 261; fax: +20-195-100 259.

Gardens surround stonework bungalows and two-story dwellings at this seaside resort. Rooms are spacious and well equipped, with air-conditioning and generous terraces. The resort has two beaches, two swimming pools, a gym, tennis courts, three restaurants, and three bars. $$

Marsa Shagra Safari Camp

Red Sea Diving Safari, 53 El Hussain Street, Dokkey, Cairo, Egypt; tel: +20-2-337 9942; fax: +20-2-349 4219; web: www.egypt.com/redsea

This long-established safari camp is situated on a small private bay, with easy access for dive boats going to offshore reefs and excellent snorkeling and diving on the house reef. Facilities are fairly basic but comfortable. Accommodations include tented sites on the water's edge and simple domed lodges overlooking the sea. $

TOUR OPERATORS

Hayes and Jarvis

Hayes House, 152 King Street, London W6 OQU, UK; tel: +44-870-898 9890; fax: +44-20-8741 0299; e-mail: diving@hayes-jarvis.com

Tours feature many options in the Red Sea, including live-aboard boats and explorations of the "deep south."

Oonasdivers

23 Enys Road, Eastbourne, East Sussex BN21 2DG, UK; tel: +44-1323-648 924; fax: +44-1323-738 356; e-mail: info@oonasdivers.com; web: www.oonasdivers.com

This diving operator works with several Red Sea resorts, live-aboard boats, and the safari camp at Marsa Shagra.

Red Sea Desert Adventures

Marsa Shagra Safari Camp, Southern Red Sea, Egypt; tel: +20-195-100 262.

A Dutch geologist and explorer

runs desert safaris from her base at Marsa Shagra. The most popular is a half-day excursion into the foothills of the Eastern Desert mountains, followed by a camel ride through a spectacular gorge and tea in a Bedouin tent. Other options include a stargazing tour in the desert, an overnight excursion to the top of Mount Igla, and tours to ancient emerald mines and associated shrines in Wadi Jamel.

Red Sea Diving Safari

53 El Hussain Street, Dokkey, Cairo, Egypt; tel: +20-2-337 9942; fax: +20-2-349 4219; web: www.egypt.com/redsea

This long-established dive operation manages the dive facilities at Marsa Shagra Safari Camp and Kharamana Resort. A wide range of instruction is available from beginner level up to dive master, and equipment can be rented.

Regal Diving

22 High Street, Ely, Cambs, CB6 2RB; UK; tel: +44-1353-778 096; fax: +44-1353-777 897; e-mail: andy@regal-diving.co.uk; web: www.regal-diving.co.uk

This dive tour operator organizes worldwide diving holidays and comprehensive options in the Red Sea, including live-aboard boats and reef exploration in the "deep south."

Excursions

Nile River

Egyptian Tourist Office, 630 Fifth Avenue, Suite 1706, New York, NY 10111; tel: 212-332-2570; fax: 212-956-6439.

The Nile, Africa's longest river, supports a wealth of bird life. Look for bulbuls, bluethroats, wheatears, hoopoes, turtle doves, redstarts, and dark-backed stonechats. Common birds of prey include hawks, kestrels, and falcons. Waders such as egrets and purple gallinules can also be seen. Most Nile cruises offer a three- or five-day trip between Luxor and Aswan.

Sinai Desert and St. Catherine's Monastery

Egyptian Tourist Office, 630 Fifth Avenue, Suite 1706, New York, NY 10111; tel: 212-332-2570; fax: 212-956-6439.

Situated between Asia and Africa, the Sinai Desert has been a pathway and battleground between empires for millennia. Now demilitarized, its 24,000 square miles (62,000 sq km) are open to camel treks and four-wheel-drive safaris. The interior is a wilderness of towering dunes and wind-sculpted rock formations, punctuated by lush oases and isolated springs. In the south, Mount Sinai is revered as the site of God's revelations to Moses. In the valley below, St. Catherine's Monastery is the main focal point for pilgrims and tourists alike. There are regular tours from the Sinai dive resorts and Cairo.

Western Desert Oases

Egyptian Tourist Office, 630 Fifth Avenue, Suite 1706, New York, NY 10111; tel: 212-332-2570; fax: 212-956-6439.

Egypt's harsh Western Desert is interrupted only by a series of oases, isolated pockets of human habitation where date palms, olives, and fruit trees are intensively cultivated. Some have been occupied since 5000 B.C., linked by camel trains to the Nile Valley. Today, the four major oases – Bahariya, Farafra, Dakhla, and Kharga – can be visited as part of a Great Desert Circuit trip from Cairo; two others, Fayoum and Wadi Natrun, are accessible on day trips from the capital. Visit in spring or autumn, when the orchards are in bloom or being harvested.

SECTION THREE

•

Resource
Directory

CLIMATE

In southern Africa, summer (November–March) is also the rainy season and can be hot and humid with daily thunderstorms. Some parks, such as Mana Pools in Zimbabwe and parts of the Okavango Delta in Botswana, are closed. Winter (June–August) can be pleasant in the northerly areas, with clear skies and mild temperatures. Winter in the far south and along the Namib coast can be bitterly cold, and snow is not uncommon in the mountainous parts of South Africa. Equatorial East Africa has warm weather year-round; the rains come in two bites – the "little rains" in October and November and the "long rains" from March to early June.

September is perfect almost everywhere, with clear skies, temperatures that are warm but not too hot, and superb game viewing as the animals mass around water holes and rivers. October is wonderful in the far south but searingly hot inland, farther north, and in the deserts, where it is known as "suicide month."

COMMUNICATIONS

The postage system in most of Africa is slow and unreliable. It is strongly suggested that contact be made via fax, phone, or e-mail. Use Federal Express or DHL to ship anything valuable.

On the whole, phone systems have improved, though land lines across most of Africa are still subject to regular crashes due to lightning strikes, damage caused by elephants, and other problems. Many people rely on mobile phones, but travelers should verify that their phones will function abroad. Many game lodges don't have phones; their only link with the outside world is by radio. Satellite phones can be used, but most lodges ask you to limit use to the privacy of your room; half the point of going to the bush is to be out of contact with the outside world.

Internet access is spreading in Africa. Many towns have Internet cafés, and hotels with phones allow guests to plug in laptop computers.

TRAVELING WITH CHILDREN

Travelers with young children should keep several safety considerations in mind. For the most part, only fenced lodges and camps will accept responsibility for small children. Many upmarket lodges refuse to take children under 12, and even then, travelers with children will be expected to pay for a private vehicle, as children may disrupt game viewing. It is inadvisable to take children under five; the cry of a child is said to resemble that of a wounded animal and may attract predators. Ideally, wait until children are nine for their first safari. Then choose a child-friendly camp with a pool and play area, so kids can let off steam between game drives. Arm yourself with hats, sunblock, motion-sickness pills, and plenty of drinks and snacks. It is also worth having a child's safari guide and camera so children can really take an interest. Several excellent books published in South Africa, such as the *When Hippo was Hairy* series, combine details about the animals with entertaining local legends.

HANDICAPPED TRAVELERS

Safaris are ideal for handicapped travelers, because they require little or no walking to get into the bush. Large hotels at well-developed reserves such as Masai Mara, Kruger, or Chobe have suitable facilities. Some small lodges may be properly equipped, but disabled travelers are advised to check directly with the lodges or book through a reputable specialist agent. Few lodges have specially adapted safari vehicles for game drives, so getting in and out may require assistance.

SAFARI ETIQUETTE

The following rules apply to most game-viewing in Africa and are designed to ensure the well-being of both visitors and wildlife:

• Stay in your vehicle, except in designated areas. Avoid making any sudden movements or waving your arms out the windows.

• Never attempt to feed wild animals.

• Never drive off roads unless explicitly permitted by park authorities.

• Never park in a position that obscures the views of others.

• Turn off your engine when parked (even if the air-conditioning is on), and keep your voice down, especially if the windows are open.

• Minimize disrupting wildlife by waiting for a lull in activity before leaving.

• Carry binoculars, a camera, and field guides to identify the species you see.

• Allow plenty of time to return to camp before the gates close.

DOCUMENTS

All travelers need a passport valid for at least six months. You may also be asked to show your return ticket and proof that you can support yourself financially during your stay (a recognized credit card will do). Visa requirements vary from country to country. Check with your travel agent, tour operator, or nearest embassy well in advance of your departure. Photocopy important documents and keep them separate from the originals in case of theft. Carry official identification with you at all times.

DRIVING

Renting and driving your own vehicle is more practical in some countries than in others. In all cases, you should be able to use your driver's license for three months, but it is sensible to acquire an international driver's license before leaving home. There may be restrictions on driving a rented vehicle across international borders. Check with your rental agency before departing.

South Africa, Zimbabwe, and Namibia have excellent roads. In Botswana, you can expect to reach only the northern fringe of Chobe National Park. Driving in Zambia and Malawi is possible, but the quality of the roads varies enormously. The quality of roads in Kenya, Tanzania, Uganda, Madagascar, and Ethiopia is often poor, and it may be difficult to reach the best game-viewing areas under your own steam. A four-wheel-drive vehicle with high clearance is essential for driving on rough terrain and also affords better visibility.

Before embarking on any bush trip, drivers should ensure that their vehicle's brakes and tires, including at least one full-sized spare tire (not a "doughnut") are in good condition. Make sure you have the tools necessary to replace a tire and consider taking a second spare. Other essentials include a spare fan belt, emergency fuel, water for passengers and your vehicle, extra food, blankets or sleeping bags, and flashlights. If your vehicle breaks down, it may be a long time before another vehicle passes to help, and you may be marooned overnight. Be sure that someone knows when you left, which route you plan to follow, and when you are scheduled to arrive, so search parties can be dispatched if necessary.

ELECTRICITY

Most countries in the region use 240V electricity, but the shape of the plugs varies. Bring an international adaptor, although most hotels can provide one. Service may be intermittent in remote areas; a flashlight is a useful addition to your luggage. Many safari lodges do not have electricity, except for a single socket in the office available for recharging batteries.

INSURANCE

Travel insurance is essential. Make sure your policy provides adequate health coverage, including the services of an air ambulance, and covers you while engaged in outdoor activities such as bush walks and canoeing.

HEALTH AND SECURITY

Contact the Centers for Disease Control for health advisories well before your departure. Few inoc-

ulations are mandatory, although you may need a yellow-fever certificate in some countries. Most travelers will have been vaccinated against typhoid, polio, and tetanus as children, but it's best to confirm your vaccination history with your physician. An additional vaccination against hepatitis A is advisable; allow two months for the full treatment.

Malaria is a concern at virtually all game reserves, and the risk is heightened in the rainy season, when mosquitoes are breeding. Ask your physician for up-to-date information on which prophylactic to take and stick rigidly to the regime. Medications are not completely effective, so take other common-sense precautions. Mosquitoes are most active between dusk and dawn, so wear long trousers, long-sleeved shirts, socks, and covered shoes, and use plenty of insect repellent during these hours. If possible, sleep under a mosquito net. If you develop any flulike symptoms within six months of your visit, ask your doctor to test for malaria.

Take all prescription medications with you; the nearest pharmacy may be hundreds of miles away. Carrying a letter of authority from your doctor will avoid complications at Customs.

Drinking water is usually safe (except in Egypt and Ethiopia), but it's always advisable to drink bottled water and avoid ice. Do not swim in fresh water. Crocodiles inhabit rivers and water holes and will attack humans. Fresh water that is not treated with chlorine may be contaminated with schistosomiasis (also known as bilharzia), a disease caused by parasitic worms.

Venomous snakes, spiders, and scorpions are common throughout Africa and are fond of hiding under rocks and branches, in crevices, and in other dark, sheltered places. A good rule of thumb is to keep your hands and feet where you can see them. Wear proper shoes and socks, shake out your shoes and sleeping bag before getting into them, and, yes, check under the toilet seat before sitting down. If you are bitten or stung, summon aid immediately. If you are bitten by

a snake, try to remember what it looked like, so that identification can be made and the proper antivenin administered.

Apply antiseptics to cuts and abrasions. Infections can become serious quickly, so seek medical attention at the earliest signs of trouble. If you are bitten by an animal, you must seek immediate treatment for rabies.

HIV and AIDS are pervasive throughout southern and eastern Africa. Practice safe sex at all times and avoid blood transfusions unless absolutely necessary, except in South Africa, where hospital standards are excellent and blood is properly screened.

The following resources provide travelers with up-to-date information on medical issues, political stability, crime, and personal safety:

U.S.

Centers for Disease Control
1600 Clifton Road, Atlanta, GA 30333; tel: 877-394-8747 or 800-311-3435; web: www.cdc.gov/travel

The CDC provides comprehensive information on vaccinations and other travelers' health issues.

U.S. Department of State
Office of American Citizens Services, Washington, DC 20520; tel: 202-647-5225; web: www.travel.state.gov/ travel_warnings.html

The State Department posts its current travel warnings on this site.

U.K.

Foreign and Commonwealth Office Travel Advice Unit
1 Palace Street, London SW1E 5HE, England; tel: +44-20-7238 4503; fax: +44-20-7238 4545; web: www.fco.gov.uk

This site has security updates from around the world.

Medical Advisory Services for Travellers Abroad (MASTA)
tel: +44-906-8224 1000; web: www.masta.org

MASTA offers a massive online database with up-to-the-minute information on 250 countries. For a small fee, the telephone information service will provide you with a medical plan of action for your trip.

AMERICAN AND BRITISH EMBASSIES IN AFRICA

Embassies are a reliable source of up-to-date information on visa requirements and security issues and should be notified in the case of a lost passport.

Botswana

U.S.
P.O. Box 90, Gaborone, Botswana; tel: +267-353 982; fax: +267-356 297 or +267-312 782; e-mail: uscomml@mega.bw

U.K.
P. Bag 0023, Gaborone, Botswana; tel: +267-3-52841; fax: +267-3-56105.

Egypt

U.S.
5 Latin America Street, Garden City, Cairo, Egypt; tel: +20-2-355 7371; fax: +20-2-357 3200.

U.K.
Ahmed Ragheb Street, Garden City, Cairo, Egypt; tel: +20-2-354 0850; fax: +20-2-354 3065.

Ethiopia

U.S.
P.O. Box 1014, Addis Ababa, Ethiopia; tel: +251-1-550 660; fax: +251-1-551 328; e-mail: usembassy@telecom.net.et

U.K.
Fikre Mariam Abatechan Street, P.O. Box 858, Addis Ababa, Ethiopia; tel: +251-1-161 2354; fax: +251-1-161 0588; e-mail: b.emb4@telecom.net.et

Kenya

U.S.
P.O. Box 30137, Nairobi, Kenya; tel: +254-2-537 800; fax: +254-2-537 810.

U.K.
Upper Hill Road, P.O. Box 30465, Nairobi, Kenya; tel: +254-2-714 6199; fax: +254-2-719 082; e-mail: bhcinfo@iconnect.co.ke

Madagascar

U.S.
14–16 Rue Rainitavo, BP 620, Antsahavalo, Antananarivo, Madagascar; tel: +261-20-222 1257; fax: +261-20-223 4539.

U.K.
1st Floor, Immeuble Ny Havana, Cité de 67 Ha, BP 167, Antananarivo, Madagascar; tel: +2612-20-222 7749; fax: +2612-20-226 690; e-mail: ukembant@simicro.mg

Malawi

U.S.
P.O. Box 30016, Lilongwe 3, Malawi; tel: +265-783 166; fax: +265-780 471.

U.K.
P.O. Box 30042, Lilongwe 3, Malawi; tel: +265-782 400; fax: +265-782 657.

Namibia

U.S.
14 Lossen Street, Ausspanplatz, Windhoek 9000, Namibia; tel: +264-61-221 601; fax: +264-61-229 792.

U.K.
116 Robert Mugabe Avenue, Windhoek 9000, Namibia; tel: +264-61-223 022; fax: +264-61-228 895.

South Africa

U.S.
877 Pretorius Street, Arcadia, P.O. Box 9536, Pretoria 0001, South Africa; tel: +27-12-342 1048; fax: +27-12-342 2244.

U.K.
91 Parliament Street, Cape Town 8001, South Africa; tel: +27-21-461 7220; fax: +27-21-461 0017.

255 Hill Street, Arcadia 0083, Pretoria, South Africa; tel: +27-12-483 1200; fax: +27-12-483 1302; e-mail: britain@icon.co.za; web: www.britain.org.za

Tanzania

U.S.
36 Laibon Road, P.O. Box 9123, Dar es Salaam, Tanzania; tel: +255-51-666 010-4; fax: +255-51-666 701.

U.K.
Hifadhi House, Samora Avenue, P.O. Box 9200, Dar es Salaam, Tanzania; tel: +255-51-117 659; fax: +255-51-112 951; e-mail: bhc.dar@raha.com

Uganda

U.S.
Parliament Avenue, P.O. Box 7007, Kampala, Uganda; tel: +256-41-259 792; fax: +256-41-259 794.

U.K.
10–12 Parliament Avenue, P.O. Box 7070, Kampala, Uganda; tel: +256-41-257 054; fax: +256-41-257 304; e-mail: bhcinfo@starcom.co.ug

Zambia

U.S.
Independence Avenue, Lusaka, Zambia; tel: +260-1-250 955; fax: +260-1-254 861.

U.K.
Independence Avenue, P.O. Box 50050, Lusaka, Zambia; tel: +260-1-251 133; fax: +260-1-235 798; e-mail: brithc@zamnet.zm

Zimbabwe

U.S.
172 Herbert Chitepo Avenue, Harare, Zimbabwe; tel: +263-4-703 169; fax: +263-4-796 488.

U.K.
Corner House, Samora Machel–Leopold Takawira Streets, P.O. Box 4490, Harare, Zimbabwe; tel: +263-4-772 990; fax: +263-4-774 617.

AIRLINES

Major international airlines with regular flights to Africa from North America, Great Britain, and continental Europe include British Airways, Virgin Atlantic, Air France, Lufthansa, Swissair, Sabena, KLM, and TAP. The main African airlines include:

Air Botswana
Sir Seretse Khama Airport, P.O. Box 92, Gaborone, Botswana; tel: +267-351 921; fax: +267-353 928.

U.K.
177–178 Tottenham Court Road, London W1P 9LE, England; tel: +44-20-7757 2737; fax: +44-20-7757 2277; e-mail: bpsales@flightbookers.co.uk

Air Namibia
Gustav Voigts Centre, Ground Floor, Independence Avenue, P.O. Box 731, Windhoek, Namibia; tel: +264-61-298 2552;

fax: +264-61-221 382; e-mail: air_namibia@hotmail.com; web: www.airnamibia.com.na

U.K.
Beaumont House, Lambton Road West, London SW20 0lW; tel: 020-8944 0188; fax: 020-8944 7199; e-mail: frank@london.ins.co.uk

U.S.
c/o Kartagener Associates, 12 West 37th Street, New York, NY 10018; tel: +1-212-465 0619; fax: +1-212-868-1654.

Air Zimbabwe
Redbridge, 2nd Floor, Eastgate, Harare, Zimbabwe; tel: +263-4-794 481; fax: +263-4-796 039; web: www.airzimbabwe.com

U.K.
52–55 Piccadilly, London W1V 9AA; tel: +44-20-7491 0009 or +44-20-7491 3783 (reservations); fax: +44-20-7491 3164.

Ethiopian Airlines
Churchill Road, P.O. Box 1755, Addis Ababa, Ethiopia; tel: +251-1-517 000; fax: +251-1-611 474; web: www.ethiopian-airlines.com; e-mail: info@ethiopian-airlines.com

U.K.
Foxglove House, 4th Floor, 166 Piccadilly, London W1V 9DE; tel: +44-20-7491 2125; fax: +44-20-7491 1892.

U.S.
405 Lexington Avenue, New York, NY 10174; tel: 800-445-2733 or 212-867-0095; fax: 212-692 9589.

Kenya Airways
Nairobi Airport, tel: +254-2-823 000; fax: +254-2-823 488; web: www.kenyaairways.co.uk

U.K.
Bedfont Road, Heathrow Airport, Staines TW19 7NL; tel: +44-1784-888 233; fax: +44-1784-888 300.

South African Airways (SAA)
Airways Park, 1st Floor, Block C, Johannesburg International Airport, Jones Road, P.O. Box X13, Johannesburg, South Africa; tel: +27-11-978 1762; fax: +27-11-978 1795; web: www.flysaa.com

U.K.
St. George's House, 61 Conduit Street, London W1R 0NE; tel: +44-20-7312 5005; fax: +44-20-7312 5008; e-mail: info@lon.flysaa.com; web: www.saa.com

U.S.
515 East Las Olas Boulevard, Suite 1600, Fort Lauderdale, FL 33301; tel: 954-769-5000 or 800-722-9675; fax: 954-769-5079; e-mail: sausa@fll.flysaa.com

TOUR OPERATORS

Safari operators offer a wide range of travel options, from luxury to low budget. Below is a sample of the many operators in North America, the United Kingdom, and Africa. See "Travel Tips" at the end of each destination chapter for additional listings.

Abercrombie & Kent
Sloane Square House, Holbein Place, London SW1W 8NS; tel: +44-20-7559 8600; fax: +44-20-7730 9376; e-mail: info@abercrombiekent.co.uk; web: www.abercrombiekent.com

1520 Kensington Road, Oak Brook, IL 60523-2141; tel: 800-323-7308 or 800-757-5884 (brochure request); e-mail: info@abercrombiekent.com
This global giant has 32 offices operating in 100 countries as well as a large safari program.

Africa-Adventure Company
5353 North Federal Highway, Suite 300, Fort Lauderdale, FL 33308; tel: 800-882-9453 or 954-491-8877; fax: 954-491-9060; e-mail: noltingaac@aol.com; web: africa-adventure.com
Mark Nolting, a leading American travel writer, arranges custom tours.

Africa Travel Center
P.O. Box 1918, Boulder, CO 80306; tel: 800-361-8024; fax: 303-546-0875; e-mail: info@africatvl.com; web: www.africatvl.com
The company offers customized safaris to various destinations in eastern and southern Africa, including Malawi, Kenya, South Africa, and Tanzania.

Philip Briggs and Ariadne Van Zandbergen
P.O. Box 2636, Bedfordview 2008, South Africa; tel/fax: +27-11-792 6736; e-mail: philari@hixnet.co.za
These experienced African travel writers and photographers arrange and lead customized tours and safaris throughout Africa.

CCAfrica/Afro Ventures
CCAfrica, P Bag X27, Benmore 2010, South Africa; tel: +27-11-809 4300; fax: +27-11-809 4400; e-mail: bookings@ccafrica.com; web: www.ccafrica.com
CCAfrica and Afroventures operate an extensive collection of luxury lodges and mobile safaris in some of the best wildlife destinations on the continent.

Field Guides Incorporated
9433 Bee Cave Road, Building 1, Suite 150, Austin, TX 78733; tel: 800-728-4953 or 512-263-7295; fax: 512-263-0117; e-mail: fgileader@aol.com; web: www.fieldguides.com
This operator specializes in bird-watching trips to Kenya, Tanzania, and South Africa.

Geographic Expeditions
2627 Lombard Street, San Francisco, CA 94123; tel: 415-922-0448; fax: 415-346-5535; e-mail: info@geoex.com; web: www.geoex.com
Trips to Kenya, Tanzania, and other destinations range from mobile and fly-in safaris to backpacking safaris in national parks.

International Expeditions, Inc.
One Environs Park, Helena, AL 35080; tel: 205-428-1700 or 800-633-4734; e-mail: nature@ietravel.com
Naturalists lead trips to Uganda, Tanzania, and Kenya, with an emphasis on natural history and conservation.

Ker & Downey
P.O. Box 27, Maun, Botswana; tel: +267-660 375; fax: +267-661 282; e-mail: safari@kerdowney.bw; web: www.kerdowney.com

2825 Wilcrest Drive, Suite 600, Houston, TX 77042-6007; tel: 800-423-4236; fax: 713-917-0123; e-mail: info@kerdowney.com
This upmarket safari operator has safari camps and mobile safaris throughout southern and eastern Africa.

Mountain Travel-Sobek
6420 Fairmount Avenue, El Cerrito, CA 94530; tel: 888-687-6235 or 510-527-8100; fax: 510-525-7710; e-mail: info@mtsobek.com; web: www.mtsobek.com
This leading American tour operator specializes in trips for small

groups and offers an array of game-viewing trips to Africa, with destinations in Zambia, Madagascar, Malawi, Kenya, South Africa, and Botswana.

Okavango Tours and Safaris
Marlborough House, 298 Regents Park Road, London N3 2TJ; tel: +44-20-8343 3283; fax: +44-20-8343 3287; e-mail: info@okavango.com; web: www.okavango.com

Customized itineraries make use of small bush lodges and exclusive hotels.

Safari Consultants
Orchard House, Upper Road, Little Cornard, Suffolk CO10 0NZ; tel: +44-1787-228 494; fax: +44-1787-228 096; e-mail: bill.safcon@pop3.hiway.co.uk

2038 North Clark Street, Chicago, IL 60614; tel: 312-573-0125.
Seasoned guides offer a variety of travel options, from tourist bungalows and bed-and-breakfasts to luxury lodges.

Unusual Destinations
P.O. Box 97508, Petervale 2157, South Africa; tel: +27-11-706 1991; fax: +27-11-463 1469; e-mail: unusdest@global.co.za; web: www.unusualdestinations.com

This sensibly priced company specializes in customized tours to some of Africa's out-of-the-way destinations, such as Madagascar, Eritrea, and Ethiopia.

Wilderness Safaris
c/o Outposts, Narracott, Drewsteignton, Exeter, Devon EX6 6PU; tel: +44-164-728 1665; fax: +44-164-728 1288; e-mail: outposts@usa.net

c/o Tim Farrell & Associates, P.O. Box 7300, Wilton, CT 06897-7300; tel: 203-762-8050; fax: 203-762-7323; e-mail: safaritim@aol.com
This company is one of the leading operators of exclusive, upmarket lodges in some of the continent's finest reserves. It also operates package tours and mobile safaris and will provide customized tours with private guides throughout southern Africa.

CONSERVATION ORGANIZATIONS

Through the organizations listed here, you can pursue your interest in natural history, learn about volunteer opportunities, and find out more about the status of conservation efforts throughout Africa.

Durrell Wildlife Conservation Trust
Les Augres Manor, Trinity, Jersey, Channel Islands JE3 5BP; tel: 01534-860 000; fax: 01534-860 001; e-mail: jerseyzoo@durrell.org
The trust is one of the world's foremost centers for captive breeding of rare and endangered animals.

Environmental Investigation Agency
P.O. Box 53343, Washington, DC 20009; tel: 202-452-8661; fax: 202-452-8663; e-mail: eiagency@email.msn.com
Founded in 1984, the EIA investigates illicit trade in wildlife products and ozone-depleting substances, and illegal logging.

Feedback Madagascar
Westering, Crinan, Argyll PA31 8SR, Scotland; tel/fax: +44-1546-830 240.
This small but effective Scottish charity promotes conservation in rural communities on the edge of the rain forest.

Friends of Conservation
Riverbank House, 1 Putney Bridge Approach, London SW6 3JD; tel: +44-20-7731 7803; fax: +44-20-7731 8213; e-mail: focint@compuserve.com
This organization supports much-needed conservation projects in East Africa, including rhino protection in the Masai Mara.

Hurghada Environmental Protection and Conservation Association (HEPCA)
P.O. Box 144, Hurghada, Red Sea, Egypt; tel: +20-65-445 035; fax: +20-65-445 035.
HEPCA campaigns on all aspects of reef conservation and has installed more than 250 mooring buoys along the coastline to help prevent anchor damage caused by dive boats.

International Cheetah Research and Education Centre
Cheetah Conservation Fund/WILD, P.O. Box 1380, Ojai, CA 93024; tel: 805-640-0390; fax: 805-640-0230; e-mail: info@cheetah.org; web: www.cheetah.org

The organization operates a cheetah research and captive-breeding center.

Tusk Trust
19 Amner Road, Battersea, London SW11 6AA; tel: +44-20-7978 7100; fax: +44-20-7223 2517; e-mail: sales@tusk.org; web: www.tusk.org
This UK-based conservation group raises funds for endangered-species projects in eastern and southern Africa.

World Conservation Monitoring Centre
219 Huntingdon Road, Cambridge CB3 0DL; tel: +44-1223-277 314; fax: +44-1223-277 136; e-mail: info@wcmc.org.uk; web: www.wcmc.org.uk
The organization provides information on conservation and the sustainable use of the world's living resources.

World Wildlife Fund for Nature
1250 24th Street, N.W., P.O. Box 97180, Washington, DC 20077-7180; tel: 202-293-4800 or 800-225-5993; fax: 202-293-9211; web: www.panda.org
This is the world's largest non-profit organization aimed at the preservation of wildlife, with 4.7 million supporters in more than 100 countries.

USEFUL WEBSITES

Check these sites for helpful links to safari operators, lodges, parks, and sources of travel information and regional news.

www.go2africa.com
This site is a useful safari planner with travel ideas and links to tour operators.

www.iafrica.com
The site features news, travel, sports, dining, and entertainment in southern Africa.

www.safariafrica.com
This search engine specializes in links to safari camps, lodges, and tour operators.

www.safarilink.com
This search engine features links to safari operators, lodges, parks, and airlines.

www.travelsa.com
The site provides in-depth infor-

mation on tourist facilities throughout southern Africa.

www.webrite-zw.com
This search engine covers select websites in southern Africa.

FURTHER READING

The following list contains a small selection of essential titles. At the very least, travelers should carry a field guide to assist in wildlife identification.

General Titles

Among the Elephants, Ian and Oria Douglas-Hamilton (Viking, 1985).

The Big Cat Diary, Brian Jackman and Jonathan Scott (BBC Books, 1996).

Born Free, Joy Adamson (Collins & Harvill, 1960).

Cry of the Kalahari, Mark and Delia Owens (Houghton Mifflin, 1992).

Elephant Memories, Cynthia Moss (University of Chicago Press, 2000).

The Eye of the Elephant, Mark and Delia Owens (Houghton Mifflin, 1993).

Fantastic Invasion, Patrick Marnham (Harcourt, Brace, Jovanovich, 1980).

Gorillas in the Mist, Dian Fossey (Penguin, 1983).

The Great Migration, Carlo Mari and Harvey Croze (Harvill Press, 1999).

The Great Migration, Jonathan Scott (Elm Tree Books, 1988).

A Hunter's Wanderings in Africa, Frederick Selous (Macmillan & Co, 1919, reprint Wolfe Publishing, 1986).

In the Shadow of Man, Jane Goodall (Phoenix, 1996).

The Last Wilderness, Nicholas Luard (Simon & Schuster, 1981).

Lost World of the Kalahari, Laurens van der Post (Hogarth Press, 1958).

Maasai, Tepilit Ole Saitoti and Carol Beckwith (Elm Tree Books, 1991).

The Marsh Lions, Brian Jackman and Jonathan Scott (Elm Tree Books, 1982).

Okavango: The Miracle Rivers, Peter and Beverley Pickford (Southern Books, 1999).

Okavango: Africa's Wetland Wilderness, Adrian Bailey (Struik, 1998).

Okavango: Jewel of the Kalahari, Karen Ross (BBC Books, 1987).

Okavango: Sea of Land, Land of Water, Peter Johnson and Anthony Banister (Struik, 1977).

On Safari in East Africa, Ernest Neal (Harper Collins, 1991).

Reason for Hope: A Spiritual Journey, Jane Goodall (Warner Books, 1999).

Roaring at the Dawn, Brian Jackman (Swan Hill Press, 1995).

Safari, Bartle Bull (Penguin, 1992).

Travel Guides

Discovering Southern Africa, T. V. Bulpin (Discovering Southern Africa Productions, 1992).

Exploring South Africa, Melissa Shales (Fodor's, 2000).

Madagascar: The Bradt Travel Guide, Hilary Bradt (Bradt, 1999).

Malawi, Mozambique and Zambia, David Else (Lonely Planet, 1997).

Ngorongoro Conservation Area Guidebook, David Bygott (David Bygott & Co., 1990).

Southern Africa, David Else (Lonely Planet, 2000).

Traveler's Companion Kenya, Jack Barker, Peggy Bond, and Michael Bond (Traveler's Companions, 1999).

Traveler's Companion South Africa, Jack Barker (Traveler's Companions, 2000).

Traveller's Guide to Kenya, Melissa Shales (AA/Passport, 1996).

Trekking In East Africa, David Else (Lonely Planet).

Zimbabwe and Botswana: The Rough Guide, Barbara McCrea and Tony Pinchuck (Rough Guides, 1996).

Zimbabwe, Botswana and Namibia, Deanna Swaney (Lonely Planet, 1999).

Wildlife Guides

Birds of East Africa: Collins Safari Guide, David Hosking and Martin Withers (Harper Collins, 1996).

Birds of the Indian Ocean Islands, Olivier Langrand and Ian Sinclair (Struik, 1998).

Cichlids and Other Fishes of Lake Malawi, by A. Koning. (TFH Publications, 1990).

A Field Guide to the Larger Mammals of Africa, Jean Dorst and Pierre Dandelot (Collins, 1970).

A Field Guide to the Mammals of Africa, Theodor Haltenorth and Helmut Diller (Collins, 1977).

A Field Guide to the National Parks of East Africa, J. G. Williams (Collins, 1967).

Field Guide to the Trees of Southern Africa, Eve Palmer (Collins, 1977).

Guide to Mammals of Southern Africa, Chris and Tilda Stewart (Ralph Curtis, 2000).

Guide to the Common Trees of the Okavango and *Guide to the Common Flowers of the Okavango*, Veronica Roodt (Shell Oil, Botswana, 1998).

Madagascar Wildlife, Hilary Bradt, Derek Schuurman, and Nick Garbutt (Bradt, 1996).

Mammals of Madagascar, Nick Garbutt (Pica Press, 1999).

Newman's Birds of Southern Africa, K. B. Newman (Southern Books, 1999).

Robert's Birds of Southern Africa, Gordon Maclean (New Holland, 1988).

Two Oceans: A Guide to the Marine Life of Southern Africa, G. M. Branch, C. L. Griffiths, M. L. Branch, and L. E. Beckley (David Philip, 1994).

The Safari Companion: A Guide to Watching African Mammals, Richard D. Estes (Chelsea Green, 1999).

PARKS AND RESERVES

Avid travelers may want to explore the many other parks and reserves throughout the continent. Here are a few of the best, with an emphasis on West and North Africa.

Benin

Parc National de la Pendjari
Embassy of the Republic of Benin, 2737 Cathedral Avenue, N.W., Washington, DC, 20008; tel: 202-232-6656.

Encompassing 1,062 square miles (2,750 sq km), bordering the Pendjari River and the Parc National d'Arli in neighbouring Burkina Faso, the park is primarily wooded savanna, with some of the best game viewing in West Africa. Elephants, lions, large herds of buffalo, antelope, hippos, and crocodiles are often sighted.

Cameroon

Dja Wildlife Reserve
Ecofac Regional Coordinator, BP 15115, Libreville, Gabon; tel: +241-73-2343; fax: +241-73-2345; e-mail: coordination@ecofac.org

Dense rain forest and swamp dominate this 2,031-square-mile (5,260-sq-km) reserve which lies within a loop of the Dja River. Rich in biological diversity, it supports more than 100 mammal, 320 bird, and 1500 plant species. The swampy regions are home to otters and sitatungas, while lowland gorillas, chimpanzees, mandrills, elephants, and talapoin monkeys inhabit the forest. Between a dense network of waterways are grass-covered rocky outcrops, the haunt of buffalo.

Canary Islands

Whale-watching
Spain Tourist Office, 666 Fifth Avenue, New York, NY 10103; tel: 212-265-8822.

Although Spanish, the Canary Islands are located off the northwest coast of Africa. During the year, one-third of all cetacean species, including blue and sperm whales and numerous dolphin species, pass through the waters of Tenerife, making it a prime site for whale- and dolphin-watching. Short-finned pilot whales and bottlenose dolphins are permanent residents. The Tenerife ports of Los Gigantes, Playa San Juan, Playa de las Americas, and Los Cristianos offer whale-watching excursions.

Comoros

Scuba Diving
Indian Ocean Commission, 203 Sheen Lane, London SW14 8LE; tel: 020-8876 2407; web: www.ioc-tourism.com

Set off the East African coast at the northern end of the Mozambique Channel, the Comoros are renowned for some of the best wall dives in the Indian Ocean, with sites ranging from coral reefs and shipwrecks to night and drift dives. The best sites are found on Moheli Island, a 15-minute flight or four-hour boat trip from Moroni on the largest island, Grande Comoro. Because of political unrest, visitors should consult their embassies for the latest travel advisories.

Democratic Republic of the Congo

Virunga National Park
Embassy of the Democratic Republic of the Congo, 1800 New Hampshire Avenue, N.W., Washington, DC 20009, tel: 202-234-7690; fax: 202-686-3631.

The park sprawls over 3,088 square miles (7,998 sq km) along the Rwanda–Uganda border. Most people come to visit the endangered mountain gorillas at Djomba and Bukima, but lions, buffalo, antelope, and elephants can be seen farther north, while Lake Edward has varied bird life. Climbing excursions of Nyiragongo (11,385ft/3,470m) and Nyamulgira (10,023ft/3,055m) can be arranged. At the time of this writing, the park is closed for security reasons. Visitors should consult their embassies for the latest travel advisories.

Gabon

Lope-Okanda Wildlife Reserve
Ecofac Regional Coordinator, BP 15115, Libreville, Gabon; tel: +241-73-2343; fax: +241-73-2345; e-mail:coordination@ecofac.org

Most species typical of West African rain forests are found here, with large numbers of primates and forest elephants. One gorilla family is being habituated to humans.

More than 1,500 plant and 350 bird species have been recorded. There are archaeological sites from the stone and iron age, and walking and boating excursions.

Gambia

Abuko Nature Reserve
Gambia Embassy, 1155 15th Street, N.W., Suite 1000, Washington, DC 20005; tel: 202-785-1399; fax: 202-785-1430.

Remarkably diverse with savanna and forest, this tiny reserve has an excellent network of bird-watching trails. More than half of Gambia's 500 recorded species can be seen here, together with green, red colobus, and patas monkeys as well as duiker, bush babies, and crocodiles. Excursions on the Gambia River upstream from Banjul give the opportunity to explore creeks by pirogue or to take a motor cruise to the old French trading post of Albreda, followed by a visit to James Island, one of the main trans-shipment points during the slave trade. Farther upstream, one finds sitatunga, clawless otters, and Pel's fishing owls at the Baobolong Wetland Reserve. Also in the region, River Gambia National Park is the site of a private chimpanzee rehabilitation project.

Ghana

Mole National Park
Ministry of Tourism, P.O. Box 4386, Accra, Ghana; e-mail: mot@ghana.com; web: www.est.ghana.gov.gh

Remote, lightly visited, and accessible only with a four-wheel-drive vehicle, Mole encompasses 1,868 square miles (4,840 sq km) of savanna and rocky outcrops. Elephants and plains game are among the 93 mammal and 300 bird species recorded in the park. Guided walks are available.

Kakum National Park
Ministry of Tourism, P.O. Box 4386, Accra, Ghana; e-mail: mot@ghana.com; web: www.est.ghana.gov.gh

A highlight of the park is the treetop canopy walkway, 200 feet (60m) high in some places. The 139-square-mile (357-sq-km) park combines virgin rain forest and semideciduous forest. Specialties at the park include walking tours to view forest medicinal plants, birds (300 species) and butterflies (600 species). Wildlife is diverse, from forest elephants and shy bongo to nine species of primates.

Ivory Coast

Parc National de la Comoe
Tourism Information, Ivory Coast Embassy, 2424 Massachusetts Avenue, N.W., Washington, DC 20008; tel: 202-797-0300.

The largest game park in West Africa encompasses 4,440 square miles (11,500 sq km) of savanna and riparian forest, with three mountains – Yevele, Potrou, and Boutourou – averaging 2,000 feet (609m) tall. The Comoe River runs through the park. Wildlife includes elephants, lions, hippos, waterbuck, and roan antelope. Bird life is excellent, with more than 400 species recorded. Game drives and pirogue trips on the Comoe River are available, but no walking is permitted.

Kenya

Kakamega Forest National Reserve
Kenya Wildlife Service, P.O. Box 40241, Nairobi, Kenya; tel: +254-2-501 081; fax: +254-2-504 171; e-mail: kws@kws.org; web: www.kws.org

Kenya's only tropical rain forest has excellent bird-watching. Some 350 species have been recorded, including rare snake-eating birds normally seen only in West Africa. Four miles (6km) of trails through magnificent stands of trees gives the opportunity to see a variety of primates, including black and white colobus, blue, and red-tailed monkeys. Other forest animals include bush pigs, clawless otters, porcupines, civets, suni, ground pangolins, and gray duiker.

Saiwa Swamp National Park
Kenya Wildlife Service, P.O. Box 40241, Nairobi, Kenya; tel: +254-2-501 081; fax: +254-2-504 171; e-mail: kws@kws.org; web: www.kws.org

This tiny park, only one square mile (3 sq km), is the only place in Kenya to see the sitatunga antelope. There are nature trails and a boardwalk around the swamp with several viewing platforms. Other species include endangered de Brazza monkeys,

otters, giant forest squirrels, black and white colobus monkeys, bushbuck, and gray duiker.

Kisite Marine National Park
Kenya Wildlife Service, P.O. Box 40241, Nairobi, Kenya; tel: +254-2-501 081; fax: +254-2-504 171; e-mail: kws@kws.org; web: www.kws.org

Boasting some of East Africa's finest coral gardens and shallow reefs, the park covers 11 square miles (28 sq km), stretching some four miles (6 km) out to sea. More than 250 fish species in prolific numbers and vibrant colors and 45 varieties of coral have been recorded. Staghorn, mushroom, brain, and pencil corals are common. Sport fishing, snorkeling, and dolphin-watching excursions by motorboat or traditional dhow can be arranged from Shimoni.

Meru National Park
Kenya Wildlife Service, P.O. Box 40241, Nairobi, Kenya; tel: +254-2-501 081; fax: +254-2-504 171; e-mail: kws@kws.org; web: www.kws.org

Famous as the setting of Joy Adamson's *Born Free*, Meru encompasses 336 square miles (870 sq km) of mixed habitats, including woodlands, open plains, and palm-fringed riverbanks. The park suffered from severe poaching in the 1980s, but the elephant population is now stable. Large lion prides and buffalo herds are common; cheetahs, leopards, lesser kudu, dik-dik, duiker, hippos, and crocodiles are often sighted. More than 300 bird species have been recorded, including the Pel's fishing owl and Peter's finfoot. Kora National Reserve, the site of George Adamson's camp, is also in the region. Bordered by the Tana River, the reserve encompasses 690 square miles (1,787 sq km), where the plains are studded with inselbergs. Wildlife includes lions, elephants, lesser kudu, wild dogs, striped and spotted hyenas, leopards, and cheetahs.

Libya

Sahara Trek
Caravanserai Tours, 1–3 Love Lane, Woolwich, London SE18 6QT; tel: +44-20-8855 6373; fax: 020-8855 6370; e-mail: info@caravanserai-tours.com; web: www.caravanserai-tours.com

The desert proper begins at Ghadames, a former stopping point on the trans-Sahara caravan route from Timbuktu to the Mediterranean. The finest desert scenery is found in the Acacus region, reached from the Tuareg town of Ghat. Enormous sand dunes, dramatic wind-carved rock formations, and prehistoric cave paintings are found in this 58-square-mile (150-sq-km) wilderness. Safaris are available using four-wheel-drive vehicles or camels. Excessive heat and sand-storms make travel impractical in June, July, and August.

Morocco

Atlas Mountains
Moroccan National Tourist Office, 20 East 46th Street, Suite 1201, New York, NY 10017; tel: 212-557-2620; fax: 212-949-8148.

The best trekking is in the 435-mile (700-km) High Atlas Range, which has more than 400 summits above 6,650 feet (2025m). Among them is 13,671-foot (4167-m) Mount Toubkal, North Africa's highest peak. A network of mule trails crisscross the mountains, giving access to Berber mountain villages. Visitors can hire local guides and pack mules or join an organized trek. Ski touring is possible from February to April.

South Africa

Itala Game Reserve
South African Tourist Board, P Bag X164, Pretoria, South Africa 0001; tel: +27-12-482 6200; fax: +27-12-347 8753; web: www.satour.co.uk

Encompassing some 115 square miles (298 sq km), this park contains some of the oldest geological formations in the world, dating back three billion years. Wildlife is varied – black and white rhinos, elephants, buffalo, giraffes, and antelope – but no lions. Large birds include lappet-faced and white-backed vultures, black eagles, and secretary birds. Day and night drives and self-guided trails are available.

Madikwe Game Reserve
South African Tourist Board, P Bag X164, Pretoria, South Africa 0001; tel: +27-12-482 6200; fax: +27-12-347 8753; web: www.satour.co.uk

The fourth-largest game reserve in South Africa was established on former farmland in 1991. Operation Phoenix, the largest game relocation program in the world, released 10,000 animals of 28 species into the park. Wildlife includes South Africa's second-largest population of elephants, endangered Cape hunting dogs, black and white rhinos, buffalo, lions, cheetahs, and leopards.

Addo Elephant National Park
South African Tourist Board, P Bag X164, Pretoria, South Africa 0001; tel: +27-12-482 6200; fax: +27-12-347 8753; web: www.satour.co.uk

Addo is regarded as South Africa's best elephant park, with a breeding herd of about 300 animals. Other wildlife include black and white rhinos, buffalo, eland, kudu, red hartebeest, grysbok, and duiker, and more than 185 bird species. Day and night game drives, hiking, and horseback riding are available.

Mountain Zebra National Park
South African Tourist Board, P Bag X164, Pretoria, South Africa 0001; tel: +27-12-482 6200; fax: +27-12-347 8753; web: www.satour.co.uk

The park was established in the 1930s to protect endangered mountain zebras; 200 now inhabit this 324-square-mile (840-sq-km) reserve, along with eland, red hartebeest, caracal, and bat-eared and Cape foxes. The dramatic mountain scenery has sweeping views across the Karoo plains and wooded valleys. More than 200 bird species have been recorded; raptors such as black eagles, booted eagles, Cape eagle owls, and chanting goshawks are often sighted. Hiking, mountain biking, horseback riding, and game drives are available.

Richtersveld National Park
South African Tourist Board, P Bag X164, Pretoria, South Africa 0001; tel: +27-12-482 6200; fax: +27-12-347 8753; web: www.satour.co.uk

About a third of South Africa's succulent plant species, including a variety of quiver trees, is found in the volcanic mountains and gravel plains of this austere and remote desert park. Wildlife viewing is limited, although rock hyrax and baboons are often spotted along the Gariep River. The

only practical means of traveling in the park is by four-wheel-drive vehicle or by canoe on the Gariep River. Namaqualand, to the south of the park, is renowned for its spectacular profusion of springtime flowers, which carpet the desert in August and September.

Table Mountain and Cape Point
South African Tourist Board, P Bag X164, Pretoria, South Africa 0001; tel: +27-12-482 6200; fax: +27-12-347 8753; web: www.satour.co.uk

Table Mountain (3,500ft/1,066m) towers over Cape Town. A variety of walking routes lead to the top, but most visitors take the easy option and go by cable car. The mountains stretch south from the Table to Cape Point in 29-square-mile (77-sq-km) Cape of Good Hope Nature Reserve, which has more plant species than the entire British Isles as well as antelope, Cape mountain zebras, and baboons. More than 200 bird species have been recorded here, including seabirds such as albatross, shear-waters, and Cape gannets.

Tanzania/Zanzibar

Jozani Forest Reserve
Zanzibar Commission for Tourism, P.O. Box 1410, Zanzibar, Tanzania; tel: +255-54-33845; fax: +255-54-33448.

A 10-square-mile (25-sq-km) remnant of the forest that once covered Unguja (Zanzibar's largest island), this reserve is the only place to see the endangered Zanzibar red colobus monkey, of which 500 survive. Other rarely seen animals include the endemic Ader's duiker, suni, and leopard. Nature trails lead through the forest; guides are available.

Chumbe Island Coral Park
P.O. Box 3203, Zanzibar, Tanzania; tel/fax: +255-54-31040; e-mail: chumbe.island@raha.com

The first marine park in Tanzania boasts some of the best-preserved shallow reefs in East Africa, with more than 200 species of coral and 370 species of fish. Snorkeling trails illustrating the variety of marine life have been developed. The island itself is a nature reserve encompassing a little more than half a square mile (1.6 sq km). The forest is home to the rare, nocturnal coconut crab, the endangered

Ader's duiker, and a variety of birds. Guided walks are available.

Zimbabwe

Chizarira National Park
Zimbabwe Department of National Parks and Wildlife Management, P.O. Box CY 140, Causeway, Harare, Zimbabwe; tel: +263-4-792 783; fax: +263-4-724 914; e-mail: nationalparks@gta.gov.zw

A deep gorge bisects this rugged and remote park, whose 741 square miles (1,920 sq km) take in floodplains, miombo and mopane woodlands, savanna, and grassland. Chizarira is renowned for its large buffalo herds, but elephants, black rhinos, lions, leopards, zebras, and a variety of antelope may also be encountered. More than 480 bird species have been recorded here, including the rare taita falcon, narina trogen, broadbilled roller, Livingstone's flycatcher, and Angola pitta. Wilderness trails and escorted walks are available.

Nyanga Mountains National Park
Zimbabwe Department of National Parks and Wildlife Management, P.O. Box CY 140, Causeway, Harare, Zimbabwe; tel: +263-4-792 783; fax: +263-4-724 914; e-mail: nationalparks@gta.gov.zw

Primarily a scenic park, Nyanga encompasses Zimbabwe's highest mountain, Inyangani, at 8,507 feet (2,593m). There are several lakes and waterfalls, including dramatic Pungwe and Honde Falls. Wildlife includes blue and common duiker, servals, otters, waterbuck, and kudu, as well as a variety of forest birds. Trout fishing, hiking and horseback riding are available.

PHOTO AND ILLUSTRATION CREDITS

Theo Allofs 18B, 35T, 37T, 46-47, 57M, 72B, 88T, 97T, 99B, 109B, back cover top

Peter Arnold/Peter Arnold, Inc. 149M, 177M

David M. Barron/Oxygen Group 136T, 137B, 139T, 139B

Peter Blackwell 40B, 90T, 144, 146, 149B, 160, 163B, 164T, 164B, 166B, 169T, 186, 188T

Robin Brandt 82, 113T

Camerapix 169M

Roger de la Harpe/Africa Imagery 22, 28T, 42, 51B, 52T, 53B, 54B, 57T, 64T, 67T, 77T, 85B, 90B, 93B, 99M, 104B, 110, 115M, 117T, 117M, 155B, 165B

Nigel J. Dennis 9B, 36T, 39B, 50, 58, 60, 61B, 65B, 73T, 77B, 89T, 93T, 96, 104T, 106TR, 126, 128, 129T, 130T, 131B, 142, 147B

Dian Fossey Gorilla Fund International 182B

Gerry Ellis/ENP Images 26, 30T, 44, 57B, 70T, 181B, 185M, 207B

Everett Collection, Inc. 156T

Dave B. Fleetham/Tom Stack & Associates 200, 203B, 204T, 204B, 205

Nick Garbutt/Planet Earth Pictures 131T

Chris & Sheila Hillman/Camerapix 197B

J&B Photographers 30B, 37B, 51T, 63B, 70B, 85T, 98T, 147M

Gavriel Jecan/Art Wolfe, Inc. 18T, 35B, 52B, 91, 122, 150, 167

M. Jelliffe/Trip Photographic Library 136B

Wolfgang Kaehler 1, 4, 30M, 40T, 71, 72T, 74T, 74B, 88B, 98B, 101B, 133M, 156B, 173T, 173B, 207M

Kitchin & Hurst/Tom Stack & Associates 130B, 145B

Thomas Kitchin/Tom Stack & Associates 138B

Frans Lanting/Minden Pictures 85M, 101T

Tom & Pat Leeson 147T, 152, 153T

Craig Lovell 68, 81T, 117B, 125M

H. Luther/Trip Photographic Library 45

Mary Evans Picture Library 190T, 190M

Buddy Mays/Travel Stock 156M

Joe McDonald/Tom Stack & Associates 123B, 177B

Colin McRae 8T

Carol Polich 5B, 109M

Kevin Schafer 10-11, 86, 114, 166T, 191T

John Shaw/Tom Stack & Associates 6-7

Martin Sutton/EarthWater Stock Photography 203T

TC Nature/Animals Animals 73B

Tom Till 16

Heinrich van den Berg/HPH Photography 25, 31, 63T, 65T, 77M, 78, 113B, 115T

Ingrid van den Berg/HPH Photography 61T, 62T, 62B, 64B, 112

Philip van den Berg/HPH Photography 36B, 53T, 89B, 101M, 109T, 115B

Ariadne Van Zandbergen 24T, 24B, 105, 106B, 120R, 137T, 141T, 141M, 141B, 159T, 185T, 185B, 188B, 190-191B, 193T, 193B, 197T, 199M

Nik Wheeler 34T, 157T, 208-209

Duncan Willetts/Camerapix 177T, 193M, 194, 199T, 199B

Art Wolfe/Art Wolfe, Inc. front cover, 2-3, 5T, 8L, 9T, 12-13, 14-15, 19, 20-21, 28B, 29, 32, 34B, 38T, 38B, 39T, 41, 48, 54T, 55, 67M, 67B, 75, 80, 81B, 83T, 83B, 93M, 94, 97B, 99T, 102, 106TL, 107T, 107B, 118, 120L, 121, 123T, 123M, 125T, 125B, 129B, 133T, 133B, 134, 145T, 149T, 153B, 154T, 154B, 155T, 157B, 159M, 159B, 162, 163T, 165T, 169B, 170, 172, 174T, 174B, 175T, 175B, 178, 181T, 182T, 183, 189, 207T, back cover bottom, spine

C. Zocher/Trip Photographic Library 138T

Design and layout by Mary Kay Garttmeier

Maps by Karen Minot

Indexing by Elizabeth Cook

INDEX